The Adventures and Confessions of an American Drama Queen in Turkey

Barbara A. Lawrence

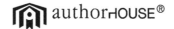 authorHOUSE®

AuthorHouse™ LLC
1663 Liberty Drive
Bloomington, IN 47403
www.authorhouse.com
Phone: 1-800-839-8640

Published by AuthorHouse 02/17/2014

ISBN: 978-1-4918-5967-4 (sc)
ISBN: 978-1-4918-5966-7 (hc)
ISBN: 978-1-4918-5965-0 (e)

Library of Congress Control Number: 2014901995

This book is dedicated to the late Dr. Caroline Loose, my mentor, my guide and my dear friend. Her unconditional love and unwavering support were the catalysts in my journey of self-discovery. I will never forget her or the gifts she so generously bestowed upon me. Hopefully, through the writing of this book I will be able to pass on some of the wisdom that she shared with me.

ACKNOWLEDGMENTS

I want to thank all of my friends who read my *Letters from Tarsus* and encouraged me to write this book. Without their unwavering support and encouragement, I would never have had the courage to believe I could do this.

I'd like to thank the late Dr. Caroline Loose for the lessons she taught me and the strength she gave me. It enabled me to weather the many storms in my life and, eventually, to come to the realization that nothing was going to change until I changed.

I'd like to thank Veronica Van Dalen for listening to me, night after night, as I struggled to find my way in a new culture and in new relationships.

I'd like to thank my friend Hatice Gezer for listening to me and giving me the Turkish man's perspective on things. I'm also grateful for the many times she graciously agreed to act as my "official translator" when I found myself in over my head.

I'd like to thank my friends and neighbors Mustafa Cortanciolu and Patrice. They have been among my greatest supporters during the past three years of my struggle. In addition, Patrice was responsible for helping me recover the rough draft of my manuscript after it was accidentally deleted at the computer "hospital." She also helped me do the first edit of the original manuscript.

I'd like to thank Can Yesirgil for his emotional support and technological services. He helped me with more computer problems than I care to count.

Last, but certainly not least, I'd like to thank Metin for being the catalyst in my battle for self-discovery. I've been told that the Universe sends us many teachers. Those of us who refuse to learn our lessons are condemned to repeat them, and each time we resist, the Universe sends a more persuasive teacher. By the time I had gone through my third divorce, it was obvious that I was a reluctant learner, so I was presented with a teacher and a variety of situations so bizarre and outrageous that, eventually, even I could no longer ignore the obvious.

All of these people have played important roles in my spiritual and emotional development over the past eight years. I would never have been able to write this book without the support they gave me, in one way or another, as my situation changed and evolved into what it is today. I will be eternally grateful to each of them for their invaluable contributions.

INTRODUCTION

True intimacy with another human being can only be
experienced when you have found true peace within yourself.
—Angela L. Wozniak, *Each Day a New Beginning*

In order to understand why a woman who seems to have everything would suddenly decide to pack up and move to the other side of the world, one has to know where this woman came from. Who were her parents? What happened in her formative years to create a hole in her soul that no one and no amount of excitement could seem to fill? Why would she leave her comfortable home, husband of twenty years, fulfilling job, and all her worldly possessions to pursue a brand-new life in a third-world country? While these are interesting questions to ponder, even more interesting is learning how she eventually navigated her way through the many storms she encountered and found the inner strength necessary to build a life of her own. What did she find that, at long last, gave her happiness and a sense of being "whole" that she was never able to find in her conventional midwestern setting? This is a true story of one woman's journey into her soul. Some of the names have been changed to protect the confidentiality of the people involved. However, other than that, this is a true story of how I came face-to-face with my inner demons and what it took for me to become "whole." It's humorous and painful and requires great courage to share with you. I invite you to accompany me on my "great adventure."

CHAPTER 1

The Formative Years

God grant me the serenity to accept the things I
cannot change, the courage to change the things I
can, and the wisdom to know the difference.
—Alcoholics Anonymous, "Serenity Prayer"

I was the oldest child of an alcoholic father and a seemingly helpless, codependent mother. They were grossly mismatched from the beginning. Both my mother and father were first-generation Americans born to immigrant parents who arrived in this country penniless, but who managed to amass small fortunes in the land of golden opportunity. However, that's where the similarities end. My mother was a high school dropout. Her brother became seriously ill in high school, and because both of her parents were busy running their small business, my mother left school to help nurse him back to health. By the time he had recovered, she decided she'd lost too much time to try to pick up where she left off, so she left school permanently and went to work in her father's tavern.

My father, on the other hand, graduated from Notre Dame and attended law school at the University of Wisconsin in Madison. Considering that he and his four siblings were able to attend prestigious, and expensive, universities during the height of the Depression gave my father a false sense of superiority and entitlement, which he clung to until the day he died.

In addition, my mother's parents were not religious in any sense of the word, while my father's parents lived next to the largest Catholic church in Racine, Wisconsin, and were avid churchgoers and supporters. His parents were also socially prominent, and up until the time when my grandmother became seriously ill and was confined to bed, they hosted lavish dinner parties in their luxurious and well-appointed home. They were complete with bootleg liquor brought up from Chicago in long, sleek black limousines driven by petty gangsters armed with submachine guns. Once again, the stark contrast between them and my mother's parents—who worked day and night, seven days a week in order to survive in their adopted country—couldn't be ignored.

There was no time for anything as frivolous as a social life. Considering how diametrically opposed these two people were, I still find myself wondering what the common thread was that brought them together and, even more importantly, that kept them together for almost fifty years. As a child, I used to think it was because they were Catholic and lived in a time when divorce was social suicide. However, in retrospect, I have come to believe that, at least on some level, they must have loved each other. Unfortunately, I'll never know.

My parents' first few years together were a constant financial struggle. My father was the youngest of five children and, as such, was cajoled and coddled his entire life. He never came to grips with the fact that he was expected to go out into the world and become the breadwinner for his family. Because my mother never finished high school, she was unskilled and unemployable. My father resented her for this and constantly berated her for her inability to contribute, financially, to their relationship. He drifted, unsuccessfully, from one job to the next, feeling that his education, coupled with his family name, would certainly open doors for him. However, his lack of follow-through combined with his problems with alcohol resulted in his spending almost as much time in unemployment lines collecting his monthly checks as he did in the local tavern bemoaning his fate.

Finally, this well-educated man from a socially prominent family found himself working in a tiny office of a small local foundry.

To our family, it was just another blow in a series of embarrassing situations. We lied and made excuses to try to minimize the damage it was doing to our family name, but it was hopeless. Just when we thought it couldn't get any worse, it did. The time he spent at that factory marked the end of family life as we knew it. More importantly, however, it also paved the way for my later bouts with depression, alcoholism, overeating, and obsessive-compulsive behaviors of every description. Although I didn't know it at the time, I was on the way to becoming a woman who would be unable and uninterested in forming normal relationships with men.

I would suffer from extreme abandonment issues, which would render me incapable of giving or accepting unconditional love. I would find myself always waiting for "the other shoe to drop." It would be decades before I would learn that there wasn't another shoe. As I grew into womanhood, I would wonder why I was addicted to drama and excitement. I would wonder why I was never interested in the so-called nice boys at school. I would always wonder why I gravitated toward the ones whom most girls shied away from. *They don't know what they're missing,* I thought to myself. Being with the boys who lived on the edge was as good an adrenalin rush as a drug. It was, in fact, my drug of choice. It would take another forty-five years for me to realize how misguided my thinking was and to learn that what had happened to me as a very young girl was actually at the root of my problems.

Working in the same foundry as my father was a woman named Shirley. She was attracted to my father, and he was attracted to her. She was the antithesis of my mother. She was single, independent, and skilled enough to get a job outside of the home. Although she was not highly educated, for some reason my father found her company fascinating. To my mother, my sister, and me, she was the woman responsible for my father's transformation into a complete stranger.

In record time, he went from the smartly dressed man we knew who wore expensive clothes purchased from the best stores to someone none of us recognized in his cheap polyester pants and shirts and even more hideous leisure or, in our words, "loser" suits. He began to talk more like a drunken sailor than a college graduate, and he started to chain smoke and guzzle quarts of beer, straight out of the bottle, at an alarming rate. When he got drunk, which was every night, he would become physically violent and verbally abusive. My younger sister and I retreated, frightened and confused, to our rooms in order to stay out of the line of fire. We would lie on the floor with our ears flat against the heat register, trying to hear all of the details of the arguments going on below us. There never seemed to be any logical reason for his outbursts. To us, it seemed he was angry simply because he was where he really didn't want to be, and that was at home with us. We cowered under the protection of our blankets and cried ourselves to sleep at night, wondering what would become of us.

By this point in time, the only joy left in our family life was our Saturday morning outings with our father. This was the day he took us to the local candy store to pick out precious pieces of penny candy. We stood spellbound with our noses pressed against the glass case, our mouths watering, staring at the delectable display before us. We carefully considered our choices before making our final selections. As our father and Shirley became closer, she began to resent even this small amount of time he spent with us, because it took away from their time together. Suddenly, the trips to the candy store became biweekly, then monthly, and pretty soon they stopped entirely. The trips that we so anxiously looked forward to were replaced by Saturday morning trips to the Taylor Street Orphanage.

We sat wide-eyed and terrified, afraid to move, as our father brandished his fist at us and shouted insults about our mother. He threatened to pack my sister and me up and send us to the orphanage if our mother didn't shape up. We had heard stories about life in the orphanage, and our blood ran cold as we worried and wondered what we could do to try to make our father happy and to avert this horrible fate. These confrontations soon became daily occurrences, which left us stunned, confused, frightened, and desperately searching for something stable we could cling to in this midst of all this chaos.

These early years became the basis for my eventual undoing. At age seven, I was in the kitchen, standing next to my mother, when she opened a bill from a local gynecologist. Shirley had become pregnant by my father and had lost the baby. "Tubular pregnancy" the bill read, and as a result of a clerical error, the bill for the doctor's services had come to our family's home. The look of anguish on my mother's face was unforgettable as she dropped the envelope on the floor and ever so slowly collapsed. Her body was shaking, and she was sobbing uncontrollably. She pulled at her hair and let out screams of disbelief. At that point, I was too young to even guess what was going through her mind, but I knew what was going through mine.

What would my friends at school say? We were Catholic, and I went to a Catholic grade school. I was sure that my friends would no longer be able to associate with me because of the shame that my father had brought upon our family. At that moment, I hated my father and what he had done to us. Little did I know that very shortly, instead of getting better, things would, once again, get worse. Suddenly, and without warning, I became the lady of the house and, as such, I became responsible not only for protecting my younger sister from my father's violent outbursts but from my mother's frequent bouts of depression. My sister and I were alone. There were no adults in our home who were interested, or capable, of taking care of us. I lied and cajoled to keep my little sister from feeling as frightened as I was. I had to appear to be strong enough to keep things from falling apart even though I didn't have the slightest clue as to how I was going to go about doing that.

The next eight or ten years are a complete blur. I have absolutely no memory of the chain of events that transpired during that time. Isolated instances stand out because they were so horrific. However, beyond that, I have no recollection. People have told me that this is comparable to what women experience when they go through childbirth. The pain is so debilitating that if women were to remember it, they would probably never have another child. If I could recall the specific events of that terrible period in my life, I don't know where I would be today. My memory lapse is a blessing, because it allowed me to move on, albeit like a wounded bird. The only thing I knew for sure was that immediately after high school graduation, I was going to leave the house that had stolen my childhood from me and begin anew. No matter what happened,

I reasoned, it couldn't be any worse than what I'd already lived through.

In 1965 I graduated from high school, left home, and never went back. I still wasn't aware of how deep the psychological damage was that I had endured. I had no idea that it would result in three failed marriages and hundreds of unsuccessful love affairs. Nor did I realize that I too would suffer bouts of depression and struggle with both alcoholism and food addictions. During the next thirty-five or forty years, I paid a heavy price for what I experienced in those formative years. However, people much wiser than I maintain that when a soul incarnates, it chooses who its parents and friends will be, knowing that each of these people will have something to offer in terms of life lessons that need to be learned.

As I matured and grew into an adult I didn't have the slightest clue what lessons I was supposed to have gleaned from my chaotic and trauma filled childhood. However, to prevent myself from plunging into the depths of despair and self-pity, I choose to look upon my early years as the springboard that was necessary for me to become the person I am today. The journey has not been easy, but then again, anything worthwhile usually comes with a high price attached to it. I have paid that price and am finally in a position to reap the rewards. If any part of my life had been any different from what it was, I probably wouldn't be sharing my story with you now.

CHAPTER 2

"How in the Hell Did My Life Become Such a Mess?"

If you're going through hell, just keep going.
—Winston Churchill

I had escaped. I had graduated from college with honors, gotten my master's degree with highest honors, and, to summarize, became an overachiever par excellence. No one had a clue that just under the surface of my perfect facade was a woman who was still as insecure and unsure of herself, and her surroundings, as she had been when she was seven and became the lady of the house.

On the outside, everything looked great. I had a wonderful career as an educator. I was loved by the students, parents, and professionals in my community. The walls in my home were covered with awards I had received from local and national organizations. I was recognized as one of the best in the business. Why then did I decide to retire early and, at age fifty-five, pursue a career in an entirely different field?

I had a wonderful home in an affluent suburb of a major midwestern city. It was filled with all the "creature comforts" a person could hope for. The rooms were decorated with furniture and accessories from my travels all over the world. My closets, which were the size of small bedrooms, were overflowing with designer shoes and clothing. Gold and diamond jewelry was spilling from my many jewelry boxes, and my walk-in closet in the basement contained enough fur coats, vests, and capes to hold a private trunk show for my friends. I was on my third husband, which, in and of itself, should've been a clue that I struggled with relationships. When friends remarked about my penchant for falling in and out of love, I joked that I was going to give Elizabeth Taylor a run for her money. However, everyone said that the third one is always the charm, so I was hopeful that, although there were significant differences between my third fiancé and I, this marriage was indeed going to last. Once again, I had chosen a man who was remarkably similar to my father in many respects, so I shouldn't have been surprised that after spending twenty years together, we too would eventually divorce.

My husband was handsome, impeccably well dressed, and extremely attentive. On the outside, it appeared as though we had the perfect marriage. He was thoroughly amenable to my every suggestion and was an "above average" helpmate. We traveled the world together, made home improvements together, and put forth a conscious effort to develop common interests. I took up hunting and joined a bowling league to please him, and he tried skiing and ice skating to please me. We dined out two or three times a week and entertained frequently in our comfortable and inviting home.

On the surface, it appeared as though we had found the secret to marital bliss. We had no children to tie us down, so we enjoyed a carefree and exciting lifestyle. We were the envy of all of our friends. However, what the outside world didn't know was that we were harboring a secret, a secret so deep and so dark, a secret so intimate, that it was taboo to discuss with even one's closest friend. What the outside world didn't know was what went on—or, in this case, didn't go on—behind closed doors. We were living in a completely sexless marriage. There was no kissing except for the occasional peck on the cheek, no hugging, and certainly not even any mention of sexual intercourse. We still slept in the same bed but rarely, if ever, went to bed at the same time. I was usually the first one to retire, so by the time my husband eventually crawled into bed, I could pretend to be asleep. As time went on, he did the same. I was still young and vibrant enough that I desperately longed for the warmth and intimacy that's a natural by-product of a mutually satisfying sexual relationship.

Is this normal? I kept asking myself. *Do other women live in sexless marriages? Can a woman ever be completely fulfilled without sexual intimacy? If not, why am I still here?* Although these questions plagued me from time to time, it's amazing how easily they can be pushed to the back of one's mind. If we keep ourselves in perpetual motion, it's relatively simple to blame the lack of closeness on any number of other factors. Consequently, my list of accomplishments continued to grow. I looked better and better professionally, but I was dying emotionally, physically, and spiritually.

Eventually, I could no longer ignore the unwelcome truth that something was seriously lacking in my life. However, to come to grips with the ugly reality would necessitate monumental changes. They would rock the very foundations of my life. I was never one who was fond of change, so I decided to explore alternative solutions. I found a "spiritual mentor" and tried to use mediation and a variety of other techniques to ease my emotional pain. I read every New Age self-help book that hit the bookstores. I learned the jargon, went to the lectures, and utilized every technique any professional I met suggested. I quit drinking and smoking in an effort to get closer to my inner self. I checked myself into a local treatment center for depression and stayed a month. I communed with nature and took up some creative pursuits to try to exorcise my demons. I retired early, determined to devote my every waking moment to discovering true happiness, but my demons still haunted me. As a result, I found myself being perfectly miserable living my seemingly perfect life.

I felt like life was passing me by. Instead of communing with nature, I was watching grass grow. When I ended my teaching career prematurely, I gave up my lifeline. Gone was the rush that came from confronting new problems every day and solving them; daily contact with students, parents, and colleagues; the satisfaction that comes from having a difficult job to do and doing it well. The nagging emptiness that comes from having a hole in your soul continued to plague me. *What next?* I wondered.

I made a seamless transition into a new career in an entirely different field. I became a manager with an international women's clothing company. It gave me an opportunity to reinvent myself. I had never done anything but teach middle school, which meant I had really moved out of my comfort zone. I had moved so far out of my box there were nights I couldn't sleep. I wondered what would happen when everyone discovered how little I knew about what I was doing. As usual, I threw myself into my new endeavor with the same enthusiasm and gusto with which I approached everything else. As a result, it didn't take long before I had also overachieved in my new profession. I kept asking myself how it was I could do so well in my professional life and be suffering so much personally.

For the next two years, I experimented with the idea of reinventing myself. I changed my hairstyle and decided to get in shape. I justified my determination to be the best I could be physically by reminding myself I was in the fashion business. Why would women come to me for advice and clothing tips if I didn't look the part? I joined a health club and took a part-time job at a second one. I worked out every day and had expensive facial treatments guaranteed to impart a more youthful appearance without surgery. I took singing lessons and flew to Palm Springs to audition for the *Follies*.

I managed to find clients and women from all over the country who were interested in working with me. I scheduled fashion shows and presentations from California to New York. I was on a plane once or twice a month, which kept me so busy that, once again, I didn't have to address my emotional void. My friends thought I had found the pot of gold at the end of the rainbow. When I was offered a chance to work for this same company in Italy, I believed my friends were right. I had struck gold. My dream had always been to work overseas, and at that time, Italy was definitely my country of choice. I was so preoccupied with the professional part of my life that I was able to lose sight of everything else. At long last, I thought, I had found my bliss.

While I waited for the company to open their Italian division, I continued to travel for them in the States. On one of my last trips, serendipity struck. I reconnected with an old college flame. The fact that he was interested in getting together again, after our forty-year hiatus, was all I needed to fill my emotional void at that time. If I had known then what I know now, I'd have to ask myself whether I would've actually agreed to meet him.

His name was Terry, and I was in Louisville. It was October, and I was in town for a manager's meeting with the clothing company I represented. The evening before I left to return to Milwaukee, I found myself alone in my room with a few minutes of downtime. I never handled those times very well. They provided a rare moment of quiet that might ultimately lead to some self-reflection. Once again, I would have to confront the nagging question: Why did I continue to stay in a loveless marriage? My life was quickly passing me by. *Is this all there is?* I kept asking myself. This idea was so repugnant to me that I always managed to fill my alone time by turning on the TV, reading a magazine, or doing some much-needed paperwork. This time, however, was different. *Why not call and see if Terry still lives here?* I thought. It had been at least ten years since I'd heard any news of him, and I couldn't resist the urge to pick up the phone and see for myself.

Knowing that he was an attorney, I reasoned he would probably be listed in the phone book. Sure enough, I found his number, called, and got his voice mail. The voice was unmistakable. Although I realized that he must have changed a lot in the past forty years—after all, hadn't we all—his voice hadn't. He still had the unmistakable twang in his voice that is so characteristic of people in that part of the country, and I could actually hear the glint in his eyes. I left a short, sweet message that I had been in town and thought of him. I wished him well and hung up. I didn't leave any of my contact information, reasoning that if he had any interest in contacting me, he certainly would've done it before now. Looking back, I realize that the real reason I didn't leave the information was the fear that he wouldn't contact me.

Two and a half months later, I was preparing to leave for a three-week European holiday with my husband. Our house phone rang, and I heard the unmistakable twang of the voice I knew so well.

Terry thanked me profusely for calling him and apologized for letting forty years pass with no contact. He told me that he was extremely frustrated by the fact that I hadn't left any contact information and explained all of the hoops he had to jump through in order to find me. He had called the hotel, but because I was there as part of a company function, they didn't have any registration information for me. He contacted the company I was working for and explained that years ago he had been my attorney and I had visited his office to catch up on old times. He said that while I was there I had forgotten some important papers that he desperately needed to return to me. After many frustrating attempts, he was eventually able to get my home phone number from them. He asked if I would be willing to have lunch with him sometime. I eagerly accepted his invitation but explained that I was leaving for Europe in two days. I said that I would call him when I returned.

CHAPTER 3

Coming Alive Again

Don't ask yourself what the world needs; ask yourself what makes you come alive. And then go and do that. Because what the world needs are people who have come alive.
—Harold Whitman

The period of change and self-reflection that was touched off by our lunch together in Chicago can only be likened to opening Pandora's Box. The eight and a half years that have passed since that fateful afternoon have forced me to confront my greatest fears, to delve into the darkest places in my soul, and to examine the best and the worst of what makes me who I am. It was a time of ecstasy and bliss, as well as heart-wrenching disappointments. My time with him empowered me to embark on a journey from which there was no return. I wouldn't be where I am today, living the life I'm living now, if it weren't for the love and the confidence that Terry so unselfishly showered on me. He made me realize that I was entitled to a lot more happiness and fulfillment than I was getting from the way I was living my life. For this, and for so much more, I owe him a debt that I can never repay.

The lunch itself was just that—lunch. He had checked out of his hotel room on our way to the restaurant, so it was apparent there would be no "afternoon delight." *How strange*, I thought, *for a man who was one of the best sexual partners I had ever had the pleasure of being with.* Was it because he had such great respect for me, or was it because he wasn't interested in rekindling our sexual relationship? More insecurity, more rejection, and more abandonment issues were rearing their ugly heads. However, sex or no sex, that first meeting was the match that reignited the flame that had always burned so brightly between us. The chain of events that followed couldn't have been predicted at that point. If either one of us could have foreseen what was to come, I'm sure one of us would've had to good sense to stay home that fateful day.

Since the crux of my emotional evolution has taken place in Turkey, Terry's involvement in my story is limited to a great extent. However, he was the catalyst that set the chain of events into action. We continued to meet for the next three years. Because we lived in different states, our meetings were infrequent, clandestine, and charged with enough electricity to light an entire city. Despite the fact that we were both forty years older, my heart still beat with excitement every time I spoke to him, and the feelings that ran through me when I was on my way to meet him sent tingles through my entire body. The sexual energy between us had not diminished over time. In fact, if anything, it was heightened. Whether he was waiting for me in an airport terminal or a hotel lobby, my heart started to race in anticipation at the very thought of lying next to him again. Every muscle in my body tensed, and my breathing quickened at the mere sight of him.

Once we were together again, we embraced and kissed so passionately that I prayed the moment would never end. I could feel his penis pulsating against me, and all I could think of was the bliss that we'd both experience as soon as he entered me again. We kissed in elevators, taxi cabs, and restaurants. We kissed in parks, on the street, and in department stores. We were in a world of our own, and when we were together, we were oblivious to everything around us. My palms grew sweaty and my pulse quickened every time he reached for my hand or cupped my chin to pull me closer to him. We wrapped our naked bodies around one another and slowly, ever so slowly, made passionate love for hours at a time. When we were finally sated, we would lie in each other's arms and fantasize about what life would be like if we were both free of our obligations and could be together like this forever. However, in our heart of hearts, we both knew that this was never to be.

The times we were together reminded me how much I used to enjoy kissing, cuddling, enjoying sex, and experiencing the warmth of an intimate relationship. I wondered, over and over, how I could continue to live in a loveless marriage. My husband and I were more like brother and sister than husband and wife. Initially, I believed my time with Terry was all I needed to satisfy my natural urge to form an intimate bond with someone. I tried to convince myself that I could go back home and be satisfied with my life as I knew it if I knew that Terry and I could be together periodically. However, the more I had of him, the more I wanted. I never intended to be unreasonable or demanding. I never intended to put his marriage, or mine, in jeopardy. However, it didn't take long for him to feel the pressure that's a natural byproduct of having an affair with someone like me who is suffering from severe abandonment issues.

I tried to tell myself I had made great progress in my emotional development. After all, I had discovered I had a hole in my soul and admitted it. I talked about it and professed to be coming to terms with it. Unfortunately, my heart and mind were not one on the subject. As a result, my words sent one message and my actions quite another. Terry started to pull away. His calls became less frequent, his voice less loving. He became more and more consumed with his law practice and family. He became more and more concerned about being discovered. His responsibilities increased, and as a result, his time with me decreased. Eventually, he learned he had a heart problem and had open heart surgery. Although we continued to try to maintain some semblance of a relationship, it was clear that things were not the same, and our relationship would never be the solution to my problem.

During this same period, things changed for the worse in my professional life as well. After September 11, 2001, retail businesses all suffered. The clothing company I worked for was no exception. With declining sales came the decision to halt all expansion. The company would not be opening an Italian division; therefore, my dream of living abroad would not be realized by continuing to work with them.

The dissatisfaction I felt with life in general accelerated. I'm not sure if my marital situation began to deteriorate more rapidly or if it just seemed that way. I wasn't happy, and my husband wasn't happy—life wasn't good. My first impulse was, as it had always been, to run. I decided that a divorce was the only solution. I spent five thousand dollars and got the advice of two different attorneys. Both of them agreed that divorce would be financial suicide. I was a retired teacher with a pension, a house, and a Mercedes. My husband, like my father, had bounced from one job to another, never finding his niche. He had no pension and, because he had never held a real job for any length of time, would receive a minimal social security benefit. Was I willing to share half of my assets with him and incur half of his debt? Was I willing to pay alimony because I made more money than he did? *What a ridiculous idea,* I thought.

I was no longer a champion of women's rights. I was fifty-seven years old, and I was in a rut! I was desperately seeking a way to fill the hole in my soul. Obviously, Terry wasn't the answer. Perhaps, I reasoned, returning to teaching would be the best thing to do at this point. If I could find a job overseas, I could leave Milwaukee with my house and my pension intact. This seemed like the most logical solution. As a result, I got on the Internet and started to search. This is where my story really begins.

CHAPTER 4

Taking the Plunge

To improve is to change, to be perfect is to change often.
—Winston Churchill

My soul searching and journey of introspection had unleashed a monster. It became impossible for me to continue with life as I knew it. I had to escape. The only thing I knew for sure was that I felt like I was standing on the edge of a precipice. Below me was a dark abyss—the unknown. The only way to move forward was to go across this abyss. I was going to have to trust that rather than falling into this bottomless black pit, I was going to be supported and uplifted on angels' wings. My only choice was to let go and let God. The sheer thought of what might lie ahead nearly immobilized me. However, the thought of continuing on the same path was enough to move me into action.

It was in the fall of 2004 when my dear friend Anne and I met, once again, to complain about our miserable existences. It was our favorite pastime. We were both depressed, dissatisfied, and disgruntled. We lived in adjoining suburbs of Milwaukee, Wisconsin. Anne lived in the most exclusive suburb in the state and enjoyed a life of luxury and privilege. Her husband was a partner in a local law firm and provided her with a lifestyle that most could only imagine. My husband, on the other hand, had bounced from one job to another, never able to find exactly the right fit. Nevertheless, Anne and I were like sisters and, as such, shared our innermost thoughts, secrets, and desires.

Both of us, for entirely different reasons, suffered from terminal boredom and were convinced that if nothing changed, we would each die a premature death. It was only a matter of time before we would be shipped off to some retirement home in Florida and left to die alone and unfulfilled. We had tried a variety of things to increase our excitement from compulsive shopping and, in my case, extramarital affairs. Nothing worked, and we were determined to change things at any cost. We made a pact that by June of 2004 we would have taken some positive steps to produce a significant change, or we would forfeit our right to complain about anything.

I started frantically surfing the Internet in search of an idea. I was a retired teacher and decided that my best chance lay in finding a teaching position in an exotic foreign land. However, I didn't have the slightest clue how to go about doing that. As my intention became clearer, I realized there were two criteria my search had to meet. The first was finding a recruiting agency that would receive its payment from the employer rather than the employee—namely, me. The second was finding a free and easy form I could use to update my employment information. By this time, I had been married three times, so none of my college records were in the correct name. In addition, all of my references were more than thirty years old, and many of the people who had written them for me were either no longer alive or in contact with me. Much to my surprise, I found both of these things on the Internet in a relatively short period of time.

I connected with a gentleman at COIS, the Council of International Schools. He was an American who had lived abroad for more than thirty years. We were very close in age, so I began to believe that perhaps one could teach an old dog new tricks. After weeks of soul searching and hundreds of e-mails, he gave me the courage to take that all-important leap of faith. He was an avid fisherman, so it wasn't surprising that he used a fishing metaphor to reel me in. He said that if I didn't throw my line into the water, I'd never know whether I would have gotten a bite. It made sense to me so, in January of 2005, Anne and I boarded a flight to London to attend a job fair. After all, I mused, if all else failed, we could always go shopping.

My dream destination was Italy. My third husband and I had honeymooned there and fell in love with the country and all things Italian. We took language courses when we returned home and enjoyed, in quick succession, twelve more visits there. In my mind, there was only one place I would consider working, and Italy was it.

I found the job fair to be very disappointing. There were only three schools there from Italy, and none of them had an opening that matched my qualifications. I berated myself for succumbing to such a silly pipe dream and decided to return to the room, get Anne, and go shopping.

What happened next was surely divine intervention. As I walked toward the exit, I had to decide whether to turn right or left. Because I'm left-handed, I invariably turn left. It was a few minutes before noon, so my stomach was growling. As I turned, I noticed what appeared to be a basket of Perugina chocolates on a table. Perhaps because I was still dreaming of finding a teaching position in Italy, I naturally mistook the bright silver and blue colors that I saw for their signature packaging. The woman holding the basket didn't miss a beat. She saw that something had caught my eye and motioned for me to approach the table.

As it turned out, the few steps it took me to reach the table were going to be life altering. If I had known what lie ahead, perhaps I would have foregone the chocolates. Then again, perhaps I would have welcomed the changes and challenges that were to come. It's a moot point now, because without a moment's hesitation, I was in front of the table with my hand in the basket. However, what I held in my hand was not a Perugia chocolate. In fact, it wasn't a chocolate at all. It was an evil eye bracelet that Tulin, the woman at the table, explained was a good-luck talisman guaranteed to ward off any and all evil spirits. She was warmhearted and engaging and asked me if I had ever considered working in Turkey. *How absurd,* I thought. *She obviously doesn't know that my heart's desire is to live and work in Italy.* As we talked, I explained my passion about all things Italian. Tulin then pointed out that Italy and Turkey share many similarities. As she rattled them off, I began to think that, perhaps, she may have a point. I rushed up to the room to discuss it with Anne and to get her opinion.

We sat on the bed and giggled like schoolgirls. We were thoroughly amused, not only by the idea of me moving to Turkey but by the fact that someone was interested in hiring me. Yes, I was a seasoned veteran of the classroom with a string of prestigious awards to document my thirty-one years of service. However, I was also a fifty-seven-year-old woman with no international teaching experience. By the time the next school year began I would be fifty-eight! Was it truly possible that someone would be interested in hiring a teacher who had already retired twice? As if this notion wasn't amusing enough, Anne and I giggled about the fact that, two women who had graduated from prestigious universities with honors, given a blank world map, would not have been able to put our fingers on Turkey. We would probably have settled on a spot somewhere near the Mediterranean Sea, but that's definitely as close as we would have come. We called Anne's husband to get his opinion, and he was extremely supportive. He reminded me that it was only a two-year commitment and asked what I had to lose. If I didn't like it, I could leave at the end of my contract. That settled it. I signed a contract to begin teaching in September 2005.

I had kept my part of the pact with Anne. I was definitely doing something life altering. I was not going to continue life as I knew it. This decision would guarantee that, at least for the next two years, my life would be exciting and different. I wouldn't be sitting on the deck in my backyard watching the grass grow or commiserating with Anne about our miserable existences. I was heading to points unknown.

At the time, little did I know that this decision would alter the course of my life. It would change my financial situation and my marital status, as well as my core values. My life would never be as I knew it before. This was truly the beginning of a great adventure.

CHAPTER 5

Where in the World Is Tarsus, Turkey?

Life is either a daring adventure or nothing at all.
—Helen Keller

The big day finally arrived. In late August 2005, I kissed my husband good-bye and boarded a Turkish Airlines flight in Chicago bound for Istanbul and then Adana, Turkey. Adana is the city closest to Tarsus with an airport. As we flew over the Atlantic, I became very introspective and kept asking myself what it was that had made me so discontent that I was willing to give up my comfortable life, my friends, and all of my creature comforts in order to start all over in a third-world country six thousand miles away from home.

If I were perfectly honest, I would have to say that my marriage was in shambles. This one was my third, and each one had been progressively worse. My first husband was my childhood sweetheart, and we stayed together for ten years. He was a workaholic who was more interested in amassing millions than in spending time with me. He was incredibly successful at what he did and eventually reaped the benefits of his hard work. He became a multimillionaire and turned what I considered to be a character defect into his greatest asset. My second was an alcoholic, and I knew I had made a mistake even before we walked down the aisle. However, I rationalized that the invitations were in the mail, and being the superwoman that I was, I was sure I could fix everything that was wrong with him in short order, and we would live happily ever after. After all, hadn't fixing things always been my specialty? His penchant for the "good life" killed him shortly after I divorced him. My third husband was also a man who thoroughly enjoyed his drinks and who never quite found himself. He had a realtor's license, but in the twenty years we were married, he sold fewer than ten homes. He had inherited a large sum of money and relied on that to see him through. We both contributed equally to the upkeep of the house, but other than that, our money was our own.

I'd been financially burned in my two previous divorces and didn't intend to go down that road again. As a result, we paid our own way when we went out to dinner or took a trip. When his money ran out, the big problems really began. We could no longer go out for expensive dinners or jet around the world unless I paid his expenses as well. I desperately missed the diversions that this lifestyle afforded. Since my retirement, I had lost my sense of purpose. I was searching desperately for something to make me feel alive again.

There's a song that asks: Is that all there is? I found myself asking the same question over and over and over again, and frankly, I didn't like the answer. *If this is all there is,* I told myself, *I may as well curl up somewhere and die.* I was determined that I was not going to spend my golden years like my mother did, alone in front of the boob tube watching soap operas. I decided that no matter what I found when I arrived in Tarsus, it would be better than the alternative.

As we soared over the Atlantic, I was lost in thought. Putting my thoughts on paper has always been very cathartic for me, so I wrote the following poem in the margins of our in-flight magazine. I've kept it all these years to remind me what I was feeling at the time.

A woman bound for distant lands, alone yet unafraid
Not knowing if the choice to leave was the one she should have made.

She agonized for weeks and months about what she should do
Feeling trapped, she'd lost all hope, she felt her life was through.

Every day was just the same, then came the endless nights
The thrill was gone, she plodded on, she'd lost her zest for life.

Things must change and quickly, or surely she will die
Sitting in a rocking chair, watching wet paint dry.

And so today, without regret, she packed her bags and left
Searching for new things to do and friends she hasn't met.

In time she'll know if what she did was right or was it wrong.
Right now the only certainty is that she's feeling strong.

She took the job and left behind everything she had.
And, in the end, hopes she'll look back and say, "I'm really glad."

She faced the fears that haunted her and kept her stuck in time
She cut her ties, is moving on, and cannot look behind.

I ripped the page out of the magazine and put it in my purse. Then I sat back, closed my eyes, and waited to see what the next day would bring.

As I reminisce about the first few days and weeks in Turkey, I am still amused by my first impressions. I had left a suburb of manicured lawns, stately homes, and two-, three-, and four-car families in search of something different. I was looking for change and great adventure. Within moments of landing in Adana, it became obvious I would get both!

When I arrived in Adana, I was met by a representative of the school for which I would be working. There were a few other people who had arrived on other flights. We all piled into the school van and headed for Tarsus.

Tarsus is a small city about half way between Adana, which is a huge metropolis, and Mersin, a lovely seaside city. In ancient times, Tarsus was also on the sea, and there are many legends about St. Paul and the time he spent there. However, the sea has long since receded, leaving a dusty and brutally hot little city in its wake. It's filled with ancient reminders of its glorious past and fabulous homes and buildings that, even in their current state of disrepair, leave one with a feeling that this city had a wonderful legacy to share with us.

The road into Tarsus was full of potholes and clogged with horse-drawn carts, donkeys, entire families on motorbikes, and ancient automobiles with brand names I had never heard of. The landscape was dotted with shacks in need of repair and old people, both men and women, in shalvars (very baggy pants with crotches that hang down to one's knees) tending the fields. The heat was debilitating and the dust blinding. The sweat was pouring off of me. There was no way to camouflage my discomfort. As we pulled into Tarsus, I felt that I had been catapulted back in time—no McDonald's, Burger King, Domino's, or Starbucks and only one supermarket! The school was one of the more modern and better maintained buildings in the city, and it dated back to 1888. This was obviously a place where I was going to have to learn some new survival skills. I was exhausted after the flight and prepared to go to bed early. However, before turning out the light I wrote another poem.

A stranger in a foreign land excited and alone
Trying to remember why it was that she left home.
Had marriage lost its sparkle, was life flying by too fast?
Did she want to build a future or hide a sordid past?
Did adventure call from distant shores, or did the calling come
From a heartfelt need to do some good before her life was done?

Questions, questions, and more questions. Hopefully, my experience here would provide the answers I was looking for.

Within a very short period of time, it became obvious that the school was a well-respected and revered part of the town. Because I was a teacher there, I was also well respected and revered. Tarsus is so small that it was only a matter of weeks before I found my way around and truly immersed myself in it. The kindness and generosity of the people was indescribable. I made friends with everyone from the butcher to the shoe repair man. I never stopped marveling at the warm welcome I received and at the long-term friendships I forged with some of the townspeople. Everyone was interested in knowing where I came from and why I was in Tarsus. Because few of the townspeople spoke English, our conversations were sometimes laborious but always tinged with a mysterious and exotic flair that left me spellbound and eager to come back for more.

Life in ancient Tarsus turned out to be a great adventure. Saint Paul's Church is there, as well as an ancient road that Marc Anthony and Cleopatra reportedly strolled down. Cleopatra's gate is on a main thoroughfare, and recently, they stumbled upon Daniel's tomb as they attempted to restore an ancient mosque. There are so many remnants of ancient buildings that townspeople use fragments of the pediments as supports when they restore their shops and homes. St. Paul's courtyard is littered with pieces of ancient columns, and security guards at the college use them to rest their bicycles and motor scooters against. Clearly, the sheer numbers of ancient sites makes it impossible to police and/or preserve all of them.

While I was a university student, I had seriously contemplated becoming an archaeologist, so without any effort at all, Tarsus had me under its spell. I was ecstatic to learn that my apartment was in a historical building right across from the school. There are even rumors that Ataturk may have slept there. While I'm not sure about that, I do know that during World War I soldiers used the building as a barrack. This was a long way from the sprawling ranch with a beautiful garden that I left behind in Milwaukee.

I went to sleep the first few nights in my new home content that, although I wasn't in Italy, I was exactly where I supposed to be. Most good teachers are lifelong learners, and it was clear from the start that there was a lot to be learned about my adopted country.

CHAPTER 6

East Meets West

It's true that we don't know what we've got until
we lose it, but it's also true that we don't know
what we've been missing until it arrives.
—Unknown

Before I left Milwaukee, I had read several books, spoken to friends, surfed the 'net, and even attended social events at the Turkish American Association in my community in order to learn as much as I could about Turkey and its customs, food, and people before I arrived. My goal was to make my transition into this new life as smooth as possible. However, in retrospect, I realize that nothing could have prepared me for what I was going to find when I actually arrived. The clothing, the attitude of the people toward foreigners, and the food are just some of the things that are distinctively Turkish and things that one must experience firsthand in order to understand.

Well-meaning friends who had traveled or worked in the Middle East offered advice on what to wear and how to behave so I wouldn't be considered a decadent Westerner or, worse yet, an infidel! One good friend even flew up from Miami to help me pack. She was determined that I would be regarded as the consummate professional that I was and not a lewd and lascivious foreign hussy. As a result, my luggage was filled with modest ankle-length skirts, long-sleeved blouses, and jackets that were long enough to camouflage any hint of a derriere. Much to my surprise, my wardrobe could not have been more out of step with the climate in Tarsus or the times. In my first week, I saw more belly buttons and bare midriffs than I cared to count, and the front pages of the local newspapers looked more like pages out of a *Playboy* or *Penthouse* magazine than the front pages of Islamic newspapers. Clearly, my well-intentioned friends had erred on the side of staunch conservatism, and I was going to have to reoutfit myself immediately if I ever hoped to blend in with the locals.

Another big surprise was the incredible warmth of the welcome I received. I had been warned that Turkey, because it was an Islamic country, considered us "dangerous" because of our political and religious differences. In fact, other well-intentioned friends warned me that I was probably taking my life in my hands by going there. Once again, nothing could have been further from the truth.

The English teachers at the college were the only foreigners in town, so we created quite a stir wherever we went. The people literally bent over backward to help us. We were treated like visiting royalty. If we eyed something in a pastry shop window, the owner came out and gave us a sample. If we looked hot, someone handed us a cold drink or invited us to sit and have a cup of chai (tea). If we looked lost, someone took us by the hand and led us to our destination. If we were in a shop and appeared confused, the store manager and two or three clerks came and acted as our personal shoppers. Perhaps the best evidence of their sincere affection for us was their generosity. If we admired something that someone was wearing, eating, or holding, the person gave it to us without hesitation. If we refused to accept it, it was considered an insult. I've traveled all over the world and have never experienced anything like this. Because of this unusual custom, I learned very quickly to keep my compliments to a minimum to avoid stripping my Turkish friends of all their worldly belongings.

In the first two weeks I was there, the only food I recognized was hummus. Every bite of Turkish food was an adventure. Yogurt is everywhere, even in soups and cold drinks. *Ayran* is a drink made from yogurt and water, and it's amusing to see young people pushing and shoving to be the first in line to get theirs. Can anyone imagine children in the United States fighting over a glass of yogurt and water? Having said this, the national drink here seems to be tea, because it's also everywhere. Every shop owner offers it while customers are browsing. It's even available at gas stations where people frequently sit and relax while their gas tanks are being filled. The question I kept asking myself was, "Why does everyone talk about Turkish coffee, when everyone here drinks tea?!" Every region of Turkey has its own culinary specialty so, until a person has explored this country from one end to the other, there's always another delicious culinary surprise on the horizon.

The dawn of each day in my new surroundings brought with it the opportunity to learn new things and meet new people. At first, I was amazed that with my background and experience, life could still hold so many surprises. However, I quickly learned to embrace the differences.

CHAPTER 7

Observations of a *Yabançi* (Foreigner) in Turkey

The wise man belongs to all countries, for the
home of a great soul is the whole world.
—Democritus

As Dorothy in *The Wizard of Oz* observed, I was not in Kansas anymore! There were new sights, tastes, and smells, as well as some very interesting behaviors, and I wanted to know about all of them. For instance, why do people here eat carrots served in a glass of water and lemon juice with their drinks when they go to a bar or nightclub? Why do men eat *suzme* yogurt with *raki*, an anise-flavored alcoholic drink? Why are most of the toilets holes in the ground, but more importantly, why, when I find a familiar-looking European one, does it always have, for lack of a better term, a butt washer? Why do men hold hands when they walk down the street? Why aren't there any self-service gas stations here? Why is gas so expensive, often twelve or thirteen dollars a gallon? Why do they call private elementary and high schools colleges? Why don't the restaurants serve butter with bread? Why do Turkish people love to eat hot soup for breakfast, even in the summer? Why are there so many stores that don't refrigerate milk and eggs? Why do Turkish people simply say thank you when asked how they are instead of actually explaining how they feel? Why do students who attend expensive private schools have tutors and attend special after-school programs every night and every Saturday to make sure that they are getting a proper education? Why are exam grades posted on the wall for everyone to see? Why are grades negotiable? Why do Turkish teachers use a check mark to indicate a correct answer and an *X* for answers that are wrong? Why is there such animosity toward Kurdish people? Why doesn't the Turkish language have words for *private* and the verb *to like* (as we use it)? Why do some men still have more than one wife? Why is there social pressure for a successful man to have a second wife or a mistress as a testament to his success? Why is prostitution legal? Why are parents still arranging marriages for their children? Who was Kemal Ataturk?

What is Ataturk Death Day? Why do people have decals of his signature and his profile put on their car windows? Why can I only shower in some hotels from five o'clock in the evening until midnight? Why do some hotels with state-of-the-art bathtubs and sinks put a trash can next to the toilet because guests are not allowed to put paper of any kind in the toilets? Why is there so much hugging and kissing going on in the schools? Why were we warned not to use the words *sick* and *peach* in the classroom? Since the lights on all of the police cars are always flashing, how does a person know when to pull over and stop? Questions, questions, and more questions. In this chapter, I will answer a few of the more significant ones.

Situated as it is between the East and the West, Turkey is truly unique. It is a bridge between the two and, as such, has adopted elements of life from both sides. However, the contributions Kemal Ataturk made to shaping modern Turkey have set it apart from the rest of the Middle East and resulted in the establishment of a secular state that differs significantly from the governments in Syria, Iran, and Iraq. For this reason, Ataturk's life and memory are celebrated with a solemnity I've never seen bestowed on any other political figure. He is the Turkish equivalent of George Washington, Abraham Lincoln, Thomas Jefferson, John F. Kennedy, and Martin Luther King Jr. all rolled into one.

November 11 is Ataturk's Death Day, but ironically, it's more a celebration of his life than the mourning of his death. It's not within the scope of this book to discuss his list of contributions. However, life in modern Turkey has been shaped by him. As a result, his portrait hangs in, literally, every business and office in the country, from the local barber shop to the government buildings in Ankara. On November 11, everyone, young and old, pin a picture of him on their clothing, and at 9:05 in the morning everything stops for a moment of silence followed by the singing of the national anthem. Special programs remind young people of his contributions during the war and after. There are monuments in his honor scattered throughout every city and village, and a person can be imprisoned for speaking of him in a negative manner. Schools hold flag ceremonies every morning followed by a pledge to uphold the principles set down by him. There can be no denying that modern-day Turkey is what it is in large part because of the changes that Ataturk implemented. He is responsible for catapulting Turkey into the twentieth century.

A foreigner here would also notice significant differences in the educational system. The national Ministry of Education regulates all aspects of what goes on in the schools, including what teachers can and cannot wear. During what is considered to be the winter season, female teachers must wear nylon stockings and shoes that cover the back of their heels. Men must wear a tie and a jacket. When the Ministry declares that it is springtime, these regulations no longer apply. Granted, the intensity with which these mandates are carried out varies from school to school and city to city. However, there is always the feeling that Big Brother is watching. The atmosphere is very Orwellian.

There are few, if any, educational programs for children with special needs, so regular classroom teachers are expected to have the skills necessary to deal with any and all exceptional needs. It is often assumed that misbehavior is the result of a child feeling that the teacher doesn't love him enough. Perhaps because of this, or perhaps because Turkish people are naturally much more affectionate and demonstrative than in some other cultures, there is an inordinate amount of hugging and kissing that goes on in Turkish schools. Having spent my entire career in a society where touching a student could result in a lawsuit, it took me awhile to become accustomed to this kind of public display of affection. Needless to say, once I knew I wouldn't be sued, I plunged right in with the best of them and enjoyed my daily dose of TLC. It was wonderful, and I began to tell my students that I wasn't working for money; I was working for hugs. In retrospect, I have to admit that being able to freely exchange feelings like this made going into the classroom every day a joy. I looked forward to getting my morning hugs and to giving them in return. When students and teachers relate to one another on this level, the positive feelings spill into every aspect of their relationship, and it brings out the best in everyone. When I reminisce about my teaching experience in this country, these moments will always be among my fondest memories.

Another big difference that a foreigner can't help but notice is the way teachers are treated in Turkey. Teaching is considered to be a very honorable profession, and teachers, as a result, are treated with tremendous respect. November 24 is Teacher Appreciation Day, and like Ataturk's Death Day, it's marked with special celebrations and assemblies. Teachers receive roses and bouquets of flowers and a festive atmosphere prevails. My first year here, I was at the ceremony when a primary student read a poem that she had written. I was so touched by it that I asked if I could have a copy. At the program it was read in Turkish and English. Admittedly, something is lost in the translation. However, I think it speaks volumes about how important both a teacher's role is here, as well as the contributions that Ataturk made to modern Turkey.

The right, the beautiful, the good, the brotherhood and love
You taught me, my beloved teacher.

You told me about Ataturk, the Turk with the golden mane
And the Turkish song upon my lips
My beloved teacher.

I want to kiss your caring hands for you took me forward.
You taught me and guided me to knowledge
My beloved teacher.

Wishing to spend days and nights
Yearning to learn more of what you've got to teach me
My beloved teacher.

I do not want any dark nights
I am wishing to learn more as Ataturk desired

You provide the unique opportunities
My beloved teacher.

A new teacher here must also be very vigilant about their use of certain English words in the classroom. Some of them have an entirely different meaning in Turkish, and a foreign teacher can unwittingly create chaos in a classroom by using them. For example, *piç*, which, in Turkish, is pronounced "peach" means a bastard, so I quickly learned the Turkish word for peach, because I truly enjoyed peach-flavored ice tea. *Sik*, which in Turkish is pronounced "sick," means penis, so my students were never sick, they were ill. A foreign teacher only has to mistakenly use the wrong word once before quickly coming to the realization that she has made a major cultural faux pas!

My first December here also brought with it another completely different set of surprises. Since Turkey is a Muslim country, I didn't expect to see or hear anything that would remind me of Christmas. Wrong again! Demre, a city in western Turkey, was once an important member of the Lycian League, and St. Paul is said to have stopped there on his way to Rome in 61 AD. However, the city is better known as the diocese of St. Nicholas, also known as Santa Claus, who was born in Patara sixty kilometers west of Demre. Today, there is a partially restored church that stands as his burial site. Primary students in schools all over Turkey fill their classrooms with drawings of Santa and his reindeer. Many have Christmas trees as well, a tradition that was abandoned in US schools long ago in an effort to become more politically correct.

School children draw names for Secret Santas just as students in the United States used to do, and life-size Santas stand in storefronts in cities large and small. Colored lights decorate store windows and major thoroughfares. A local radio station plays Christmas carols twenty-four hours a day, and store shelves are stocked with ornaments and colored lights to decorate all the Christmas trees. The trees are put up a few days before New Year's Eve. I asked some of my students if they knew why people put a star on top of their trees. Not surprisingly, they thought it was up there simply because it was pretty. When I explained that the star led the three wise men to Bethlehem, it didn't change anything. The stars stayed.

Perhaps the biggest shock a foreigner has after arriving in Turkey comes the first time they travel in a taxi or a private car. Turkey is a country where traffic laws are merely suggestions. I have driven in most major European cities, yet continue to be amazed at the absolute chaos that reigns on Turkish roads. Lane markers and red lights are totally ignored, and no speed limits are posted. Pedestrians run for their lives and there's "open season" on people on bicycles and motor scooters. Potholes are everywhere, which makes driving down the street as treacherous as trying to cross a minefield uninjured. Well-intentioned people often mark the potholes with piles of rocks, which makes driving a car at night like a Kamikaze pilot flying a plane blindfolded. Not only do you hit the pothole but the pile of rocks as well. Motor scooter drivers are referred to as organ donors, and up until ten years ago, it was de rigueur to carry a body bag in the trunk of your car. That certainly speaks volumes about the danger of driving here.

I've learned to "walk and run like a Turk" and look for any opening in traffic to cross the street. Needless to say, I was shocked when I was stopped by a policeman, who was talking on his cell phone and smoking a cigarette, for crossing the street on a red light. When I darted into traffic, I was part of a pack of four other people, all Turks. Why, I wondered, had this man singled me out? When he approached me, I pretended I didn't understand what he was talking about. When I could see he wasn't going to write my transgression off to sheer stupidity, I responded in my best Turkish and apologized profusely. He continued to hold me "captive" on the corner. As the conversation unfolded, it became obvious that he knew I worked at the Koleji and simply wanted to chat. He told me to "stay put" (not his words), and I waited, apprehensively, for what was to come. People here ignore all speed limits, run red lights, and weave in and out of traffic as though they were on a skateboard rather than behind the wheel of a car. I couldn't even imagine getting a ticket for jaywalking. The next thing I knew, the policeman reappeared with two chai (glasses of tea) and chairs. We sat down and drank our tea together like old friends. All he was really looking for was an opportunity to speak with a foreigner. The next thing I knew he gave me his schedule and asked how often I crossed this intersection. He wanted to set up a weekly tea time, so he could have all his questions about the United States answered. The encounter reminded me how special foreigners are in this country. It's part of the charm of being here and the reason why I've coined the term "princess treatment" for the way in which the people here treat us. It's also a reminder that I may be the only American some of these people ever have a chance to speak to. As such, I feel I have an obligation to be the best ambassador I can be, and I will graciously have a chai and conversation with anyone who invites me to join him.

CHAPTER 8

Ramazan

Your true religion is the life you live not the creed you profess.
—Unknown

Turkey had, from the start, seemed to me to be more European than Middle Eastern. Sexy, partially clothed, curvaceous women adorn billboards, bus terminals, magazine covers, and the front pages of newspapers. Bare midriffs and halter tops are everywhere. People smoke, and there are bars and nightclubs on every corner. Covered women are few and far between. If I had lived in Istanbul, this probably wouldn't have been so surprising. However, I lived in the "Bible Belt" of Islam, a very conservative city that, despite its size, seems more like a large village than an actual city.

However, each year the coming of Ramadan, or Ramazon as it's called in Turkey, changes at least some of this. It's a period of fasting and sacrifice that precedes the Seker Bayram, or Sugar holiday. Individuals choose whether they will fast or not. There is some social pressure, but there are many people who do not fast. They jokingly call themselves "bad Muslims." However, even the most liberal, or bad, Muslims usually give up alcohol for the month. The few I know who are fasting don't smoke or have any sexual intercourse during the fasting period. The time of the fast changes every day according to the time the sun rises and sets. Television channels list the names of all the major cities in Turkey, and as the fasting time ends, the name of the city is highlighted so people know when they can eat, drink, and have sex. Businessmen order their dinners and have them delivered within minutes of the breaking of the fast. In Tarsus, a cannon (Yes, a real one!) is shot at the beginning and end of the fasting time to alert everyone that it's either time to begin or to end fasting. In addition, some people even pay for a wake-up service. There are drummers who go to individual homes and wake everyone up in time to have a big meal before the sun rises and the fasting begins. This means that those of us who are *not* fasting are still awakened by the drums and the cannons.

All of this will end at sundown when the *bayram* or holiday begins. There are two major Muslim bayrams. The first is the Seker Bayram, and the second is the Kurban Bayram. Before the Seker Bayram, street vendors sell candies on every corner. Shops and stands are open until after midnight, because people are out buying the things they'll need to celebrate. *Seker Bayram* means "sugar holiday." Families buy new clothes and exchange presents. To me, it seemed like the Islamic version of Christmas. Relatives all congregate at the home of the eldest male in the family. They sprinkle lemon cologne all over everyone, and children go from house to house to get candy—an Islamic form of Halloween. When the bayram begins, there is, at least at first, a period of excess to make up for the fasting. Women will uncover a little more of their skin, and couples will be free to hold hands in public again. From what I've heard, the "after fasting" sales in Istanbul are almost as good as Macy's after Christmas extravaganza. It's always good when things get back to normal. Ramazan makes Lent, the Christian period of fasting preceding Easter, look like a walk in the park.

CHAPTER 9

Settling In

We are here on earth to do good to others. What
the others are here for, I don't know.
—W. H. Auden

My first Ramazan and Seker Bayram had come and gone, and it was time to get back into my daily routine. This meant going back to school and putting the finishing touches on my new home. Perhaps because my astrological sign is Taurus or perhaps because my childhood home was so unwelcoming, I have always placed great emphasis on my physical surroundings. I want them to be classic, elegant, and sumptuous, yet comfortable. I want them to reflect the kind of woman I am. My apartment was in a historical building. It had enormous rooms and twenty-two-foot ceilings. Clearly, making this seem cozy was going to require some serious efforts on my part.

Debbie, my new friend and mentor, was a teacher from Arizona. She and her husband had been on the international teaching circuit for years, and they provided me with a wealth of information on what to do, where to go, and what to buy in order to create the homey, yet sophisticated atmosphere I wanted. They maintained that no one who comes to Turkey should pass up the opportunity to buy handmade Turkish carpets. Just the thought of having a "magic carpet" of my own made my heart skip a beat. They had purchased several carpets from a shop in Adana and offered to take me there the following Saturday. I was so excited that sleep eluded me.

When Saturday morning finally arrived, we hopped into their old jalopy and headed off for Adana. The carpet shop was owned by a man named Serkan. He was breathtakingly handsome, spoke English, and gave me my first taste of true Turkish hospitality. When we arrived, the first thing he asked was if we were hungry and, with the efficiency of someone who had done this many times before, summoned his staff to set up the table, order the food, and open the wine. I was enthralled. We spent hours eating, drinking, and looking at carpets. I felt like a kid in a candy store.

The carpets were all handmade and exquisite, and even though he guaranteed that he was selling them to us at his buying price, I only had enough money to pay for a fraction of what I wanted to buy. "No problem," said Serkan, "take as many as you want, and you can pay me when you have the money." *Unbelievable*, I thought. This man, whom I had only just met, was willing to take a small deposit, let me drive off with three exquisite carpets, and wait for the rest of his money until I could afford to pay him. *He doesn't even know my last name!* I thought. We shook hands, kissed each other on the cheek, and Debbie, Dennis, and I, and my beautiful new carpets, headed back to Tarsus.

I was intrigued by Serkan. He was everything I imagined a Turkish man would be. I took advantage of the fact that I owed him money to make weekly visits to his shop. He agreed to help teach me Turkish, and in exchange, I would help him with his English. Long after I finished paying for my carpets, I eagerly continued my Saturday afternoon visits to his shop. We sat side by side and used the translator on my computer to carry on lengthy conversations on a variety of topics. I was mesmerized by him. Eventually, I became closer to him than even Debbie and Dennis had been.

He invited me to his family's home and introduced me to his youngest brother, three sisters, his mother and dad, and his wife. Before long, I was spending almost as much time at his family's home as I had spent at the carpet shop, and thankfully, because I was a foreigner, I was not governed by the same rules as a Turkish woman. I sat in the main room with the men, while the women were relegated to the kitchen. We drank wine and raki, smoked, and ate while the women scurried around serving us. It made me extremely uncomfortable, but all my attempts to help were immediately squashed. The women served us and cleaned up and, when we were all sated, finally sat on the floor of the kitchen and ate their meal. It was all new to me, and I gradually came to enjoy my hallowed position. It didn't, however, keep me from wondering why these women allowed themselves to be treated like second-class citizens. This was one of the cultural differences that, in reality, proved to be exactly as I had imagined it would be, if not worse!

The months went by, and I continued to be a frequent visitor to their family home. Eventually, I learned there was a third brother named Metin. From what I could gather, he was definitely the black sheep of the family. At age seventeen, he had married his fourteen-year-old childhood sweetheart. He had also worked in the carpet shop and was dubbed a party animal by Serkan. Before I had arrived in Turkey, most of their carpet business had been with soldiers from the Incerlik NATO base. Because Metin was considered to be the most charismatic of the three brothers, he was the one who was responsible for closing the difficult sales. If the buyer was a woman, this might involve taking her out for dinner, taking her on a tour of another city, or simply spending time schmoozing with her.

After Metin had been married only a short time, Serkan asked him to take an American woman, who had put a deposit on ten thousand dollars' worth of carpets, to Cappadocia to close the sale. Although he was reluctant, in this culture, the oldest brother calls the shots; as such, Metin was required to do what he asked. Unfortunately,

Metin's new wife discovered what he had done and, shortly thereafter, filed for divorce. It was an extremely painful time for all parties concerned. Metin tried to use their infant son, Yilmaz, as a bargaining chip. He hoped that by demanding custody of him, he could force his wife to drop the divorce proceedings. Unfortunately for him, it didn't work. His young wife agreed to let Metin keep Yilmaz in exchange for granting her a divorce.

Yilmaz, as he looks today, and me.

For the next eight years, Metin sank into a dark abyss. He gambled and drank to excess, and the only women he associated with were prostitutes. The charismatic party boy became a disgrace to his entire family, and they basically wiped their hands of him. He had fallen from grace, and his family had very little, if anything, to do with him. He moved to Istanbul where his ex-wife lived, and Yilmaz, his infant son, remained in Adana with his family. His insanity escalated, and he began to have problems with the law. Everyone thought that it was only a matter of time before Metin would either be killed in a drunken brawl or commit suicide. As I listened to his family retell stories of his escapades, I couldn't help but think that, in the past, this kind of a man would have been just what the doctor ordered for me—a wounded bird with a broken wing who I could rescue, rehabilitate, and save. Fortunately, at this point, I still hadn't met Metin.

CHAPTER 10

Sertaç to the Rescue

Things are temporary, relationships last forever. Nothing can
replace the time we spend investing in the life of another.
—Roy Lessin

Several months had passed since I had arrived in Turkey, and I was beginning to feel a little smug about my ability to "navigate solo" here. After all, I was learning the language, I had been adopted by Serkan's family, and I knew Tarsus like the back of my hand. It was time, I reasoned, to spread my wings. Since I was a child, Constantinople, now Istanbul, had been a place that I was only able to read about in books. It seemed magical, exotic, and alluring, and it had me under its spell. I had visions of magic carpets, harem girls, and genies jumping out of magic lamps. When I arrived in Turkey, I made a promise to myself that within a year I would be as familiar with Istanbul as I was with Chicago, Illinois. This, of course, would involve making several trips there—at least once a month, I thought. No time like the present to start.

I bought my ticket, and off I went to continue my great adventure. All of my friends warned me about going alone, but their pleas fell on deaf ears. After all, I was an independent American woman spreading her wings and living her dream. What did they know? As it turned out, I should have listened. Ironically, the time I spent in Istanbul was without incident. I visited the Blue Mosque, Dolmabahçe Palace, the cistern, and Topkapi Palace. I took a boat tour on the Bosphorus and shopped in the Grand Bazaar until I nearly dropped. It wasn't until my plane landed back in Adana that things started to unravel.

Everything had gone according to schedule. The plane took off and landed on time, and I was looking forward to a relaxing Sunday evening at home, "adjusting my attitude" before returning to school the next morning. I was waiting patiently at the luggage carousel in Adana for my bag to arrive when I saw a man load one onto his trolley that was remarkably similar to mine. I seriously thought about going up to him and asking him to let me check the luggage tag. However, I was leery about striking up a conversation with a strange man. From a distance, I watched carefully as he appeared to be double-checking the numbers on his claim check. He seemed satisfied the other two bags were his, so I assumed the red one was as well. It wasn't until I was the only person left at the carousel that I realized he had indeed mistaken my bag for his. Granted, normally, this would have been a problem but not a cause for major panic. However, I had shopped extensively in Istanbul, and after mentally reviewing what was in my bag, I immediately went from being mildly inconvenienced to full-blown panic. Among other things, I bought an incredible white leather and fox-trimmed coat for which I paid a thousand dollars. In addition, I had taken an expensive pinstripe mink vest to wear because I knew evenings in Istanbul would be chilly. I also knew I'd suffocate if I wore it back to Adana, so it was folded nicely and put inside the new coat. There were several other items, which brought the total value of things in this bag to approximately $5,500.

As I stood at the carousel, dumbfounded and incredulous, an airline employee approached me to ask if there was a problem. I was so stunned I couldn't speak. No one spoke English, so I quickly phoned Gulcan, a good friend and fellow teacher at the college, and asked her to explain what had happened. The woman in the lost-and-found department insisted that it was too late, and she was entirely too busy to deal with what she considered to be a minor problem. She had the name of the culprit who had taken my bag, because he had left his behind. In spite of this, she refused to contact him and told me to return the next day. She dismissed me with the wave of her hand, and another airline employee walked me to a cab. He told the driver I was having a bad night, which, at this point, made him the master of understatement. I asked him to take me to the bus station so I could catch a bus back to Tarsus. The airline employee told me that after having had such a traumatic experience, I should let the taxi driver take me back to Tarsus. The cost of the cab would have been seventy-five Turkish liras. I told him that was too much, and he lowered the price to sixty—still too much. However, since we didn't seem to be communicating very well, and the taxi driver seemed adamant about taking me to Tarsus, I called my friend Gulcan again, and, once again, she told the driver to take me to the bus station and drop me off.

Perhaps because he didn't understand or perhaps because he was angry about losing a hefty fare, he did *not* drive me into the bus station itself. Instead, he dropped me off on the edge of the highway where I found myself the only foreigner among a group of at least twenty-five Turkish peasants who had just finished working in the fields. My heart beat faster as I clutched my purse and pulled it close to me. My eyes were cast downward to avoid making any eye contact that could be misconstrued by the throng of men ogling me. Eventually, another taxi stopped, and I ran toward it so quickly I'm not sure my feet even touched the ground. Much to my chagrin, we began the negotiations all over again! Finally, he wore me out. He came down to fifty liras, which, although still expensive, seemed reasonable in the wake of all that had just happened. I jumped into the cab, and, before I could digest what was happening, I was followed by three Turkish field hands.

Once again, my heart beat faster, and my mind was reeling as I tried to grasp the meaning of what was going on. Apparently, they were going in the same direction and were more than happy to have their fare paid by a foreigner. I was so shocked by this turn of events that it took me a few minutes to realize that in addition to losing my suitcase, I had left the bag of fragile gifts I was carrying by hand in the airline lost-and-found office. I was down to one bag, and I was riding in the pitch-black Turkish countryside with four strange men, none of whom spoke English. I was certain the end was near. Once again, I called Gulcan so that someone would know what happened to me if worse came to worst. She spoke to the driver and told him my tale of woe. He reduced the fare by another five liras. After dropping the Turkish workers in a neighboring city, the driver took me directly to my front door. I crawled up the steps to my apartment, dragging my one case behind me, completely dazed by the evening's events.

In the meantime, Gulcan called the airport and asked to speak to the woman with whom I had filed the report. She told Gulcan she was too busy to speak to her and hung up. Gulcan called me and said, "Don't worry, this happens all the time. Go to bed and get a good night's sleep." *Fat chance*, I thought!

I dropped off the only bag I had left and walked down the hall to see my neighbors. I knocked on their door and asked for a cigarette. They were astounded and said, "But you don't smoke."

In a voice that was barely audible, I said, "I'm smoking now." After one cigarette and serious contemplation, I decided I needed a bigger gun to go to bat for me. This is definitely a patriarchal society, and, sorry to say, I needed a man to handle this one. I called my adopted Turkish family and asked Sertaç, the youngest son, to help me. Within less than ten minutes, he had called the airport, gotten the name of the man with my bag, found his phone number, and called him. The stranger told Sertaç that the airport had just called, and he really wasn't sure what they were talking about.

He said, "There must be some confusion. I have my bag."

Sertaç called me and asked what was in the bag. When I told him the total value of the items inside, he realized why the stranger who took it was feigning ignorance. He phoned the stranger again and told him he had thirty minutes to get the bag back to the airport or suffer some dire consequences.

Sertaç called me again and told me he would be coming to Tarsus to get me. He couldn't claim the bag without me, so we would go back to the Adana airport together. He also told me he had been drinking. In Turkey, one does *not* drink and drive. Therefore, he said he would have to be a little creative. By this time, I was having a lot of trouble concentrating on anything, so when I thought he said, "I am sending a taxi," I went downstairs and waited in front of my building for the taxi to arrive. Within less than five minutes, a taxi came screaming down the road. The driver slammed on the brakes and screeched to a halt right in front of my building. He flung open the door and beckoned me to get in, so naturally, I thought he was coming for me. I jumped into the cab, and he stepped on the gas but headed off in the wrong direction.

As we tried to communicate, I asked why Sertaç wasn't in the cab. No response. After traveling a few more blocks, he asked, "Nereye?" which means "Where to?" It suddenly occurred to me that perhaps the driver hadn't spoken to Sertaç and simply stopped and picked me up because I was waiting at the taxi stand. I immediately called Sertaç again and asked why he wasn't in the cab. He asked where in the hell I was. I responded that I was in the cab that he had sent. He told me he was ten minutes away and was in his car! Because he had been drinking, he had hired a taxi driver to drive him to my apartment. He was coming with a taxi driver *not* sending a taxi. I handed the driver my cell phone so Sertaç could tell him to stop the cab and let me out. I walked the eight or nine blocks back to my apartment, went upstairs, and stayed put until I received the call from Sertaç to come down again.

A few minutes later, the car arrived. Sertaç, his cousin, and the driver were in the car. All of us headed for the airport. We parked the car and marched en masse to the airline counter. When we explained why we were there, we were told we would have to come back the next day because the person who had the key to the office had already gone home. I don't know enough Turkish to explain what happened next, but in less than fifteen minutes, both bags were back in my possession and the airline people were bowing and scraping and apologizing profusely.

As we headed back to Tarsus, I thought about all of the things that had happened within the past two weeks. I had lost all of my documents, and they were returned intact. I had lost all of my credit cards, and they were returned. I had lost my luggage, and it was recovered. I had gotten into two cabs with complete strangers in the middle of the night and in the middle of nowhere and had arrived at my destination without incident. I could only conclude I was truly surrounded by a bevy of angels who were looking out for me.

The next day I went to the school library to check out a book. Coincidentally, the librarian recommended a book titled *Tales from the Expat Harem, Foreign Women in Modern Turkey*. Jokingly, I told her, "I bet could add a chapter or two to that book that would make the others pale by comparison."

I decided that having that book put into my hands was another instance of divine intervention. Perhaps this meant that I should start keeping a journal about my experiences so that someday I would be able to put them on paper. My next "impossible dream" was beginning to take shape. That day I made a promise that before my time in Turkey was finished, I would write a book. I began to believe that everything that was happening to me here was divinely inspired. No one person, I reasoned, could be as lucky as I had been. Now, I wake up every morning and count my blessings. Eight years ago, I never could have imagined being anywhere other than Milwaukee, Wisconsin. I don't know what I did to deserve this opportunity, but I am eternally grateful for the chance to be here. The lesson to be learned is don't be afraid to dream and dream *big*!

CHAPTER 11

The Good, the Bad, and the Ugly

Some days you're the dog; some days you're the hydrant.

—Unknown

As I went over my notes and tried to decide what I should and shouldn't include in this book, I came across a few e-mails that stood out and that I felt deserved to be included. It seemed like the best way of sharing what happened to me in my first two years here. Some of the things in these e-mails will be mentioned in other parts of the book because they were instrumental in my evolution. As I read them again, they took me back to 2005 and 2006 when everything was so new and exciting. I hope they will help you experience the feelings I felt as I wrote them.

The following message was sent in November 2005:

Dear Friends and Loved Ones,

I must begin by apologizing for the amount of time that's passed since my last mail. The city of Tarsus has had some problems with their phone lines which impacted on the Internet service. The only computers working were on campus, and they all have Turkish keyboards. Need I say more? In addition, I couldn't access my address book. At long last, we seem to be "reconnected" so it's time to share the good, bad, and the very unusual events which have transpired in the last few weeks.

Last Thursday, November 10, was Ataturk Death Day. At 9:05 a.m., 67 years ago, Kemal Ataturk died. He's responsible for bringing secularism to Turkey. One can't adequately express to someone who hasn't been here the honor Turkey has bestowed on this man. His picture is in every office, building, classroom, etc. in the country. Every courtyard, city square, school campus, shopping mall, etc. has a statue of him. Reproductions of actual photos of him adorn fences, walls, airports, hospitals, etc. Clocks in Dolmabahçe Palace, the place where he died, all read 9:05. On the actual day of his death, known as Death Day, there are solemn parades, speeches, dedications, and more speeches. All movement literally comes to a grinding halt. We sang the Turkish national anthem three times that day. This continues for an entire week. It's the most incredible display of respect and admiration I've ever seen. He is the George Washington, Abraham Lincoln, Martin Luther King Jr., and JFK of this country all rolled into one! I'm tempted to add, and then he sprouted wings and flew but, in Turkey, criticism of him is punishable by a jail term! How's that for patriotism?

For the "good part" of this mail, I have another incredible "it could only happen in Turkey" story. Yesterday was the three-month anniversary of my arrival in Turkey. It seems like so much longer than that. I decided to celebrate, so the day, quite naturally, included the purchase of a special gift for me! I bought the most garish camel-shaped lamp that one could possibly imagine. It looks like it came right out of a sultan's tent complete with gilding and fake jewels. The camel and I are currently bonding, but that's not where the story is going. I had a lovely day and went to bed last night not knowing anything was amiss. As I headed to lunch today, one of the security guards cut me off at the pass and pulled me aside to hand me a small package. In it were all of my documents! My platinum credit card, driver's license,

ATM cash card, insurance papers, and on and on and on! My first question was, "Where in the world did you get these?" In his broken English, he explained that everything was found in the street last night by two young boys who figured out I worked at the college by going through the documents. They returned everything intact! I can't say things like this only happen in small cities in the south of Turkey, but I'm thinking it! I can definitely say that is the best part of this mail.

Now, lest you think everything here is always a bed of roses, let me tell you about some of the interesting "challenges" I've experienced lately. In addition to having Internet problems all week long, I had an electrical fire in my apartment last week. The building I live in is between 150 and 200 years old. *Very* charming but filled with the kind of problems one would expect to find in a 200-year-old building. Electrical sockets fall out of the wall, and there definitely aren't enough of them. As a result, I was running my TV, computer, printer, heater, and three lamps off of one socket. I created a Rube Goldberg type of connection with adapters stacked one on top of the other. My ingenuity finally caught up with me when the cords ignited. I have always believed in angels, but the experience surrounding this event was almost bone chilling. At approximately 3:00 a.m., every light in my kitchen went on. It was so bright it woke me up. Naturally, I thought there was an intruder in the apartment, so I prepared to meet him head on. When I got to the kitchen, I saw the sparks coming from the cords in the living room. I'd like to send a special thank you to whoever sent the angel to turn on my lights!

As if all of this wasn't bad enough, I discovered I have mice! It's either an entire family or one *really* big one who poops a lot. I tore my kitchen apart and even washed under the sink with bleach. While doing all this, I realized there was a false floor under my sink. I tried to rearrange the boards to close up the openings and pounded my finger so hard the knuckle was purple.

Haste was making waste, so I took a break to go outside and repot some of my plants. My garden trowel had disappeared, so I weeded the roses instead and ended up bleeding all over because of the thorns. My roses are nearly five feet tall, and the thorns are the size of small finishing nails. Finally, I admitted that in order to do anything else in the way of gardening I was going to have to replace my trowel. My neighbor and I went out to try to find one. We spent three hours and no luck. We didn't know the Turkish word for *garden trowel*, so we were offered everything from a shovel to a dustpan. The language continues to be a challenge. We were never successful but did finally manage to get some mouse poison. Hopefully, the mouse will have the courtesy to die in the hall or courtyard rather than my apartment.

After that, we went to Gima, the only supermarket in a city of nearly three hundred thousand people. People cruise the aisles at Gima like we do the malls in the US.

They're so in awe of all of the products being displayed that there are frequent hit-and-run accidents in the aisles. I have personally been rear-ended more than once! I was experiencing a domestic streak—not sure where it came from, but I decided to try to cook my first meal. As I looked at my choices, lamb seemed like the best option. Since I've never cooked lamb, I wasn't sure what to ask for. However, since I didn't know the Turkish for any of the pieces, it didn't seem to make much difference. I pointed at a leg and tried to explain that it was way too large. I asked if they could cut it, but instead of getting it in one piece, they chopped it all into little pieces and pounded it to death. After spending fifteen minutes at the meat counter trying to get it sorted out, I called a Turkish friend on my cell phone to translate for me. It was too late. I had lamb pieces. I wasn't sure exactly how to cook a leg of lamb, and I certainly didn't know what to do with what appeared to be pieces of stew meat. When I tried to ask for cooking directions, they misunderstood and thought I wanted to buy an oven! Just another little adventure.

When I finally returned to my apartment and decided to throw the meat in the oven, I realized I had never used it and wasn't sure how to turn it on. This may sound absurd, but one can't assume that simply because they've used an oven or washing machine in the States, they'll be able to use them here. To make matters worse, I had a gas stove and had visions of blowing up the entire house. Sweat was pouring off my brow, and my hands trembled with each additional attempt to start the oven. After three different opinions, from three different neighbors, on how and where to ignite it, we finally hit the jackpot. The lamb was delicious. Another small miracle.

Every day is a great adventure. The people continue to amaze me with their kindness, and all my little "challenges" are character-building activities. The weather is glorious. Evenings and mornings are chilly, but the days are filled with sunshine and brilliant blue skies. There are oranges on the trees, lemons growing on my balcony, and roses the size of baseballs. God truly smiled on Turkey when it comes to weather.

I miss all of you and wish I could share more of what's happening here with you. I could truly write a book about daily life here. Who knows? Perhaps that will be the next great adventure.

Love and hugs to all,
Barbara

The following message was sent in January 2006:

Dear Friends,

My husband, John, was here for a little over a month. We spent his last two weeks traveling, and I continued once he left. The day after John's plane took off I was still in Istanbul, and the Ministry of Education announced they were postponing the reopening of school for another week due to the bad weather in Istanbul and the east. Since the snow ended on Friday, I really didn't understand the logic behind their decision, but far be it from me to question their wisdom. With another week off, I decided to go west.

I still hadn't been to Antalya, one of the hottest tourist spots in Turkey, so off I went, moving effortlessly from place to place and adopting new families wherever I stopped. People take care of me in every city I visit and treat me like a princess. I step off a bus wondering where and when I will find a taxi. Invariably, someone comes to my aid, runs two blocks to get a cab for me, puts my luggage in the trunk, and refuses a two-lira tip (less than two American dollars). I check into a five-star hotel and end up getting a $350 room for $75. (I spend more when I raid the mini bar at midnight.)

I have made friends in every city I have visited who insist on being my protectors when I arrive. (Since they're all tall, handsome, and between twenty-eight and thirty-six, things could be *much* worse!) I have learned how to get a bargain in the Grand Bazaar. (Most people spend a lifetime trying to do this.) In fact, on this last trip I bought another pair of gorgeous hand-embroidered boots. I am now the proud owner of three pairs—green, black, and pink! They retail in Chicago for $450. The first price I was quoted here was $300 (still a deal, they said). I ended up paying 100 YTL (about $80). On this last trip, I paid 85 YTL (less than $60). By the time I'm done, they'll be paying *me* to wear them.

Antalya was gorgeous. It looks like Genoa, Italy, only it's more sophisticated, more charming, and cleaner. The *balik* (fish) is not to be believed. I took a bus from Antalya to Konya to shorten the length of the trip home. I phoned one of my friends there. He and three buddies took me to the most incredible restaurant I've ever seen, and at my age, that's saying a lot. We drove down a one-lane gravel road that overlooked a raging river and waterfall. We crossed a swinging footbridge made out of tree branches that were tied together with rope. Since I can't swim, this was an act of true faith. We ordered fish which were scooped out of the river in front of us and grilled (still kicking) next to our table. The women were baking bread in an outdoor oven that had to be two hundred years old. The only electricity was produced by the waterfall. It ran down the mountainside and turned two huge millstones. Talk about walking back in time! If I hadn't seen it with my own eyes, I wouldn't have believed it.

I returned to Tarsus late Monday night and have spent two days in Adana since I returned. My adopted family there is determined to teach me how to cook Turkish specialties! This will be a real challenge. My first real lesson will be tomorrow.

On February 22, my friend Margery will arrive in Istanbul, so I will be returning again! My adopted family at the hotel is so excited; they're giving us the largest room (for the price of a small double) and have even offered to take us to one of the best fish restaurants Saturday night to celebrate our friendship.

Monday I'll return to school, after a month-long hiatus. I am anxious to see my students and am relatively certain that the decision has been made to move me with them next year. We've decided we like each other so much we want to stay together, so I'll be teaching grade eight instead of seven. My gorgeous principal, no one should work for someone so handsome, said, "Anything you want, my honey!" Another incredible relationship.

In spite of all this, I may have saved the best for last. I love every aspect of my apartment except the fact that I don't have a bathtub. John always says, "If you don't ask, you don't get." I thought nothing ventured, nothing gained, and before John and I left on our travels, I e-mailed the man in charge of the buildings and grounds at the school pleading my case and telling him how much I'd really love to have a tub. (He already agreed to let me have two pink walls, which are gorgeous.) Yesterday, he appeared with one of the workers and a tape measure. This is a *really* good sign! I'm hoping that in the *very* near future I will be relaxing at the end of each day in a nice, comfortable tub. I think I'll continue to dream big and pray that it will be pink and include a Jacuzzi.

Now I ask you, does life get any better than this? As I usually say before closing each e-mail, I don't know what I did to deserve this incredible opportunity. In six months

I've experienced more than most people do in a lifetime. I continue to pinch myself as a reality check. If this is a dream, I don't want to wake up. I sincerely pray that all of you will have the chance to live your dream, whatever it may be. I believe anything is possible, and no one knows what the future holds in store. Think positive, be grateful for every blessing you have, and believe you deserve to have what you want. I thought I was headed for Italy, and look what happened. Obviously, God thought I would enjoy Turkey more, and I have to believe He was right!

Love, light, and positive energy to all of you,
The Barbara

This message was sent in February 2006:

Dear Friends,

On Wednesday, February 22, my friend Margery flew in to Istanbul. She was traveling in this part of the world and decided to spend two weeks in Tarsus visiting with me and doing some volunteer work at the school. She is one of the most elegant woman I have ever had the pleasure of knowing. She teaches etiquette classes, and no one could be more suited for this. She instructs everyone from business executives to young children on the fine art of dining. She teaches her students which fork to use, when and why, and how to conduct oneself in an appropriate manner whether dining with royalty, the CEO of a company, or family and friends. She is the pinnacle of good taste and decorum. On Friday, February 24, I flew to Istanbul to meet her, and the "Great Adventures of The Margery and The Barbara" began. (Most ESL students put *the* in front of all proper nouns whether it's necessary or not. Consequently, I am now referred to as The Barbara.)

Friday night we had dinner at Kalamar, one of my favorite Istanbul fish restaurants. It's in Kumkapi, and whenever I'm in Istanbul, I never miss an opportunity to have at least one dinner there. The first question the waiters asked was, "Where are the men?" When we answered, "Yok" (i.e., there aren't any), they felt compelled to act as the stand-ins! They anticipated our every need! They began by throwing fresh red rose petals all over our table and sending out a waiter to get warm bread because they had just served the last batch and didn't want to disappoint us by giving us cold bread. The dinner was sensational, and the service was even better. I'd describe it in more detail, but I want to get to the highlight of the evening. During dinner, I was telling Margery about the sheer beauty of watching Turkish men dance. I described what I had seen at our school's Christmas party and told her it was the most sensual and erotic thing I'd ever witnessed. People here are uninhibited about their bodies, and everybody seems to be graceful and have rhythm. I swear they all emerge from the womb dancing.

Just then, Margery said, "Turn around. There are men dancing behind you as we speak."

I turned to see a man standing on a chair, waving his arms in the air, and thrusting his pelvis back and forth. I told Margery that definitely wasn't the kind of dancing I was talking about. The waiter overheard us and explained that this was a group of gay men, and we should stay to see what was coming next. We had every intention of leaving, but weren't quite fast enough.

All of a sudden, the lights went out and the waiters started lighting rockets and flares. They were exploding *inside* the restaurant and made it sound and feel like we were in the middle of a war zone. When the smoke cleared, we saw a man descending the stairs. He was dressed from head to toe in black satin, covered with silver sequins, and wearing a veil that hid all but his dark black eyes and bushy eyebrows. He moved gracefully from one table to the next, ending up in the middle of the restaurant where he did a male version of a belly dance that, even I had to admit, was so unexpected, intriguing, and mesmerizing that we stayed and watched the entire show. Only in Istanbul! They arrest people in Wisconsin for this kind of thing!

On the way back to the hotel, I told Margery that my next goal was going to be to learn to do some of these traditional Turkish dances. They're wonderful, but it's not the "do your own thing" kind of dancing we do in the States. Everyone is moving in the same direction and in unison. Obviously, some kind of instruction is needed. As I always say, be careful what you wish for because you may get it!

The next day we shopped until we dropped and were very proud of the fact that two women alone held their own in the Grand Bazaar. We bought a few things, at very good prices, and went back to get ready for dinner. The manager of the hotel sent me an e-mail informing me that I had won a prize for being the most frequent guest at the hotel. He told me we were going to have a calamari dinner and all the trimmings, which I assumed would be served in the hotel restaurant. *Wrong!* We returned to learn that we would be picked up at 7:30 and were going to be taken to a popular local restaurant, which featured dinner and a Turkish floor show. The dinner was mouthwateringly delicious, and the entertainment was incredible. At one point in the show, they pulled people out of the audience to participate in the dancing. You guessed it! The next thing we knew, The Margery and The Barbara were on the stage in Istanbul getting Turkish dancing lessons. We went back to the table, and I reminded Margery about our conversation the night before! Funny how the universe works. Before the end of the show, a woman from Russia was asked to come back on the stage. She came to our table and insisted that Margery and I to join her. The three of us were the grand finale of the evening. We danced our hearts out and had the time of our lives. Certainly an evening to remember!

Upon arriving in Tarsus, Margery began to get a taste of the Turkish hospitality I find so heartwarming. She's been invited for coffee, had people deliver food to her door, been invited into stranger's homes, and, in general, been treated like a princess. She has visited 106 countries in her life and yet finds there is something truly unique about the way foreign women in Turkey are revered. We've been invited to a friend's beach house for the weekend. I told John we would be doing some fishing. He laughed and wanted to know if I'd be baiting my own hook. I responded, "Honey, in this country I don't even shell my own pistachios!"

Margery has also personally experienced the relationship building part of the shopping experience. She was interested in buying a small carpet for a friend of hers in Milwaukee. We went to the handsome carpet dealer who serves tea and baklava to get it. After enjoying a salad, some wine, an Adana kebab, and over an hour and a half of pleasant conversation, Margery finally whispered, "When can I buy the carpet?" We had a similar experience in Tarsus. We went into a small shop to buy some costume jewelry. Margery spent five dollars, and I spent about twelve dollars. We ended up staying for wonderful conversation (limited since it was in Turkish), several Cokes, and a *very* unusual pizza. It was a "deluxe" version and included yellow kernels of corn, mustard, catsup, and mayonnaise. It was actually quite good! When we left, Margery exclaimed, "Never before have I had so much fun spending five dollars."

The high point of our week so far was our visit to Adana yesterday. I have Thursday afternoons free, so after my last class, we hopped a bus into the city. Metin picked us up at the bus station and drove us to the carpet shop. After that, he invited us to his home so Margery could meet his family. To be invited to a person's home is considered total acceptance. You truly become a part of the extended family (and this family literally extends across nations). The home is in "old Adana" in a Kurdish neighborhood. The trip from "new Adana" to "old" takes only minutes in time. However, it's a journey that transports one into another world. Both Margery and I agree that we've never been anywhere quite like this. We walked up the concrete stairs and stepped back in time. When grandma, who is eighty-nine, learned that I was scheduled for foot surgery, she was appalled. She insisted she could fix the problem, thereby saving me from undergoing another surgical procedure. Metin's three sisters assisted her like experienced nurses in an operating room. They brought a huge tub of hot water and soap, an egg, and some salt into the living room. They tore up an old sheet and made a bandage. Without going into all the details, I'm now walking around with dried egg and salt, and a homemade bandage on my foot.

Grandma says that after three days, I'll be just fine. This morning I showed my cleaning lady what grandma had done. She smiled from ear to ear and said, "Turkçe medicine." I guess I must be a little crazy myself, because I'm following grandma's instructions implicitly. I asked Margery to please let me know if and when I start smelling like rotten eggs. I'll do whatever it takes to avoid the surgery. (This isn't one that I chose!)

After this, Metin's mother read our fortunes in our Turkish coffee grounds. It was amazing! This is the third time she's done it for me so I *know* this woman has extraordinary powers that are connecting her to some kind of universal energy. She has told me things no one else in the world knows about me. I waited to see what Margery's reactions would be. When the tears started to run down her cheeks, I realized Fatima, Metin's mother, had hit a chord with her as well. Before we left their home, we were all kissing, hugging, and crying, but these were tears of joy, not sadness, that we were sharing with our new family.

It's unusual for people to have this kind of a connection, and it usually takes a lifetime to build. However, as I've said before, there's something magical going on here, and if you're open to it, you can enjoy boundless joy and unconditional acceptance. I had to travel across the world and wait fifty-eight years to get in touch with this part of my soul. It's made the experience unforgettable and irreplaceable!

It's intoxicating when a bus driver you met two months ago remembers your name or when someone you don't know, and will never see again, will stop whatever they're doing to help you, even if they have to walk you three or four blocks to do it. A cab driver won't take your money because the trip wasn't long enough. A bellboy won't take a tip because he feels helping you is his job. You spend an hour in a shop browsing, drinking tea, eating snacks, and decide not to make a purchase. The owner smiles, says "no problem," invites you back, and means it! You leave a tip in a restaurant, and the waiter chases you down the street to give it back to you. You meet a man on the bus, and he refuses to let you pay because you're a guest in his country. You visit a doctor; he performs a service or gives you a prescription and doesn't charge you. Someone stops you on the street just to tell you that you look beautiful. A woman asks to use the bathroom and a man says, "Please wait, and I will go and prepare it for you."

If I needed someone to stand in front of a speeding truck or offer to throw himself between an armed terrorist and myself, I would definitely ask one of my male Turkish friends. If I'm ever going to find the inner goddess that all women search for, this is definitely going to be the place! The question I keep asking myself is, "How did a little old school teacher from Racine, Wisconsin, end up here?" Since I don't believe in coincidences, I am certain that there are some important lessons I'm supposed to learn here. I simply have to wait for the plan to unfold.

Tomorrow we're off to the beach and more of the "unknown." The adventure continues.

Love and hugs to all of you,
The Barbara

CHAPTER 12

Princess Treatment

Life is a journey, and if you open yourself up to its possibilities, it can take you in directions you never imagined. A rich life doesn't necessarily take you there wrapped in cashmere, weighted with gold, or traveling first-class. You need not compete with anyone else. Your journey is your own.

—Suze Orman

This message was sent in March 2006

Dear Friends,

My husband has been calling me the Turkish Princess almost since I arrived in Turkey, and slowly but surely, the moniker has caught on, not only on campus but among my Turkish friends. As I thought about some of the things that happened this last week, I realized they're right! I am enjoying a "princess experience," so I wanted to share some of the highlights.

My friend Marjorie from Milwaukee paid me a visit, and we spent her last weekend in Turkey together in Istanbul. Once again, it was a grand adventure, filled with good food, wonderful friends, and incredible shopping. The high point this trip had to be our Saturday evening dinner. It was at the mansion of one of Margery's friends. We were treated like visiting royalty.

A driver picked us up and took us to Uskudar, a suburb on the Asian side of Istanbul. The home was built in 1888 and has been lovingly restored. It is a stone's throw from the Bosphorus, which means only the likes of Bill Gates can afford to live there. It was filled with museum-quality artifacts because the lady of the house is an art history major with a real love of archaeology. I admired a bowl of round objects on the cocktail table, which appeared to be some kind of rock candy. Fortunately, I didn't try to pop one into my mouth. I inquired about them and learned they

were rocks, not rock candy, uncovered at a prehistoric dig and given to the family as a gift. Icons adorned the walls, as well as antique French mirrors and chandeliers, gilded furniture, and priceless paintings. Walking from room to room was a feast for the senses. As it turns out, the man of the house is in charge of all the tourism and construction for one of the wealthiest families in Turkey.

The other dinner guest was the woman who designs all of the family's gardens. They have six homes in Turkey, so it's more than enough to keep her busy. Dinner was Turkish and included all of my favorite things and more! It was served by one of her staff, and this is the first time I actually saw someone press an invisible buzzer to summon the help. I was in awe. There are incredible details too numerous to mention. Suffice it to say, it was one of the nicest evenings I've spent in Turkey, and that's saying a lot. We were four princesses enjoying all the best the "good life" has to offer. Thank goodness I took Margery's etiquette class!

Monday morning the custodial staff at the school installed my bathtub. Up until now, I have only had a shower. Now that I know I'm staying at least two more years, I decided I had to try to convince the powers that be that I deserved a "higher standard of bathing" facility. Everyone already calls me the Turkish Princess, so I reasoned I might as well live like one. Bathtubs are not the norm here, so I was fully prepared to pay for it, and the installation, out of my own pocket. Much to my surprise, not only did the school agree to put it in, but they paid for it as well. What

a treat! I've learned that I can live without elevators, microwaves, toasters and toaster ovens, even my car! However, there are two things that are absolutely essential. One is a bathtub; the other is access to my music! This is information I didn't have six months ago, so the learning continues!

Today Fazilet, my cleaning lady, was here. She does some knitting in her spare time to make extra money. I ordered two sweaters from her last month, and they were wonderful. I was all set to order another one today when, much to my surprise, she arrived and handed me a bag. She said, "Hediye," which means gift. She knit me a beautiful long-sleeved pink V-neck. It brought tears to my eyes to think that she probably spent all the money I gave her last week to buy yarn that would be my favorite color! Needless to say, I ordered another sweater.

Later this morning, Fazilet phoned the water company and ordered another fifteen-liter bottle of water for me. When the man delivered it, she stopped him at the door, paid him, and carried it to the storage point. I asked her what in the world she was doing. It's *his* job to carry that huge thing. She looked at me and said, "And it's *my* job to protect *you*. No man will ever have a chance to look into your sleeping room while I'm here!"

She also explained that the reason she washes all my underwear by hand is that no one should see my underwear except her! If she does it in the washing machine across the hall, she's afraid someone might get a peek at them. If this isn't princess treatment, my name isn't Lawrence of Turkey!

I have a class this morning, so I have to say good-bye for now. Perhaps this e-mail isn't as exciting as some of the others because it deals with the way people have treated me here rather than some of the great adventures I've had. However, I wanted to share it because it's a way of helping me remember why I love it here so much and why I feel so at home. After spending two weeks here, Margery has a genuine understanding of why this is such a special place. My hope is that the little vignettes I share with you will give you a glimpse of the very special people in this very special place.

Lots of love, hugs, and warm wishes,
The Barbara aka Turkish Princess

Chapter 13

The Great Imposter

Real friends are those who when you've made an absolute food
of yourself, don't feel that you've done a permanent job.
—Abraham Lincoln

It was March 2006, and I finally admitted that I could no longer ignore the nagging pain in my right foot. For years, I had worn high heels in spite of all the warnings I was given by a bevy of doctors, and as a result, I struggled constantly with foot problems. If it wasn't the right foot, it was the left; if it wasn't the left, it was the right. I had already had several surgeries as a result of my predilection, and when I arrived in Turkey, nothing changed even though I no longer had a car and walked for miles every day. Consequently, I shouldn't have been surprised when my feet could no longer support me and were screaming for immediate attention. I conferred with one of the best orthopedic surgeons in Adana, and he assured me that a simple surgical procedure could correct the problem. It was settled. I would go to Adana on March 25, 2006, and have the surgery.

When I told my Turkish friends what I had planned to do, they were shocked. They warned me against going to a Turkish hospital alone and insisted that in this country a woman going to a hospital by herself was just asking for trouble. They said it wasn't safe and told me that anything could happen. "Utter nonsense," I protested. After all, I countered, I had moved across the world by myself and was doing quite nicely. Besides, I wouldn't think of imposing on anyone by asking them to give up their weekend with their family in order to spend it with me in the hospital. Consequently, in the early hours of Saturday, March 25, 2006, I hopped into a cab, alone, and headed to Adana. Little did I know, at the time, that the decision to go to alone would unleash a chain of events that would change my life forever.

Gulcan, my trusted Turkish friend, had arranged for my transportation and instructed the cab driver who was taking me to go into the hospital with me to make sure I got to the registration desk without incident. Only minutes after we arrived, things were going so smoothly. I paid the driver, thanked him, and sent him on his way. The woman behind the desk and I were communicating without any problem, and things seemed to be going very well. Less than ten minutes after I had arrived, we had completed the paperwork. I got into the elevator, and she pressed the button that would deliver me to my floor. The elevator doors opened, and I got out, never suspecting for a moment the danger that was lying in wait, literally, just around the corner.

A man standing outside the elevator doors led me to my room. Since he seemed to have been waiting to greet me when the elevator doors opened, I naturally assumed that he was there to greet me and guide me through the preliminaries. I looked at his name tag. His name was Mehmet. He ushered me to my room and reappeared moments later with a hospital gown. As he held the gown out to me, I tried to explain that I had my own pajamas and would prefer to wear them. Permission was denied. As he motioned for me to undress, I had the presence of mind to try to find out why he was in my room. When it was obvious that we were not communicating, I took out my cell phone and started to call one of my Turkish friends to translate. Mehmet grabbed the phone out of my hand, turned it off, and threw it onto the chair in the corner of the room. Next he took my dictionary and looked up the word *yardim*, which means "helper." He used hand gestures to indicate that he was there to assist me. Nothing, in this country, had ever happened to give me any reason to suspect that his intentions were anything but honorable.

I automatically assumed he was either a male nurse or, at the very least, a nurse's aide, so reluctantly, I followed his instructions.

I stood with the hospital gown in my hand and waited for him to leave. When it was apparent he wasn't going anywhere, I turned my back to him, slipped the gown over my head and, hiding under the safety of it, started to unbutton my blouse. In seconds, he was in front of me, trying to hasten the process. When I pushed his hands away from my blouse, he grabbed for the button on my slacks. When I pushed his hands away again, he started unzipping my boots. As he grabbed my foot and pulled it closer to him, I slipped and fell against the wall. Now I was lying on the floor staring up at this man who I assumed was there to help me. I was struggling to maintain my composure and to make sense of what was going on. I was shocked and frightened by his aggressiveness, but, perhaps to avert the sense of panic that was overtaking me, I tried to convince myself that we were just having a communication breakdown. I stood naked, except for my panties, clutching the hospital gown, which was at least three sizes too big, trying to figure out how to fasten the snaps.

Once again, Mehmet feigned assistance as he opened and closed the gown a couple of times, exposing my naked body. He mumbled something in Turkish, the meaning of which was clear, even though I had never heard the words before. He thought I had a great body. Now he wanted my panties! I couldn't figure out why I had to remove my underwear for foot surgery, so I clung to them for dear life, while he pulled and tugged trying to remove them. He was taller and much stronger than I, so my efforts were in vain. He tore at them with a force too great for me to overcome. I lay on the bed short of breath with tears welling up in my eyes. Was I hallucinating, or was this another thirty-year-old man making sexual advances toward me?

I tried to convince myself that I was imagining all of this, and at the same time, I wondered where the other nurses were. Why did it appear as though I was the only person on this floor of the hospital? Why wasn't there anyone here to help me? What was he going to do next? How was I going to protect myself against him? Moments later, he returned with my panties. He stood at the edge of the bed holding my underwear, which was now inside out and upside down because of the way he had torn them off of me. I tried, unsuccessfully, to grab them back from him. He pushed me down on the bed, grabbed for my ankle, and began to put the underwear back on me. As he pulled my panties up and into position, he brushed his hand deftly back and forth over forbidden territory. Now I was convinced he was a sexual predator and wondered what to do next.

I couldn't see the buzzer to call a nurse. If there was one, what would I say? No one spoke English. If I tried to tell someone what he did, what would he say and do? Clearly, he had the advantage. Another young man in blue appeared to wheel me to X-ray, and Mehmet left the room. At this point, I had been in my room for less than fifteen minutes. My surgery was scheduled for nine o'clock. I was going down for my chest X-ray, and because we had to wait for the film, time would pass. I tried to write this horrible incident off as my just reward for not listening to my friends who warned me about going to the hospital alone. With a little bit of luck, I thought, I would never see that horrible man again.

It was only moments after I returned to my room that the door opened, and Mehmet came in again. This time he was rolling an EKG machine. Still thinking he was a nurse or, at the very least, a nurse's aide, I was nervous but assumed that now he had a job to do. And with nine o'clock quickly approaching, nothing else could happen. The anesthesiologist was in the hall, and Mehmet was behaving in a very businesslike manner. When he opened the front of my hospital gown and started moving my breasts from one side to another, I assumed it was to attach the electrodes on the EKG machine. Wrong again! In seconds, a woman entered the room and performed the EKG. It was at this point that I realized I wasn't hallucinating. Mehmet was a sexual deviant posing as a professional, and he was molesting me in front of the very people who were supposed to be caring for me in this hospital.

To say I was in trouble was putting it mildly. They would be injecting the sleeping serum in moments, and I would be unconscious. I began to worry whether I would ever wake up again. I leaped from the bed with the determination of a woman fighting for her life and retrieved my phone from the chair. My hands were shaking violently, and I had trouble holding onto the phone. I fumbled but managed to turn it back on and dial a number. I needed help, and I needed it urgently. I called the only person I knew who lived close enough to the hospital to get there before I was wheeled into surgery.

Metin, the black sheep of Serkan's family, and the self-proclaimed party animal, was home from Istanbul for a short holiday. Without telling him exactly what had happened, I begged him to drop whatever he was doing and to come to the hospital immediately.

While we barely knew each other, he knew that I had become very close to the other members of his family and, because of this, he didn't hesitate to come. He arrived minutes later and could see that I was trembling and had been crying. Immediately, he asked what had happened. His English was minimal, so I wasn't sure I could even find the words to tell him. In addition, he's Kurdish, and in his culture, sexual misconduct is not looked upon lightly. Although the government doles out stiff sentences, honor killings are still commonplace. He badgered me relentlessly until I finally agreed to tell him on the condition he would keep my secret. I explained that I didn't want to cause a problem, and because it was my word against Mehmet's, I didn't think there was any point in trying to prove what he did or didn't do. Clearly, Metin didn't agree. He listened intently as I described what had happened. Then, suddenly, without uttering a word, he flew out of the room. Seconds after I finished speaking with him, the sleeping serum kicked in. I was out like a light and wheeled off to surgery.

It was several hours later when I finally woke up and found Metin and his mother standing guard in my room. He was adamant that his mother should stay with me to guarantee that nothing more happened. I told him I appreciated the thought, but I believed Mehmet's shift had ended and I was out of danger. Unlike Turkish people, I really don't enjoy having visitors when I'm ill. Although this was something neither Metin nor his mother could understand, they honored my wishes and left. Sometime later that afternoon, Metin returned with his eighty-nine-year-old grandmother, two of his three sisters, a sister-in-law, and a niece. By now, they all knew what had happened and insisted on staying to protect me.

My doctor came to see me, saw the throng of women in my room, and asked what in the world was going on. As Metin explained, the color left his face, and his expression spoke volumes. He stormed out of the room, promising to take care of the problem immediately. I was exhausted, so once again, I asked Metin to please take his family and go home. I was certain the worst was over. What I didn't know at this point was that not only had Metin alerted the entire hospital staff to what had happened, but he had also obtained Mehmet's home phone number and called him. In addition, my doctor had spoken to the director of the hospital who had, in turn, telephoned the personnel supervisor. I fell asleep not knowing that a storm of unimaginable force was brewing.

I'm not sure how much time had passed when I awoke again to find four people standing over me. Mehmet, Mehmet's pregnant wife, a floor nurse, and another young man in blue who I still assumed was part of the nursing staff were all standing next to my bed. Since no one spoke English, I wasn't sure if the hospital "staff person" was there to protect me or to defend Mehmet. Mehmet's young, incredibly stunning and pregnant wife was closest to me. She must, I assumed, have wanted to know what had happened. It was certainly one of the many questions running through my mind at the moment. Once again, I picked up my mobile and phoned Metin. I told him I wanted all of the people out of my room, and I wanted them out *now*! If they wanted to discuss anything, they were going to have to get a translator and offer me some kind of protection. I gave the phone to Mehmet's wife, and Metin told them to leave.

Moments later Metin, the consummate party animal, arrived again! He came into my room and told me that as he got off the elevator,

Mehmet pulled him aside and said, "I did something really, really wrong, and I'm so very sorry." He apparently brought his wife along to help plead his case. The director of the hospital, who was also the hospital owner's sister and in charge of hospital personnel, had driven in from her home and was threatening to fire Mehmet. Metin came back into my room twice to tell me that Mehmet would probably lose his job unless I changed my story and let him off the hook. I was furious! I told Metin that it was difficult enough to tell him, a veritable stranger, everything that had happened, and I reminded him that I had shared the information in strictest confidence and that he was the one who had reported the incident. Now that everyone in the hospital knew about it, I was not going to soften any of the details. It was not up to me whether Mehmet would lose his job. He was going to have to suffer the consequences of his actions. Metin said his only concern was Mehmet's pregnant wife. By this time, I was beginning to regret that I had confided in Metin. However, the fact that Mehmet's wife was pregnant was of little or no consequence to me. As far as I was concerned, what he had done was unforgivable, and he was going to have to deal with the consequences regardless of what they were. Finally, Metin agreed and left.

In the course of the next few hours, I had to repeat my story several more times. As a result, Mehmet was supposedly fired and escorted from the building. By nine thirty, more than fourteen hours since I checked into the hospital, a translator was finally stationed outside my door. At ten o'clock, Metin's father and mother arrived. His father used to work in a Turkish prison and still carried a gun. He came into my room, opened his coat to reveal it, and asked, "*Nerede Mehmet?* (Where's Mehmet?)" I think it was more of a show of moral support than a real threat, but the gesture warmed my heart. My extended Turkish family was defending my honor like I was really one of their own. At midnight, Metin and another man appeared, once again, at the foot of my bed to make sure everything was all right. Although I felt safer as a result of the protection Metin and his family promised me, sleep never came, and I counted the hours until I could leave the hospital and go back to Tarsus.

The next morning, the translator, who was a young single Turkish woman, was still shaking as a result of what had happened to me. She couldn't believe it. I was in one of the best private hospitals in Adana, and I had been sexually assaulted. She was wondering, out loud, what had gone wrong. I was wondering the same thing. Why wasn't there anyone stationed on the floor to greet me? Who was supposed to deliver my hospital gown and help me get into it? Why wasn't there a translator there to assist me? How could Mehmet have spent that much time in a patient's room without someone wondering where he was and what he was doing? Why wasn't someone in charge of showing me the room and explaining there was a refrigerator, closet, and, most importantly, a call buzzer? Who was in charge, and where were they?

At the time, I had absolutely no idea that this incident would turn out to be the catalyst for most of the changes that would take place in my life over the next six years. I am blessed that I didn't know what was coming, or I probably would have jumped on the next plane headed back for the United States. It would have been so much easier to return to my life as I knew it. Instead, I unknowingly chose a path that would lead me into the depths of hell and back out again.

I would experience disappointments, heartache, and emotional suffering on a level that I never imagined possible.

In order to regain some sense of balance and normalcy in my life, I would be forced to face my innermost fears and to exorcise the demons that had held me hostage since my childhood. More than once, I've asked myself if it was worth it. However, if I had taken the easy way out, I would have lost the chance to become the woman I am today. What would happen in the next six years would change the course of my life forever. It's at this point that my journey of discovery really begins, and ironically, none of it could have happened without the black sheep of his family and consummate party animal, Metin.

CHAPTER 14

The Decision

Success is not measured by what a man accomplishes, but by
the opposition he has encountered and the courage with which
he has maintained the struggle against overwhelming odds.
—Charles Lindbergh

I returned to Tarsus still shell-shocked by what had happened to me in Adana. I spent hours discussing it with my best friend, Debbie, and trying to decide what course of action, if any, I should take. What, I wondered, were my options? What had happened to me was, in my mind, heinous. The incident was something that was still hard for me to wrap my mind around. I had nightmares in which I relived the whole thing over and over. Shouldn't the perpetrator face some kind of punishment for what he had done?

I could try to find an attorney and take him to court, but that would be difficult and expensive. How much was I willing to spend to defend my rights as a woman alone in this country? What were the chances that a foreigner with limited resources could win a court case against one of the most prestigious and powerful private hospitals in southeastern Turkey? My friends and the school administration warned me that my situation could easily be compared to David's battle with Goliath. Need I say more? The chances of winning a court battle were overwhelmingly against me.

On the other hand, could I live with myself knowing that I let a man capable of such behavior walk away without suffering any consequences at all? The brazenness with which he attacked me led me to believe that he had done this type of thing before. My friends confided in me that if the same thing had happened to a young Turkish virgin, it was unlikely the incident would ever even have been reported because it would have unleashed a maelstrom of unimaginable proportions. I struggled with my dilemma for days and finally decided that if I didn't stand up for what I believe in, I stood for nothing at all.

A few days later I found myself on one of busiest streets in Adana waiting for an attorney's driver to pick me up and take me to his office to discuss a sexual assault lawsuit. Mustafa Cortancioglu, the attorney, was referred to me by an American friend who lived in Adana. She had been a bilingual teacher and ESL teacher in Arizona when she met a Turkish man, fell in love, married him, and eventually moved to Adana. After fifteen years, she decided she wanted a divorce. Turkish divorce is a nightmare. Being sentenced to murder would probably be less agonizing. Mustafa was her neighbor as well as her attorney. His English was perfect, she claimed, and his demeanor the epitome of professionalism. In addition, he fashioned himself to be a champion of women's rights—just the kind of attorney I was looking for. As it turned out, Patrice was right on all counts, and I was grateful for the introduction.

Debbie and I had driven to Adana together, and both she and Mustafa listened intently as I explained, one more time, exactly what had happened at the hospital that fateful day. After I finished, Mustafa outlined my options and the fact that if I did take legal action there could be not one, but two cases involved. One would be civil, the other criminal. Therefore, my first decision must be if I wanted to proceed, and if I did, I had to decide whether to start one or two actions. He also explained that in spite of the fact that there were no actual witnesses to the assault, he felt that I had at least a 70 percent chance of winning in court based on the fact that there was a "confession" and Mehmet had been terminated immediately as a result. I listened carefully as Mustafa explained the process involved in going to court in Turkey.

The differences between what happens (or doesn't happen) here and in the United States are daunting. The biggest of these appeared to be reluctance on the part of witnesses to testify. They are summoned, and then it's common for them to call or visit the person who has brought the suit to try to dissuade them from continuing. The potential witness will discuss the disgrace to the family and the possibility of losing their jobs or, in the most extreme cases, their lives. In addition, Mustafa explained, I could expect harassment from parents of my students who work with the hospital or one of their many suppliers. I could expect the hospital to exert pressure of its own by hiring people to threaten or follow me and to knock on my door and telephone at all hours of the day and night. I could expect local newspaper and television coverage at first and ultimately, because I am an American, national, if not international, coverage. I could expect pressure from my school because they wouldn't want their name linked with a woman who was involved in a sexual scandal. I could expect to have people "fill in their own scenarios" regarding what I did or didn't do to "encourage" this kind of "attack." I could expect stares and finger-pointing wherever I went because my photo would be splashed across front pages of newspapers and television screens. To say these were deterrents would be putting it mildly.

I began to ask myself why I was sitting in his office. Mehmet had supposedly been fired, and because of this, according to Mustafa, I was already a heroine. He praised my "courage" and willingness to come forward. He said, "No matter what happens from this point forward, you are a heroine. You have the support of every man and woman in this country, because this could have happened to their sister, their wife, their daughter." He went on to explain that, at this point, even if I did nothing more, I was already victorious. His next question was the one that went right to my core. He looked me straight in the eyes and asked me, "So what do *you* want?"

It occurred to me that I really didn't know. Mustafa explained that a case like this shouldn't be pursued in the hope of getting a huge financial settlement. At best, the settlement would be between $7,500 and $11,000, and the process could take up to three years. His expenses would be subtracted from that amount, so money would definitely *not* be the reason to go to court. In addition, he reminded me, once again, of all the potential problems and encouraged me to take a few days to think things over before making my final decision.

His driver was waiting downstairs to take Debbie and me one and a half blocks to the doctor's office. It doesn't sound like a great distance, but when you're using "sticks" (as they call crutches here), it may as well have been a mile and a half. As soon as we were settled in the car again and on our way back to Tarsus, I began to bounce ideas off of Debbie. What did she think about me becoming a crusader for women's rights in Turkey? What about a patient's advocate? Would, or could, anything I did actually change the system? Were the risks really as ominous as Mustafa had suggested? Who was responsible for what had happened to me? Was Mehmet's punishment sufficient? Why did I go to an attorney in the first place?

After three full days, and much serious soul-searching, I came to some conclusions. First, and perhaps most importantly, I felt Mehmet had received sufficient punishment. He saw a window of opportunity that never should have existed, and he took advantage of it. As a result, he lost his job and, I felt certain, had done irreparable damage to his name, his family's name, and his marriage. I didn't feel putting him in prison would have served any real purpose. If a student is injured while I'm on duty at school, my director would have to answer for my negligence. I believed that the hospital, and its director, should share the same level of culpability. If an employee does something illegal or unethical while he is working, he should be terminated, but, I reasoned, the larger question of ultimate responsibility should have to be answered by the people in charge.

Amazingly, once I left the hospital, neither the hospital nor its director had any further contact with me or anyone at my place of employment. At the very least, I expected a follow up letter, visit, or phone call. I saw my surgeon on the Tuesday after Debbie and I left Mustafa's office, and he never mentioned the incident. In Turkey, ignoring negative events is one manner of handling them. If we don't speak of something, it's as though it never happened. The fog was lifting, and the many hours I had spent contemplating the situation were allowing me to put the events into perspective and view them more clearly. My anger shifted to the hospital and its administrators who, I believe, failed miserably. There was definitely negligence on their part the day of the surgery, and their lack of follow up only served to make a very bad situation even worse. At this point, the question of who was responsible had been answered.

Getting to that point was a big step in the crystallization of my thought processes. The fog that had consumed me since all of this happened was beginning to lift, and things were starting to look a lot less murky. Mustafa had referred to me again and again as a heroine. At one point, I countered and said, "I was a very reluctant heroine." I would never have stepped forward if Metin hadn't literally opened the door and shouted the truth to the world. Once the proverbial cat was out of the bag, what choice was there? I could retract my statement and look like a raving lunatic who had been hallucinating, or I could stand firm and act with conviction and integrity no matter how embarrassing the situation was. I hadn't done anything wrong, and Metin was giving me an opportunity to do something really courageous by reporting the incident and seeing that Mehmet was punished. As I would learn later, this incident was not something even a middle-aged, married Turkish woman would have reported. The societal taboos attached to the topic are simply too overwhelming to be confronted. The only one who could ever blow the whistle, so to speak, in an instance like this would have to be a foreigner. As I thought about the accolades I had already received, I realized how misplaced they were. They really belong to Metin for clearly seeing the difference between right and wrong and forcing me to confront Mehmet.

Now the question was no longer simply, "What did Barbara want?" It was much more complicated than that. First, how could I make the hospital accept responsibility for what had happened? How could I ensure that policies would be changed to prevent this kind of thing from ever happening again? Was it business as usual at that hospital today? Had the incident been recorded anywhere, or is Barbara Lawrence a nonentity in the hospital's records? What could I do to make sure that the next woman who decides to check into a hospital by herself doesn't go through something like this?

Attorney Mustafa Cortancioglu

CHAPTER 15

The Second Visit to Mustafa's Office

Self-trust is the first secret of success.

—Anonymous

On Wednesday, April 5, 2006, I called Mustafa, the attorney, and asked whether it would be beneficial for him to speak to Metin before I decided on a final course of action. "Absolutely," he said, so my friend Gulcan and I left for Adana at noon the next day. She dropped me off at the carpet shop where Metin was waiting for me. We got into his car and drove the short distance to Mustafa's office.

Although Mustafa and Metin both speak English, they obviously communicated more effectively in Turkish. As I result, I sat quietly and listened while Metin related my story. As he spoke, his voice got louder, and his facial expressions became more intense. He gestured frantically and at one point stood up and, from what I was able to gather, asked Mustafa why he couldn't understand the gravity of what had happened to me. Mustafa was the epitome of professionalism as he sat seemingly unmoved by Metin's show of emotions and interjected a question here and there for clarification. Our time was short because I had an appointment to have my stitches removed. We thanked Mustafa for his time and prepared to leave. Mustafa reminded me again that whatever I decided to do, I had already done something noble as far as he was concerned. He expressed sincere concern over the state of the legal system in Turkey. He believed it's antiquated and ineffective, and he has vowed to do whatever he could to try to improve it. With all of this in mind, Metin and I left.

Metin took me to my doctor's office and stood next to me while my stitches were removed. He was not about to leave me alone in another hospital. He drove me to the train station where Gulcan picked me up. After introducing them, Gulcan and I headed back to Tarsus.

My friend Gulcan is a stunning thirty-six-year-old Turkish teacher who worked with me at the college. She and her husband, Alper, had become dear friends. They visited me the night of my surgery and, after learning what happened, stayed in Adana overnight so they'd be close enough to help me if I anything else happened. Gulcan wears sexy low-rise jeans and tank tops under her figure-hugging blouses. Her make-up is perfect, and her outward appearance would seem to indicate she is a modern woman in every sense of the word. However, as we headed home, she began to question the wisdom of filing a lawsuit. She wondered what would prompt someone to take on a system that's riddled with corruption and that seemed hopelessly flawed. Why, she queried, would I want to tell and retell my story? Wouldn't it be far better to bury the memory of the incident in the recesses of my mind and get on with my life? As I listened, it seemed to me that while the questions were being asked of me, she was actually examining her own conscience. What would she do in a situation like this?

I listened until she had exhausted her line of questioning. As I explained my reasoning, it became clear that there was a fundamental aspect I also had overlooked. It was the importance of taking a stand, drawing a line in the sand. My friend Kate Allister once wrote to me, "If you don't take a stand on something like this, you don't stand for anything." I talked about the importance of blazing a trail for women's rights in Turkey. I talked about accountability and the fact that many major institutions in this country don't seem to have any. Gulcan agreed. I told her about Mustafa's desire to work on a case that could be one of many that might begin to modernize the court system. That also seemed to pique her interest. And, of course, my sincere desire to help Metin and his family by giving any settlement I might win to them is something with which no one could find fault. These were, in my mind, logical reasons to proceed.

However, there was something more that I hadn't verbalized until that moment. In fact, I'm quite sure it wasn't even a conscious thought. Suddenly, without any warning, I said, "And I need to get my power back." I caught my breath, and my first thought was, *Where did that come from?* My second thought was, *I just spoke a great truth.* What renders a woman more powerless than what happened to me? Yes, there were a multitude of altruistic reasons for starting a legal action. A few of them are outlined above. However, as I struggled to decide the best course of action, the one aspect I overlooked was the impact this would have on me. Mehmet (the man) and the hospital (an anonymous bureaucratic structure) had stripped me of my power, literally and figuratively. In order to become whole again, I must regain it. The outcome really shouldn't matter.

Before Gulcan dropped me off, she agreed that this was something I must do. In fact, she admitted, this was probably something she and her family should have done when the same hospital nearly killed her sister two years prior to this. When I asked what happened and why they didn't sue, she didn't have a definitive answer. She heaved the same heavy sigh I've heard so often and said, "Perhaps because this is Turkey."

People living here share her frustration. They too feel powerless when it comes to confronting the bureaucratic institutions whether it's the courts, hospitals, or schools. I believe Gulcan's thinking has changed somewhat as a result of our conversation, and hopefully, she will change someone else's. It's a very small beginning, but it is a beginning.

Later that evening, I sent Gulcan the following e-mail.

Dear Gulcan,

Thank you again for taking me back and forth to Adana today. It certainly made my life a lot easier, and I'm sure it took some of the stress off Metin as well. I went out walking after I got home and purchased a lovely new Teflon-coated pan for making Turkish coffee. It's wonderful to know that, at my age, a person can still learn something new every day. I wrote Rana and thanked her for yet another insight!

While I was walking, I thought a lot about our conversation on the way back to Tarsus. I want you to be the first to know that I have decided to pursue the case. The more we talked, the more I realized how important it is for me to take a stand. I think people my age start thinking about what kind of a legacy they're going to leave behind. My life has been dedicated to my students. This is going to give me an opportunity to go outside the box and make an impact, be it good or bad, in a new arena. I've decided there are too many reasons why I should do this to turn my back and run away from it. I will plant my feet firmly and face whatever comes my way. I believe strongly that I was in that hospital for reasons that I will never fully understand and which go

far beyond my surgery. Wish me well, dear friend, for I will
sign the papers tomorrow.

Love,
Barbara

I believe we all have an obligation to leave this world a little better
than we found it when we entered. The majority of my life has
been dedicated to helping children. My years with the fashion
company expanded my horizons and gave me new and incredible
opportunities to continue to help people. It also gave me the courage
to do the unthinkable and move to Turkey. By pursuing this case, I
had a wonderful opportunity to leave a legacy here as well. What a
gift! I had to make the best of it.

CHAPTER 16

The First Court Appearance

Far better it is to dare mighty things, to win glorious triumphs,
even though checkered with failure than to take rank with those
poor spirits who neither enjoy much nor suffer much because
they live in the gray twilight that knows not victory nor defeat.
—Theodore Roosevelt

I marked the eight month anniversary of my arrival in Turkey by officially beginning the legal proceedings necessary to file a civil and criminal lawsuit in this country. I decided to sue the hospital in civil court and Mehmet in criminal court. I decided to pursue in spite of what the doomsayers had told me. I believed it was the right thing to do and had come too far to turn around now. Metin accompanied Mustafa and me as we began our journey through the Turkish legal system. It was laborious at best.

After spending almost two hours in the courthouse waiting to see the prosecuting attorney, we headed for the main police station. By this point, I had already repeated my story more times than I cared to recount. Each time it was to another official. They were all men, and they anxiously hung on my every word. I'm not sure if it was the fact that I was a foreigner in their country or the fact that the case involved a sexual assault that captured their attention, but it was clear that every person who heard my story felt my pain. It was also clear that they thought filing the lawsuits was a courageous thing to do. All of them remarked that this could just as easily have happened to their sisters, their mothers, or their wives.

At the police station, I waited patiently while Mustafa read the entire report in Turkish to a man whose typing skills left a lot to be desired as he entered it on the computer. By the time they finished interviewing me, we had already invested more than six hours in the process. It was after seven o'clock in the evening, so Metin decided to return the next day to give his testimony. Mustafa was going to Mersin to see his son, so he offered to take me back to Tarsus. If that day was any indication of what was to come, I anticipated a long and involved process.

It was Tuesday afternoon of the last week in May when I received a call from the school translator. She told me she had a summons from the police department. It said that I must appear at the police stations at eight thirty the next morning. She was calling to ask if I wanted her to go with me. I told her I didn't have any idea why they wanted to see me again, but I was sure it had to do with my court case. I phoned Mustafa immediately, and he assured me it was just a routine procedure. We both had busy schedules on Wednesday, so we agreed to meet after work at five thirty, which was the earliest it was convenient for both of us, and go to the police station together.

The next morning, Wednesday, I received three frantic calls from the school business administrator. She insisted that I go to the station immediately, or the police were going to come and physically pick me up. Everyone in the administration building was in a state of sheer panic. They had visions of paddy wagons pulling up to the gates of our hallowed institution and taking one of their respected foreign teachers off in handcuffs. I phoned Mustafa immediately, and he dropped everything and came to pick me up. We rushed to the police station as though my very survival depended on getting there within the hour. We arrived breathless and in record time, only to learn that it was a false alarm. It was due to a clerical error on the part of the court in Adana. The police were involved to guarantee that I knew I had to testify in Mehmet's criminal case the next day. They gave me the choice of doing it in Tarsus on Wednesday or going to Adana on Thursday and facing the accused. *Are they kidding?* I thought. I wanted my day in court, and I wanted to look the accused straight in the eyes. I'd be there with bells on!

116

Early Thursday morning, June 1, my good friend Debbie and I once again left for Adana. We planned to meet Mustafa at his office and walk to the courthouse together. When we arrived, we were shocked to learn that Mehmet had been arrested on April 21 and had already spent two months in prison. He was arrested a week after I filed the original complaint. Because the crime he was accused of wasn't of a violent enough nature, he was later released because his wife was delivering their baby. My attorney's partner didn't agree with that decision and went over the police chief's head to the next jurisdiction. The prosecutor agreed with him, and Mehmet was arrested and imprisoned again. He had been picked up immediately and imprisoned until the day of the court proceedings.

At 9:15 we walked the two blocks to the courthouse and met a representative from the US Embassy. She arrived with her translator, and we all entered southeastern Turkey's Hall of Justice. We didn't know exactly what time we would be called, so we waited in the lawyers' lounge. The furnishings were sumptuous, but the room itself was suffocating and smoke filled. It was overflowing with people waiting for their cases to come to trial. Attorneys are required to wear heavy green-and-black robes reminiscent of what was worn in twentieth-century England. The only thing missing were the powdered wigs. The judges wear long black robes with luxurious red satin and gold braided trim. The temperature was in the mid nineties, and the air conditioning was totally inadequate. It was stifling, and the sweat was pouring off of me.

Finally, Mustafa's cell phone rang, and we were called down to the courtroom. That hall was also filled to capacity. There were uniformed and undercover police everywhere. Each of them carried at least one loaded weapon. Most of them had a sidearm, but several also carried fully loaded automatic weapons. It was clear that they were prepared for trouble. My mind was racing as I wondered how I had gotten into this predicament. The only US court I had ever been in was divorce court. I had never even gotten a speeding ticket. *Is this what it felt like to stand up for one's principles?* I wondered.

All of Mehmet's family was there, as well as the hospital owner, director, head of personnel, and assorted staff members. When the courtroom door opened, I was shocked and disheartened to learn that neither my friend Debbie, the Embassy representative, nor Metin would be allowed to enter. The Embassy representative was supposed to guarantee my rights were not violated. I began to question whether I actually had any rights here. Because of the nature of the case, it was a closed courtroom. Witnesses were brought in one at a time and then ushered out. Mehmet's feet and hands were shackled, and he was brought in by three armed soldiers who stood directly behind him the entire time. He stared straight ahead hardly daring to blink.

I shot steely glances at him, hoping to catch his eye. I was prepared to look into them, because, for me, they were the inroads into the depths of hell. He was a disgusting human being, and my skin bristled at the mere sight of him. He was exactly as I remembered him, and suddenly, the urge to jump up and extract my pound of flesh from him was almost uncontrollable.

He was represented by two attorneys. Mustafa and his partner sat with me. There was a translator present who, unfortunately, was so inadequate that he had to be replaced during the lunch recess. His job was to translate my English to Turkish for the court and not, unfortunately, to translate the Turkish for me. As a result, all of the proceedings were, for me, literally lost in translation.

During the lunch recess, I learned that the hospital representatives had tried again to convince Metin he would be much better off if he decided not to testify. They offered to help him with whatever he needed if he would agree either to leave immediately or to change his story. When he told them he intended to stay and to tell the truth, Mehmet's family took over. They threatened him physically and told him they would kill him if he testified for me. Metin warned me in advance that we should expect this, so he was prepared with several supporters of his own. However, after violent threats were aimed at several of them, it was clear Metin needed reinforcements. He called his family, and before the lunch recess ended, the sides were evened out.

When we left the courthouse and walked back to Mustafa's office for the recess, we were completely surrounded by friends of the family. I thought this kind of thing only happened in mafia movies. Debbie and I giggled nervously and likened what was happening to us to an episode of *The Sopranos*. We tried to make light of it, but Metin wasn't laughing. When I saw the grave look in his eyes, I knew this wasn't a game.

We returned after lunch for three more hours of testimony. The hospital called a parade of witnesses who were not encumbered by the truth. It's a good thing I didn't understand what was being said. I wouldn't have reacted well to the gross distortions of what actually had happened. Metin was the last witness, and our testimonies matched word for word. I guess that's what happens when people tell the truth. If there was any chance of justice being done here, it would be done because of Metin's testimony.

According to the translator, a case of this nature should be heard and decided in two hours. We had already had five hours of testimony, and the court would convene again on July 27. The hospital wanted to call more witnesses. If Mehmet was convicted, they would be ruined. If they didn't actually lose their license, the scandal would destroy them. They definitely had a vested interest in trying to prove that I was either hallucinating or lying.

When we left the courtroom, I felt like we were running the gauntlet. Heavily armed police separated the families. They ushered the two sides out through different doors and followed us until we were safely out of sight. For days after that, it still felt like it was all a bad dream. I sat completely dumbfounded as the hospital witnesses told one lie after another. Although my Turkish was limited, there was no mistaking the fact that the hospital owner had lined up a parade of witnesses intended to make me look like a liar or, worse yet, a crazy old lady who had imagined all of this because of the drugs she'd been given before her surgery.

The translator who was fired after the morning session told me, "Even if you lose, you've already won." No one else would have come this far. Corruption and dishonesty run rampant here. Money doesn't talk; it screams! Once again, I likened this to the story of David and Goliath, but this match was clearly much more unequal than that. I resigned myself to the fact that we might lose and I might end up having spent a substantial amount of money to fight for my principles. However, I've said it before, and I'll say it again: if we don't stand up for what's right, we don't stand for anything.

I was grateful that I had friends like Metin who shared this philosophy. After we were safely back in Mustafa's office, Metin asked me if I knew how many people were willing to lay down their lives for me on that day. At first, I thought he was being dramatic. When he shared specific details of what had happened, I realized how naïve I had been. This really is another world, and the rules, when there are rules, are completely different. I thought the Universe sent me here to be a teacher, but at that point I felt more like a student. I was humbled by my powerlessness in the face of all this corruption. I had nothing but the truth and Metin on my side. If life were fair, that should have been enough. However, it's painfully clear that here right is not might.

CHAPTER 17

Return to Normalcy

Life is like riding in a taxi. Whether you're going
anywhere or not, the meter keeps ticking.
—John C. Maxwell

I returned to school the next day totally numb as a result of my day in court. It was Friday, and I was looking forward to the end of the day so I could retreat to my apartment and try to process everything that had happened in the past twenty-four hours. We end each week with an outdoor assembly and flag ceremony. When I arrived, I was told the vice-principal was looking for me. I didn't know why and hoped there wasn't any more bad news on the horizon. To my delight, she informed me that my request had been granted, and on June 8 I would be traveling to western Turkey with twenty-two of my best students for a long weekend. Western Turkey is where most of the famous historical sites are located, and up to this point, I hadn't had an opportunity to visit that part of the country. This was great news and a wonderful way to end an otherwise not-so-wonderful week.

The end of the year was rapidly approaching, and there were a million things that needed to be done. In addition to grades, which are a whole different story on this side of the world, there were the trips, the school carnival, the debate, commencement, and a farewell ball to look forward to. As I reflected on the past nine and a half months, I continued to count my blessings. I had laughed and cried, sang and danced, traveled, felt powerful and powerless, learned a new language, made new friends, and had adventures too numerous to detail here. What more could I want? I was grateful for all my good fortune. I was still trying to figure out what I had done to deserve all of this. I ended each day with a special prayer in which I prayed that all of my friends and family would be given a chance to live their dreams as well.

The court was recessing for the summer, so there wouldn't be any more news regarding my case until the fall. In many respects, that was a relief. It had consumed a great deal of my time and energy, so knowing that I had a three- or four-month respite from the pressures of having to deal with it was a gift in and of itself. The long arms of the hospital reached many places in Adana and Tarsus. Alumni came to the school to ask the director why he couldn't control his teachers—i.e., me! They were appalled that a foreigner would have the audacity to take on an institution as powerful and well connected as this hospital. The director of the college called me into his office twice to warn me of the perils involved in the course I was taking. Unfortunately, the die was cast. I had laid out all of my cards, and there was no recanting at this point. I was determined to let nature take its course, and I would suffer the consequences, whatever they might be.

On June 21, I boarded a plane for Milwaukee and headed back home. I fought back the tears as I got into the cab and prepared to leave the campus. The custodial staff was already busy cleaning the buildings, which were now empty. When they saw me approach the cab to leave, they stopped what they were doing and ran to the windows. They blew kisses, waved good-bye, and yelled for me to hurry back. In addition, Rudvan, my tailor and good friend, made a special point to go to work early that morning. He passed the school every day on the way to his shop. He knew I was leaving that day, and he also wanted to give me a warm send off. Tarsus and its people had me under their spell. I was intoxicated. It was my home now, and they were my people. At that moment, I couldn't imagine ever leaving that place.

CHAPTER 18

Back to School

The Chinese word for crisis consists of two characters: one
represents "danger" and the other "hidden opportunity."
—M. Scott Peck

I returned to school the following August after two rather hair-raising experiences. One had to do with some skin cancer that was found on my forehead, and the other had to do with my mammogram.

Initially, I wasn't particularly concerned about the skin cancer on my forehead. I had been a sun worshipper all of my life. If I wasn't chocolate brown by Easter, something was wrong, and achieving that goal in Wisconsin was always a stretch. I could be found in my backyard, in February or March, wearing a winter parka and lying in my lawn chair in ten inches of snow. All that was visible was my face and, at times, my hands. I put aluminum foil under my head and a combination of baby oil and iodine on my face to ensure that I would return to school after spring break looking like I had just gotten off a plane from Florida. It was an obsession, just one of many.

Someone once told me that my face was starting to look like leather. Well, at least it's Corinthian leather, I quipped. Frankly, I was more than a little surprised that I hadn't done more damage over the years. I went to my friendly plastic surgeon with what, by now, had become a familiar lesion. He immediately recognized it as a basal-cell carcinoma and, as he had done so many times before, removed it. Unfortunately, when I returned for my follow-up visit, he told me that he had to go deeper because he hadn't gotten all of it on the first attempt. We repeated the same procedure. Several days later, I returned again for my follow-up visit and, much to my dismay, learned that we were going to repeat the same procedure for the third time! I was beginning to feel like he was drilling for oil and that if he dug just a little deeper he would reveal the frontal lobe of my brain! This time he made me stay in his office until he received the results of the biopsy. It seemed like an eternity before the lab results finally came in. However, it was time well spent. Fortunately, on the third time he was able to remove all of it. I left his office with a substantial depression in the middle of my forehead and eight stitches. I would definitely have to change my hairstyle to one which included bangs. However, at least for the moment, I thought I was out of the woods.

My husband, John, and I left the doctor's office and headed for O'Hare airport where I planned to catch my flight back to Turkey. On the way, we had made arrangements to meet my dear friend, Arlene, and her husband, Earl, at a restaurant just off of the toll way. Because we had to wait for the biopsy, we were significantly behind schedule. I phoned her to tell her what had happened, and she assured me there wasn't a problem. She and her husband would have a drink and wait for us.

No sooner had we arrived at the restaurant than my cell phone rang. I didn't recognize the number, so I didn't pick up the call. A few minutes later, my phone rang again; once again, because I didn't recognize the number, I didn't pick up the call. The third time it rang I decided that someone was either very intent on reaching me or was playing some kind of a prank. Either way, it was interfering with our conversation with our friends, so it had to stop. I answered and was taken totally by surprise when the voice on the other end said, "This is Saint Mary's Hospital calling."

My mind started racing. What could they possibly want with me? The voice on the other end was gentle and compassionate, almost apologetic. She explained that they had just received the results of my yearly mammogram, and they saw something that looked suspicious. I frantically explained that I was more than halfway to O'Hare airport, and in three and a half hours, I intended to board a plane for Turkey. The voice on the other end explained that it was entirely up to me whether to turn back, but in her professional opinion, it would be the wisest course of action. I returned to the table pale, disoriented, speechless. In a halting, almost inaudible voice, I related to my husband and our friends what the nurse had told me. At this point, I couldn't imagine rearranging my flight, going back to Milwaukee, and returning to the hospital so they could run additional tests. I was in the minority. Both my husband and our friends said there was no other option. We had all lost our appetites, so we left our meal and drinks unfinished and paid the bill. My husband and I headed back to Milwaukee. A thousand scenarios were running through my mind. However, the bottom line was always, *This is not happening to me.*

I'm happy to say that, at this point at least, the story had a happy ending. I returned to St. Mary's, and they did all the tests necessary to issue me a clean bill of health. I assured all of the people at the hospital that I was too healthy and entirely too busy to have cancer. After all, I had places to go, things to do, and people to see. I thanked them profusely for all of their help and, a little over a week later, headed to O'Hare, once again, to catch my flight to Turkey.

In 2005, I knew I was running away in search of something. I didn't know what, but I was sure at that time I wasn't going to find it in Milwaukee. In 2006, my desperation seemed to have reached a new level, but once again, I wasn't sure exactly why. Perhaps it was the dramatic contrast between my life in Milwaukee and my life in Tarsus. Perhaps it was my close calls with cancer. Perhaps it was the guilt I felt at being happier six thousand miles away from home than I was in Milwaukee. At this point all I knew was that my dissatisfaction with life in Milwaukee was reaching a critical point, and although I hadn't thought a lot about the future, I felt instinctively that significant changes were in the air.

Unfortunately, the delay in my departure put a significant damper on the beginning of the school year. Instead of being ahead of the game when I arrived back, I was significantly behind schedule and had to play catch-up for weeks. John returned to Turkey with me to make sure that I followed the doctor's orders. Unfortunately, we didn't get to do any of the things that I had originally planned for us because of my late arrival. We landed on Saturday, and teachers had to report to school the following Monday. As a result, rather than being able to tour Turkey, we had to settle for a few short day trips to places close to Tarsus. This wasn't what I originally had in mind, but it proved to be incredibly satisfying in other respects.

We went to the mountains with Gulcan and Alper and, as usual, had new and exciting experiences. We picked grapes off the vine, fresh peaches, figs, blackberries, walnuts, apples, tomatoes, and pomegranates. We visited a small town with a wonderful bakery. I went in and ordered some cookies. The clerk was so enthused about having an American customer that he refused the money in exchange for a little conversation. Gulcan and Alper took us to visit a childhood friend. The woman of the house was gorgeous, so as we left, I told her I thought she was beautiful and loved her outfit. In typical Turkish tradition, she told us to wait a minute. She ran inside and emerged, seconds later, with a pair of pants identical to the ones she was wearing. Because I admired them, she felt obligated to give me a pair as a gift. One really has to be careful when giving compliments in this country!

Later that week we decided to take a bus to the mall in Adana. Since I wasn't really familiar with anything in Adana, other than Mustafa's office, I became disoriented and confused. I wasn't sure where we were or what to do next. When we got off the bus, I asked an elderly man for directions. Instead of just telling us what to do and where to go, he and his granddaughter got back on the bus, paid for our fares, and personally delivered us to our destination. Once again, I found myself asking, "Is there anywhere else in the world where something like this could happen?"

When classes actually started again, I was delighted to learn that I would be teaching seventh and eighth grades that year. I *loved* my eighth graders. That was the group I had gone to western Turkey with at the end of the previous school year. We continued to have a mutual "love affair," and it was heartwarming. The hugs and kisses always flowed freely and helped me remember why I was there doing what I was doing.

The idiosyncrasies of EFL learners continued to amuse me. Fridays were always reward day. If a class had been good and completed their work for the week, they got to spend their class time that day playing games. One of the boys was teaching me to play backgammon. They call it Tavula here. Every time he jumped me and took my stone he said, "I'm sorry I'm eating you," which, of course, made me smile. One particular week he did it twice within less than five minutes. The first time, he said, "Sorry." The second time, he said, "Double sorry." Perhaps because I had a special affinity for this student or perhaps because the expression hit a special chord with me, "double sorry" became a permanent part of my vocabulary.

Another interesting difference that was a cause for a lot of miscommunication my first few months in Turkey was the difference between British and American English. Because most of the textbooks used in Turkey are published in Great Britain, the students have been taught British English and spelling. One day, one of my eighth grade boys approached my desk during an exam and asked me for a rubber. Because my orientation is American English, I sat with my mouth gaping and my eyes wide open. I was speechless. One can only imagine what I was thinking. Because this boy was an exceptionally good student, I was certain he wasn't asking for what I understood a rubber to be, but my mind was racing trying to figure out what in the world it was that he wanted. I sat motionless, wondering what to do or say next. Fortunately, I was able to maintain my composure until he finally saw what he was looking for on my desk and grabbed it. Rubber, in British English, means eraser!

Even Turkish adults sometimes find themselves at a loss for words. One day as I was walking back to my apartment, I crossed paths with the computer technician at the college. He was one of the people I was developing a close relationship with, but we were really struggling with the language barrier. He was very polite and complimentary, and on this particular day, he was trying to come up with the right words to tell me that he thought I was thin. He knew he was trying to say the opposite of fat, but he wasn't sure what the opposite was. He ended up coming as close as he could and telling me, "You are a little piece of meat." I've known him now for eight years, and his English has improved considerably; however, to this day, memories of these moments still bring a smile to my face.

My court case was stalled indefinitely. The female judge who had heard all of the testimony in the initial hearing was suddenly appointed to a new position, which meant we had to wait for a new court date and start all over again. In the meantime, the hospital did everything in their power, once again, to try to convince Metin not to testify on my behalf. Metin has a son who was born with a congenital kidney problem. His doctor worked out of the hospital I was suing. As an incentive to abandon me, the hospital offered to give Metin's son free medical care for the rest of his life. He refused it. Next, he was offered a cash "incentive." When that didn't work, he was warned that his son and family should be careful about where they go and what they did because the hospital knew where they lived and where Metin's son went to school. Bribery, treachery, and fraud run rampant in Turkey, and especially in Adana. Because of the level of violence, it's often referred to as the Wild West of Turkey. Everything has a price attached to it, and I was beginning to get a much clearer picture of how the system worked.

CHAPTER 19

Right Is Not Might

People who have given up are ruled by their darkest mistakes,
worst failures, and deepest regrets. If you want to be successful,
then be governed by your finest thoughts, your highest enthusiasm,
your greatest optimism, and your most triumphant experiences.
—John C. Maxwell

It was sometime in December when I received a call from Mustafa, my attorney. He said he had news to share about my case and asked if we could chat for a while.

"Of course," I said, eager to hear what had transpired since our first day in court.

Purportedly, the hospital had paid a large sum of money, supposedly somewhere in the neighborhood of twenty thousand Turkish liras to secure a new prosecuting attorney. In addition, it was believed they had something to do with the appointment of a new judge. The first judge had been a woman who, for obvious reasons, would undoubtedly have been more empathetic about what had happened to me. Mustafa asked me how much money I was willing to pay to fight for my principles and then pointed out that I was totally uninformed about the ins and outs of the Turkish legal system.

If the case dragged on too long and I lost, the hospital could end up countersuing me for libel and force me to pay their legal fees as well. He reassured me that Mehmet had already been punished. Not only had his entire family been shamed by the knowledge of what he had done, but he had actually been imprisoned. In addition, in spite of the unbelievable pressure to recant my testimony, I had persevered. I had confronted the owner and director of one of the most powerful private hospitals in Adana and refused to back down. It had already cost them thousands of liras to prepare and present their defense. As far as Mustafa was concerned, unless I was willing to invest thousands of dollars to try to win the case, this was about as good as it was going to get. After some quiet reflection, I agreed that he was right, and reluctantly, we dropped the case.

CHAPTER 20

Happy Holidays!

I didn't lose the gold. I *won* the silver.
—Michelle Kwan

I had come to grips with the outcome of my court battle. The investment I'd made in terms of time, energy, and money was substantial. Initially, my only solace came from the fact that I was in a foreign country and playing by their rules, or lack thereof. David had fought Goliath and lost. However, as I replayed the events over and over in my mind, I came to the realization that the things that were lost were replaced with rewards of a different kind.

I had met many new people and strengthened my relationships with those I already knew. I had challenged one of the most powerful institutions in Adana, and although I didn't win, I had hopefully at least caused them to examine some of their practices. I had refused to let the perpetrator go unpunished regardless of the costs to me. I had done what none of my Turkish friends would have done for fear of the repercussions. The bottom line was that I had come to this country knowing I had a hole in my soul that was stripping me of my power. By going through this process, flawed as it may have been, I was beginning to get some of that power back.

Ironically, if I had been allowed to choose the month in which the verdict was going to be handed down, I would have chosen December. It had always been my favorite time of the year, because, as a child, it was the only month there was any respite from the tension, anger, and dysfunction that totally enveloped and incapacitated my family of origin. It was the only month in which my mother and father seemed able to pull themselves together long enough to do something for the good of the family. Because of this, nothing, even losing the court battle, could dampen my holiday spirit.

This message was sent on December 23, 2006:

Dear Friends and Loved Ones,

It's the eve of Christmas Eve, and as a result, I've been reflecting on all of the incredible blessings I've enjoyed this year. Whenever I do that, my dear friends come to mind. Once again, I've decided that I'd send an e-mail as opposed to an e-card. It's another opportunity to pass on some of my observations about this country, its people, and the contradictions which continue to mesmerize and confound me.

A brand-new Mercedes speeding past a donkey pulling a cart, people who describe themselves as "bad Muslims" because they smoke and drink and wear revealing clothes. Poor children selling Kleenex on the street to help support their families yet absolutely refuse to take an additional lira because they don't want pity or charity. I've listened to Christmas carols 24/7 for the last three weeks on a Muslim satellite station. The palm trees on our campus are decorated with Christmas lights, and there is a *giant* Santa welcoming students and visitors at the entrance to the school. Muslim teachers are filling in for all the foreign teachers on Monday so we can have a long Christmas Bayram. (And they don't even expect us to give them lesson plans!) Covered Muslim women stopping to admire the store windows overflowing with the scantiest, sexiest, most transparent red lingerie I've ever seen. They're even selling red bikini underwear at the grocery store. I can't get a straight answer from anyone regarding this tradition. Some people say everyone wears red lingerie on New Year's Eve. Others say it's an early display for Valentine's Day, which is quite a big event here in spite of the fact that it's *haram* (forbidden) in other Muslim countries. Perhaps the difference is they call it Lover's Day, thus no reference to a saint. One of my Turkish friends gave me a beautiful tapestry change purse with a picture of the Madonna and Child embroidered on it. Stores are overflowing with lights, ornaments, and garlands, which everyone is using to decorate their New Year's Eve trees. I can't remember the last time I was allowed to have a "holiday" tree in my classroom in the States, but they're in every elementary classroom here.

It's December 23, and one of the custodians just delivered a bag of fresh oranges to all the teachers. They were picked off the trees on the campus. I'm all alone in a country on the other side of the world, and yet I never feel alone. Tonight I'll be attending my second Christmas party this week. The first one was hosted by the director of our college. Tonight's is sponsored by the PTO and will be held in a wonderful hotel in Adana. Tomorrow morning I'm flying to Istanbul. I've heard there are three marvelous churches there, and I'm going to choose one of them for midnight services tomorrow. I imagine it will be quite an experience to do that. My guardian angel in Istanbul is a thirty-year-old Muslim man named Serdar. He is going to accompany me so I "don't have any problems." It will be his first time in a church. His comment to me was, "Maybe I will learn something too." Who would ever have believed this?

Two years ago today, I was in Bayside with John preparing to celebrate a traditional Wisconsin Christmas. I had no idea, whatsoever, that this year I would find myself on the other side of the world. To me, this is the best example I could ever give someone about miracles and God's plan for us. We truly don't know what the next day holds in store. I used to tell the women I worked with in our Weekender Unit to "feel the fear and do it anyway." I told them they wouldn't really know true freedom until they imagined themselves standing on the edge of a great precipice. Nothing but darkness loomed ahead. They had to have enough faith to step over the edge and trust that they would sprout wings and fly rather than being dashed to pieces on the rocks below. I closed my eyes, held my breath, and waited for my wings. They were my Christmas gift from God this year. They just arrived a little early.

I truly never doubted that there was a reason why I was here. Today I'm celebrating the fact that I'm flying free. My holiday wish for all of you is that you too will get your wings this year and feel free to fly wherever your heart leads you. I was once told that no one can fully experience life until they've heard their music. We're all born with a song in our hearts, and to truly live, we have to hear our music. It's frightening to take the leap but even more frightening to imagine a life that hasn't been lived to its fullest.

I wish you all of very blessed Christmas and a Happy New Year. I miss you all and hope that some of the things that I write about, and which are having an everlasting impact on my life, will also touch your hearts.

Love, light, and hugs to all of you,
The Barbara

Chapter 21

Our Last Hurrah

Find those persons in whose presence you feel more energetic,
more creative, and more able to pursue your life goals. Stay
away from persons who make you feel apprehensive, or
who influence you to doubt yourself. Especially, stay away
from those persons who drain you, so that your energy
is all used up trying to maintain the relationship.
—Dennis F. Augustine

Initially, John had fully supported my decision to go to Turkey. However, at the time, I don't think either one of us fully realized what a toll it would take on a relationship that was already strained at the seams. What was happening to me in Turkey was indeed life altering. I was doing things and experiencing things that two years earlier I would not have imagined were possible. I felt liberated and rejuvenated. I was getting my power back. I was no longer content to sit back and swallow my opinions or to let the man in my life believe that he was in a better position than I to determine what was good for *me*. I had spread my wings and flown the coop. I never imagined that this would turn out to be an irreversible move.

John was visiting me for the second time and felt like he had really learned the ropes on his first visit. Therefore, he felt obligated to try to take the lead in any and every decision about my life here. I kept my opinions to myself and played along, but it was becoming increasingly difficult for me to pretend that I was taking his well-intentioned but often misguided advice seriously. Much to his surprise, and mine, I had proved that I was perfectly capable of managing on my own. As I look back on it, the magical New Year's Eve we spent together in Adana that year was probably the beginning of the end of our marriage. It marked a turning point. Although I didn't realize it at the time, I would eventually be making decisions that would change the course of our relationship forever.

This message was sent in January 2007:

Dear Friends,

I apologize for letting the New Year come and go without a special greeting from The Barbara. I spent a *Beyaz Noel* (white Christmas) in Istanbul. However, the snow wasn't the light fluffy variety, which, in years past, made me scream with glee and magically transformed the landscape into a fairyland and my Christmas Eve into something magical. The snow in Istanbul was the heavy, wet variety, more rain than snow. It was accompanied by a bone-chilling wind and dampness that still makes me shiver when I think of it. It didn't lessen the number of people who filled the streets, but it certainly slowed me down. I came home with a cold that, three weeks later, I'm still taking medication for. I actually had two chest X-rays because I was convinced I had pneumonia again. The X-rays didn't confirm it, but my symptoms were so severe that the campus doctor ended up treating me like it was anyway. The bottom line was that I had two series of antibiotics. When the first one didn't do the trick, the doctor resorted to injections. When it was time for the first one, I rolled up my sleeve and offered my arm. He shook his head and indicated that he needed another part of my body to be bared. I can't remember when I had a shot *there*, and I sincerely hope it will be a long time before I need another one!

I did manage to get to church on Christmas. The thirty-year-old Muslim guardian angel I mentioned in an earlier e-mail found one of the only three Christian churches in Istanbul. He was gallant enough to accompany me. It was definitely the first time he was ever in a church, which was an interesting phenomenon for me to observe. The service was in Turkish, so most of it was lost on me. However, the lack of understanding was inconsequential compared to the void I felt when the service concluded and they didn't sing "Silent Night." I thought that was universal. Ah, tradition, tradition!

Istanbul itself was ablaze with Christmas lights, and shopkeepers and restaurateurs were frantically setting up oversized Santas and stringing lights the entire evening. All of this was in preparation for the New Year celebration, which is *huge* here. John arrived in time for the momentous event, so we decided to live it up. We went to Adana and spent the weekend in the most expensive hotel in the area. It's a Hilton but is extravagant by anyone's standards. We decided to have the ultimate Turkish experience, which meant we went to the *hamum*, or Turkish bath. (One of my foreign friends warned me that newbies should start with a "civilized version" of the real Turkish experience, and the Hilton seemed like *the* place.) We began with a sauna. This was followed by a scrub. The attendant gave us each what I assumed was a washcloth for my face. I was horrified, and fifty shades of red, when I realized this was my "modesty" cover. We were literally scrubbed from our heads to our toes. The finale of the scrub was being entirely covered with bubbles and then doused with bucket after bucket of ice-cold water. I decided to respect John's privacy and wait in the anteroom while he had his treatment.

Unfortunately, I didn't have the same luxury. I was instructed to lie naked on a cold marble slab that was large enough for about six people. The door opened, and the troops arrived. Although no one actually joined me on the slab, the room was ringed with observers who watched gleefully as I reacted (some would say overreacted) to every new stage in the process. The burning question I'm still struggling with is how the handsome young man, who worked himself into a sweat working on me, kept *his* modesty cover on We went from the Turkish bath to a full-body oil massage. It was decadent! After this, I was ready for a nap. Unfortunately, we only had a little over an hour to prepare for dinner.

The dinner was an extravaganza. We've been to New Year's celebrations around the world, but nothing could even compare to this! Guests entered the Grand Ballroom via a marble staircase. At the top, everyone paused to have a photo taken. Waiters circulated with trays of beverages and mouthwatering appetizers. The dining room was draped, from floor to ceiling, in gold lamé, and four-foot-high gold and crystal candelabras illuminated every table. Every chair was festooned with an enormous gold lamé bow capped with more crystals. The room literally sparkled as though it had been sprinkled with diamond dust. Some people would say it was overdone, but it was right up my alley!

The magnificent new mosque, second only to the Blue Mosque in Istanbul, was resplendent through the floor-to-ceiling windows. There was a five-course meal and an orchestra. Wine, champagne, and raki (the local favorite) flowed endlessly. A tenor sang Italian melodies (still can't figure that one out), a belly dancer gyrated energetically, and one of the most popular pop stars in southern Turkey rounded out the entertainment. John and I agreed it was worth the price of admission, which was more, per person, than an average Turk makes in a month! Ironically, there are obviously lots of people in Adana who could afford it.

There were only two other people in the entire room who spoke English, and we were sitting next to them. My only regret is that I didn't feel better. At about ten minutes after twelve, I announced, "I made it. Can we go to the room now?" My cold was moving into high gear and kept me down and out until the last couple of days. I've joked that I'm going to recover just in time to return to Istanbul to see John off.

Tomorrow is the first day of the second Muslim *bayram* (holiday). It's the *Kurban*, or sheep sacrifice. It's a day when everyone who can afford it is expected to sacrifice a lamb and give the meat to a needy family. The wealthy people don't actually do the butchering anymore, but from what I understand, there are many people who still do. It's against their religion to do it publicly, but people say if you look carefully, you can catch a glimpse of what's going on in people's gardens and backyards. I've also been told the emergency rooms will be overflowing with people who accidentally cut themselves, lose fingers, etc. A person who pays to have the animal butchered will pay anywhere from $150 to $300 per sheep, and many people order more than one. The recipients are people everyone knows are needy, and for some, it's the only time of the year they actually get meat. Things like this remain hard for me to believe because my life here at the college is so different, and the people I know, for the most part, are so privileged. Unfortunately, one doesn't have to look far to see harsh reality.

John has been here for a little over a week and seems to be enjoying his experience much more than the first visit. Perhaps it's because he knew what to expect. I think it was difficult for him the first time, because he didn't expect my adjustment to life here to be so seamless. He knows my friends now and has found places in Tarsus I didn't know existed. Tomorrow is the beginning of our semester break. We will have a three-week holiday to coincide with the beginning of the bayram. John will be here for two of those three weeks. He came early because he wanted to see my students before they left. He finds them as interesting and enjoyable as I do and attended several of my classes last week. He enjoyed it and so did the students. We plan to do some traveling in Turkey and to spend several days in Istanbul, which has become one of my all-time favorite cities. I talked to some of my friends there today, and it's still snowing! I certainly hope the weather improves before we arrive.

I am sorry I didn't send a New Year greeting. Last year I would have sent you wishes for a healthy and prosperous

2006. This year I still wish you good health. However, prosperity has taken a backseat. Instead, I wish you a spirit of adventure. May your life be exhilarating, rewarding, and take you to heights you've never achieved and, more importantly, never thought you could achieve. Get out of your box, live your lives, and cherish every new experience that comes your way. Don't turn down an opportunity to grow and be better than you were yesterday. It's *never* too late to create the life you've only dreamed you could have. You deserve to be the best you can be and to have a magical existence for the limited time we have here. Believe in yourself and your ability to create it now!

Love, light, and wishes for the best year you've ever had,
The Barbara

CHAPTER 22

Expanding My Horizons

Judgments prevent us from seeing the good
that lies beyond appearances.
—Wayne Dyer

When I first decided to leave Milwaukee for my great adventure on the other side of the world, there was no shortage of naysayers. People questioned why in the world I would want to trade the comforts of my suburban lifestyle for a stint in a third-world country. They couldn't imagine the risks I was taking by going to a Muslim country that shared borders with the "axis of evil." Didn't I know, they wondered, that I was taking my life in my hands?

All my friends knew that I had always considered myself to be a gypsy of sorts. My license plate and e-mail address were "gypzwmn," and I proudly proclaimed my predilection for travel, adventure, and excitement. After discovering that my maternal grandparents were Hungarian, I felt the spirit of adventure coursing through my blood. I openly confessed to being happier when I was on an airplane than anywhere else. I often said that I would give up my home and live out of a suitcase if I could have the luxury of getting off one plane and onto another without skipping a beat. While I was teaching in the States, I eagerly counted the days until the next holiday because it meant a chance to go abroad again. While John and I were married, we spent every one of my vacations traveling somewhere in Europe. I was a vagabond and proud of it. However, now that I was living on the other side of the world, there were new places and the promise of new adventures beckoning me. These were destinations that, in my former life, were forbidden fruit. Syria, Lebanon, and Jordon were among them and were calling my name.

Just about the time my wanderlust was crescendoing to uncontrollable proportions, I learned about a woman named Jane Digby. Given my own personal history and my insatiable taste for adventure and the fact that I was an incurable romantic, my friend Debbie was amazed that I hadn't heard about her. Debbie felt certain that there would be aspects of her life that would mesmerize me. She was right. Jane was born into the English aristocracy and possessed every conceivable advantage that a woman could have. She was undeniably one of the most beautiful women of her day. She had social position and wealth, and much like me, she spent her life searching for love. Although she lived 150 years ago, I couldn't help but feel a certain affinity for her. Admittedly, I never had the wealth or social position she enjoyed, but as I read more about her, I began to feel that, in many respects, we were kindred spirits.

Like me, she was a tortured soul, and she went from one relationship to another trying to fill the hole in it. People judged and spurned her for many of her choices and, undoubtedly, given her many advantages, couldn't fathom her inability to find true happiness. Ultimately, she gave up the Palladian mansions and gilded salons of her youth for life with a Syrian Desert prince more than twenty years her junior. It was with him that she finally found true love. I was totally intrigued by her story and determined to visit Syria in order to walk in her footsteps. She sketched at Palmyra and built a house in Damascus where she is buried. It was decided. I was going to make a pilgrimage to Syria.

At that point in time, relations between the United States and Syria were strained, so it wouldn't have been possible for me to arrange a visit on my own. However, there was a tour company in Adana that offered three-day visits to Syria, Lebanon, and Jordon. As an American, I would be allowed to enter Syria if I were part of one of these groups. Coincidentally, they were planning a visit to

Syria over my birthday weekend. I decided that I was going to book myself on this tour. Much to my delight, one of my dearest friends at the college agreed to go with me. He knew about my Jane Digby obsession and agreed that the best birthday gift he could possibly give me would be a visit to her grave.

I was absolutely thrilled that he agreed to go with me, so without hesitation, we booked ourselves on the tour. All of the people in the group were Turkish with the exception of my friend and me. He was Canadian. When we arrived at the border, everyone got off the bus and literally ran into the duty-free shop. The taxes on certain items in Turkey are staggering. Consequently, when Turkish people have a chance to buy liquor, cameras, or cell phones without paying the tax, no one misses out on the opportunity. Unfortunately, because I was an American, I did.

As soon as the bus began rolling to a stop, a Syrian soldier started making his way down the aisle. Everyone was asked to produce a passport, and they were all collected. Mine was the only navy blue one, indicating that I was the only American on the bus. As a result, after he had all of our documents, he politely asked me to follow him into a building a considerable distance from the duty-free shop. There was a translator present, and in broken English, he asked me why I wanted to visit Syria. I was pretty certain he wasn't interested in hearing about my obsession with Jane Digby, so I simply said I wanted to see Damascus. I was asked to sign a registry affirming that I had entered the country. That was it, and I was released. I rejoined the group; we boarded the bus and crossed the border. Only moments after reboarding and crossing into Syria, our Syrian tour guide began to make his way down the aisle. He paused at each row and handed the people sitting there a piece of chocolate and a fresh flower, certainly not the welcome that most of my friends in America would have expected.

Damascus was a feast for the senses. The streets were literally overflowing with people and automobiles. There was something new and exciting on every corner, and my heart was beating so fast I thought it would jump out of my chest. This was truly a great adventure. I felt like I was eating forbidden fruit. As far as I was concerned, this was a place that was even more mysterious and magical than Istanbul.

Damascus, Aleppo, Jericho, and a few other cities in the area compete for the title of the world's oldest continuously inhabited city. However, because people have always lived there, it's impossible to carry out any excavations to verify the city's exact origins. This only serves to contribute to the mystical aura surrounding these places.

We visited the Umayyad Mosque where I was required to wear an *abaya* in order to enter. This mosque is one of the most sacred places in the Islamic world. Over the centuries it has suffered damage from invasions, earthquakes, and fires, but it still inspires awe and wonder. This mosque contains the Shrine of Saint John the Baptist. It's said to contain his head, hair, and skin intact. We visited the Suleymaniye Mosque and the Mausoleum of Saladin. The mosques were breathtakingly beautiful and filled to overflowing with visitors. The Bazaar was another feast for the senses, and we stood gaping at the wide variety of exquisite goods for sale. However, the main objective of this trip was to learn more about

Jane Digby and her life, so the rest of the sites were lost on me. I was looking forward to the next day when we would have time to explore on our own.

It was May 18, and it was my birthday. My friend and I had already decided that we had two objectives for the day. The first, and most important, was to find Jane Digby's tomb and, if time permitted, the house she built in Damascus. The other was to cap off the night with a leisurely dinner in the city. Unfortunately, we had no idea how difficult our task would turn out to be.

We met in the lobby, hired a taxi, and were off on our quest. Because neither one of us spoke Arabic and our cab driver didn't speak English, we knew this wasn't going to be easy. However, we were looking for a Christian cemetery and assumed these would be few and far between. Wrong again. Much like Jerusalem, certain sections of the city are reserved for different religious groups. We had no idea how many Christian cemeteries there would be in Damascus! We drove for hours and weren't any nearer to finding Jane's tomb than when we started out. Finally, out of desperation, we pulled into a non-Christian cemetery and asked to speak to someone in charge. We explained our plight, and much to my surprise, he knew who Jane Digby was and exactly where she was buried. He gave us directions to the cemetery and agreed to call the caretaker to let us in. When we arrived, we couldn't contain our laughter. There, in *huge* letters on the front of the gate was the name and telephone number of the person to call if you were interested in visiting Jane's tomb. Unfortunately, since neither my friend nor I could speak or read Arabic, we drove right on by. Oh well, another little wrinkle in the fabric of my life.

The cemetery was small, and it didn't take us long to find Jane's tomb. It was distinctive and regal as one would expect for a woman of her station. However, we were surprised to see that she wasn't the only English noblewoman buried there. Here, in the middle of Damascus, hidden among the unobtrusive tombs of other Christians, was a small enclave of British aristocracy. Obviously, she wasn't the only one who had succumbed to the call of adventure in distant lands. It was humbling to sit under the shade of the huge tree next to her tomb and to try to imagine the things that this amazing woman experienced during her lifetime. We took photos and spent time simply soaking in the beauty and solemnity of the place.

Unfortunately, it had taken us so long to find Jane's tomb that we weren't able to continue in search of the home she built. No problem, I rationalized; after all, it gave me a good reason to come again the following year. We returned to the city center in search of a good restaurant in which to celebrate my birthday. The Christian quarter is the only one that serves liquor, so we headed in that direction in order to have a bottle of wine with our meal.

Filled with incredible memories of our lovely dinner and our great adventure in search of Jane Digby, we walked back to our hotel. We were both lost in our own thoughts, replaying our favorite memories of the past two days. We would be leaving early the next morning. The last day we would visit Aleppo, Homs, and Hama before returning to Turkey. The trip was everything I had hoped and more. I could hardly wait to see what the tour company would be offering the next year.

CHAPTER 23

What Next?

Success comes in *cans*. Failure comes in *can'ts*.

—Unknown

The end of my second year in Tarsus was rapidly approaching, and I still hadn't managed to decide what I should do to thank Metin for his loyalty and support during my battle with Mehmet and the hospital in Adana. True, we lost in court. However, without his unflappable courage and absolute insistence on doing the right thing, I doubt I would have had the courage to pursue the case. Because we hadn't won, there was no settlement to give him. The question that haunted me day and night was: What could I do to show my gratitude? I had shared my feelings with John, and although he didn't share them, he agreed that I should do whatever I could to show my appreciation.

I had a forever friend, sage, and spiritual mentor in Brookfield, Wisconsin, by the name of Dr. Caroline Loose. The best way to describe her would be to say that she was the closest thing to an angel that we mere mortals will ever have a chance to know here on earth. She was a dear friend, my counselor, and my teacher. She exposed me to truths that without her guidance would have eluded me forever. I explained my problem to her, and she suggested holding a fundraiser to try to raise some money for Metin's family. It sounded like a wonderful idea. I e-mailed her information about them and their situation that could be used in the invitation. By this time it was very clear that John was uncomfortable with the closeness of the relationship that had developed between Metin and me. However, even he supported this. Unfortunately, the idea, as good as it seemed at the time, never really got off the ground, and I'm not sure why. Perhaps the distance between Milwaukee, Wisconsin, and Adana, Turkey, was just too great. In spite of this, Cary, out of the goodness of her heart, wired Metin one hundred dollars. That was a heartwarming gesture that still brings tears to his eyes. However, it was obvious that I was going to have to start thinking outside of the box if I was ever going to be able to do anything meaningful to repay him.

Dr. Caroline Loose, myself, and Veronica Van
Dalen on Thanksgiving Day, 2008.

As the weeks and the months passed, I began to spend more and more time at Metin's family home. I shared dinner with them and became closer and closer to everyone in the family, especially Fatma, Metin's mother. I went through my closets and took his sisters and sisters-in-law clothing, shoes, purses, and jewelry I no longer used. I bought fish for the barbecues and raki for his father. I did whatever I could to try to make things a little easier for them. However, I began to feel as though I was losing sight of my mission, which was to do something to repay Metin.

By the end of the school year, a plan was beginning to crystallize. Metin had always dreamed of opening a restaurant or a café. If I gave him the seed money to open his own place, perhaps it could be a source of additional income for me as well. I would have my own special Turkish retirement plan. Metin preferred Istanbul to Adana, and I had begun to think that when my contract in Tarsus was finished, perhaps I would move to Turkey permanently. Istanbul would be an amazing retirement haven, I thought. As a matter of fact, when John had been in Turkey in January, we had actually looked at a house that was for sale there.

Not surprisingly, the tension between Metin and John was escalating, because I was spending more time with Metin than with him. If John and I had any hope of staying together, this was going to have to be resolved. Metin was, by comparison, a child and still the consummate party animal. I was twice his age and ten years older than his mother! *Could this really pose a serious threat to John?* I asked myself.

As I was writing, this seemed like a good place to insert another e-mail. This one was sent to my friends at the end of my second year in Tarsus. It's evidence (How's that for throwing in a little courtroom lingo?) that as important as my court case was, it wasn't all-consuming. I have many fond memories of this time to help offset the disappointments of what happened in the courtroom. Yes, the court case was a wrinkle in the fabric of my life. I knew that my chances of being victorious were small, and as a result, I had to be careful about how vested I became in the outcome. There's an expression: let go and let God. I had no other option at this point. Although the details of this period of time are still clear in my mind, the intensity of the emotions I was feeling have long since dissipated. This message, I believe, still contains them.

This message was sent on June 11, 2006:

Dear Friends,

I started this e-mail on May 28. Today is June 11, so if I don't finish it soon, I'll be able to deliver it to all of you in person when I arrive on July 20.

As usual, things are never dull. Our school held a week-long International Folk Festival, and the PTA hosted a magnificent end-of-the-year ball for the teachers. I celebrated my sixtieth birthday in grand style with all of my dearest friends. At the same time, we're frantically preparing for the eighth grade graduation ceremony and ball and, just to prove that life isn't chaotic enough, I'm moving!

I continue to learn something new every day and am still exhilarated by that. I also continue to be amazed at the contradictions in this society. After living here for almost two years, I didn't think there was much left that could surprise me. On the contrary! The more immersed I become in the culture and the closer I get to the people, the better understanding I have of how truly unique this country is. The increased awareness is humorous and daunting at the same time. I continue to strengthen my relationships with my Turkish friends, and this, in itself, is a gift.

The end of every school year is a challenge. However, the end of the year in a private Turkish school that's still under the auspices of the Turkish Ministry is an adventure in and of itself. The paperwork is overwhelming, and the grading system is far from perfect. I've come to the realization that teaching in a foreign country requires the ability to put all preconceived notions about what's right and wrong to rest. One has to learn to go with the flow or go home.

The International Folk Fair was marvelous. Groups of dancers came from all over Turkey and several European countries. It was an incredible event, and as usual, the school rolled out the red carpet. They get an A+ for the grand scale on which they entertain guests. The celebration lasted four days and was memorable in every respect. Surprisingly, the most memorable moment for me didn't have anything to do with dancing but certainly goes back to the cultural differences. Several of my seventh-grade girls were determined to teach me how to do the traditional Turkish dances. I'm convinced both boys and girls here come out of the womb dancing! Suddenly, two of the girls pulled me aside and frantically started asking me about orchids. We were having a small communication breakdown, and I thought they were asking me if I was growing them on the balcony of my apartment, which was visible from where we were standing. As it turned out, Orkid is a brand name for what we call Kotex. One of the girls discovered she needed one immediately and assumed I would have one in my purse. I giggled as I explained that a sixty-year-old woman doesn't have a ready supply and sent her off to the school doctor's office. Now, every time I pass the display in the grocery store, I giggle.

The ball the parents hosted for the teachers was also a grand event. If there's one thing Turkish people know how to do, it's throw a party. It was comparable to one of the nicest weddings I've ever been to in America. It was held at a hotel owned by the family of one of our students. The room was done in cream and gold, and the meal was mouthwateringly delicious. In addition to a wide variety of *meze* (Turkish appetizers), they served one of the best cuts of beef I've ever had, and a good cut of beef here is worth its weight in gold.

The highlight of the evening was the fact that many of our eighth graders' parents came. It's wonderful to see Turkish parents interact with their children. The children truly are the jewels in the family crown. I tried to imagine a group of American eighth graders warmly welcoming their parents to their graduation party. We were entertained by several of the students. They've formed a band and performed along with our principal and one of the fifth-grade teachers. The students, as well as their families, treat their teachers like extended family members. In all my years of teaching, I've never experienced anything quite like this. It's one of the most rewarding parts of being here.

Last week, I had a similar experience. It was additional proof that a teacher here, especially a foreign teacher, is considered a special gift. One of my students gave me a beautiful necklace for my birthday. I asked her for the name of the shop where she bought it and told her I definitely wanted to pay them a visit. She suggested we go one day, the following week, after school. When the next week arrived, we jumped into my car together (unheard of in America because of the potential legal problems) and drove to Adana where the shop was located. We walked around after we finished shopping and stopped for ice cream. When I returned from paying the bill, Asli, my student, was holding a dozen red long-stemmed roses for me. I was flabbergasted. She explained that her dream, ever since I arrived last year, was to go shopping me. She wanted to show her appreciation for the fact that I made her dream come true! Once again, I felt like a princess.

My sixtieth birthday party was, as usual, an international gathering of people, which made it really special. My cleaning lady, Fazilet, prepared all of the food this year, and it was some of the best I've had since I arrived. She came the day before to prepare everything and the day after to clean up. I don't know what I'd do without her. My guests consumed twenty-six bottles of wine and twenty-four bottles of beer, and I thought Turkey was a strict Muslim country!

I signed a contract for a third year and reaped the rewards as a result. I had requested a larger apartment, because I'd outgrown my closet space. Since I arrived at the college, I had lived in the same building. It was a historic old mansion directly across from the school. It was huge and only had four apartments. I didn't want to leave the building and requested the apartment that's usually reserved for a married couple with children. I never imagined they'd grant my request, but miracles do happen! I will start moving in two weeks. I think it has as many square feet as our home in Wisconsin. It has two bedrooms, one of which is large enough to rollerblade in. It has a large salon and a kitchen that's as big as my living room and dining room combination in Milwaukee. The terrace is twice as big as the one I currently have, and there are three sets of French doors leading outside. I think I've died and gone to heaven.

In addition, I've decided to take up tennis. Our school physician and several other alumni pooled their resources and opened a private tennis club. It has clay courts and a small clubhouse. They have a resident pro who gives lessons and several other amenities. The problem was the fact that the annual membership is 2,000 Turkish liras (approximately $1,400). I thought that was a hefty price to pay to take lessons. Much to my surprise, Dr. Ali, the school physician, informed me that membership is free for any teachers or students who live on campus in the dorms. How's that for a "beni"? I also received a $1,000 signing bonus and my airfare home for the summer. They're making it very difficult to leave!

I continue to enjoy my seaside retreat and having a car at my disposal even though gas is incredibly expensive. According to most sources, it's the most expensive in Europe. Depending on the exchange rate, it varies from $9 to $10 a gallon! $2.50 in the States is going to look like a bargain. After my first year, I received an $11,000 raise. Unfortunately, most of it is being eaten up by my additional expenses. I guess the only consolation is that it's not costing me money to have this great adventure.

As usual, I've saved the best for last. Most foreign teachers, regardless of their placement, move on after the second year of their contract. Most of them are young people whose primary goal is to see the world. They country hop until the novelty wears off, and then they go home. As a result, although they're respected as professionals, they aren't afforded the same level of prestige and acceptance as Turkish teachers. *Hocam* is a Turkish word that's always used when addressing Turkish teachers but, seldom, if ever, a foreigner. Last week, I knew I had arrived when I was walking down one of the main city streets and a chicken vendor (cooked, not live) called me *hocam* and not Barbara. The thrill I felt at this show of respect is hard to explain, but suffice it to say, I had the feeling I had arrived.

My last bit of news is along the same lines. I mentioned that we are frantically preparing for the eighth-grade graduation and the ball that will follow two nights later. Once again, it's hard to explain what a monumental event this is. The amount of pomp and circumstance is normally reserved for university graduations in the States. At the beginning of the year, I promised my eighth graders that if they would study their English, I would learn enough Turkish to be able to give a farewell speech to them in Turkish. As it turns out, I will be honored by being the only foreign teacher included in the graduation program, and I will wish them all the best in Turkish! Who would have thought this could ever happen? Words can't express what an honor it is to have this opportunity.

It's been another rewarding and eventful year, and it's sometimes hard to remember what my life was like before I came here. There are obviously many things I miss about my life in the States, but I can't imagine what I could do there that would be as rewarding as teaching here has been. I had no idea what to expect when I arrived here, but my actual experience far exceeded my wildest expectations. I know I'm making a difference, and I'm thrilled to have this opportunity.

I look forward to seeing as many of you as possible when I return in July. I will be home from July 20 until August 17.

I hope you're all living your dreams and enjoying all the blessings that the Universe offers.

Love and lots of Turkish kisses,
Barbara

In July I flew back to Milwaukee for a month, and by then, my plan for how I would thank Metin had taken shape. I had a teacher's retirement account that I had contributed to for almost thirty years. I decided I would close the account and withdraw all of the money. I would give a portion of it to Metin so he could open his café or bar, and I would keep a little nest egg for myself in case of emergencies. I was so excited that I was ready to burst. I could hardly wait to tell him.

My plane landed, and within a week, I had withdrawn the money, phoned Metin to tell him about my plan, and made arrangements to meet him in Istanbul at the end August. Normally, a month wasn't nearly long enough for me to see all of my friends, go to all of my doctor appointments, and do all the things I wanted to do while I was in Wisconsin. However, now I had bigger fish to fry.

Notice that by the second summer I'd been in Turkey I was no longer referring to Wisconsin as home. This is a hint of what was to come. Days dragged by, and I could hardly contain my enthusiasm about the upcoming project. To say that John didn't share my feelings would have been putting it mildly. Unbeknownst to me, by this time, he was experiencing severe financial problems. We never talked about money. This was a lesson I had learned from my parents. In their almost fifty years of marriage, my mother never knew how much money my father made or how he spent it. She was given an allowance, and whatever she or my sister, my brother, or I needed was expected to be paid for out of that. I had learned my lesson well, and on the rare occasions that the subject of money came up, I was told it was none of my business. I worked and had my own money, and although John never held a steady job, he had his inheritance to fall back on. We each contributed a set amount each month to cover the household expenses. Little did I know at this point how infuriated he was about my plans to help Metin and how he had already begun to even out the score.

CHAPTER 24

The Beginning of the End with John

You will be as small as your controlling desire,
as great as your dominant aspiration.
—James Allen

I never suspected for a moment that as Metin and I were planning how to create a brighter and more secure financial future for each of us, John was plotting my undoing.

When I returned to Turkey, I flew into Tarsus before boarding another plane for Istanbul.
I wanted to lighten my load, literally. My luggage, as usual, was bursting at the seams. I couldn't imagine living out of the same suitcase for another two weeks, so I took a couple of days to unpack and repack before meeting Metin.

When I returned to the school campus, the guards were waiting for me at the gate. They were talking a mile a minute, and although my Turkish was progressing nicely, I couldn't understand what they were trying to tell me. I summoned help and listened carefully as they listed all of the problems they had encountered while they were babysitting my car.

After the end of my first year in Tarsus, I decided, for several reasons, that it was time to invest in a car. I was spending entirely too much time and energy traveling back and forth to Adana on the bus. I had splurged and rented a fabulous getaway apartment on the shores of the Mediterranean thirty-five kilometers from Tarsus. I planned to spend every weekend there, and because it was relatively close, I even envisioned being able to spend an occasional night there during the week. Although public transportation here is efficient and easy to use, it would obviously be a lot easier to jump into my own car and come and go as I pleased. However, perhaps most importantly, I decided I was going to stay a third year. That meant I was going to want to expand my horizons and travel to places that, up until that point, had been out of my reach. I didn't want to spend a lot of money, especially if I decided to leave Turkey after my third year. As a result, I decided to visit the car gallery in Tarsus that specialized in secondhand cars. I took two good friends with me, and because they were men, I automatically assumed they would have much more knowledge in this area than I. Either I was wrong again, or my powers of persuasion were so formidable that I was able to convince even them that the only car everyone warned me against should end up being the one I would buy.

It was a red Spanish Seat. *What's that?* you're probably wondering. First of all, it's pronounced "say at" (with a short *a* in "at"), and my friends told me it was comparable to a Polish Volkswagen. It had been lovingly customized by a young Turkish man. That meant he had added a spoiler on the back, changed the suspension so he could outfit it with racing tires, equipped it with a special muffler that made it sound like a Ferrari, installed a CD player and special speakers, and added brand-new tweed seat covers. All of this information, which I should have taken as a warning of the problems to come, went in one ear and right out the other. The car was red and had a CD player and a sunroof. That was all that mattered. I didn't test drive it. In fact, I didn't even sit in it, or I would have seen that the seat covers were installed to cover all the damage to the original upholstery. My friends told me to sleep on it. I wouldn't hear of it. It was a Sunday and the busiest day at the car gallery. I was afraid someone would snatch it out from under me, so I immediately agreed to pay slightly more than the asking price, which was already much more than the car was worth, and left a deposit. I agreed to return the next day to seal the deal.

To describe in detail the problems I had with my Seat would necessitate writing a separate book on the dangers of letting your emotions cloud your judgment when buying an automobile. Driving in Turkey is like trying to run across a minefield uninjured. There are potholes everywhere. In many instances, people put a pile of rocks in front of them to warn oncoming traffic. Unfortunately, when it's dark, not only does one hit the pothole but the pile of rocks as well. Every time I hit one, I blew a tire, and the replacement cost was 175 Turkish liras.

The first time I returned to the tire store a week after having purchased four brand new tires, I inquired about a guarantee. The man just smiled politely and looked at me like I had just arrived from another planet. I could have made a small down payment on another car for what I spent on tires the first six months I owned my "boy toy." *Oh well*, I rationalized, *it's only money.* And, at least for the moment, that wasn't a problem. I should remind the reader, lest you forget, that my friends had always told me I gave new meaning to the title drama queen. While they were reveling in the joy of becoming grandparents for the first time and settling comfortably into their retirement routines, I was living on the edge. I was basking in the thrill of discovering new places, immersing myself in foreign cultures and responding to the siren's call for adventure and romance. Therefore, one can only imagine the thrill I got revving the engine in the center of the city and having everyone's head turn. All the young men I knew, and I knew a lot of them, were scrambling to stand in line for a chance to sit behind the wheel. (If only I'd done that before driving it off the lot!)

Unfortunately, the young man who customized the car obviously didn't have a degree in electrical engineering. The CD player turned itself on and off regularly, and the horn had a habit of going off in the early hours of the morning, thereby waking up the entire campus. The headlights also had a mind of their own and frequently drained the battery of all of its life. On three different occasions, there was a fire in the engine. While driving in Adana one day, I suddenly found myself struggling to breathe because of the heat. I knew Adana was always a little warmer than Tarsus, but this was ridiculous. Even after another driver caught my attention and told me to pull over immediately, I didn't grasp the severity of what was happening. My engine was on fire! Luckily, I happened to be directly in front of the carpet shop owned by Serkan, Metin's brother. After analyzing the situation, he called the nearest mechanic who towed it away, once again, to repair. Every mechanic who worked on the car told me that Allah was smiling on me because I was driving "the car from hell," and I should have died many times over.

One evening while I was at a stop sign in Adana, a young man came running up to me and proudly announced that the used to be his. I offered to sell it back to him, on the spot, for half of what I paid. He just smiled and walked away. By this time I had literally replaced every movable part on the car at least once, if not twice, and had spent almost as much money repairing it as I had originally paid for the car!

You're probably wondering what the car, and all my little horror stories about it, had to do with my deteriorating relationship with John. As I said, when I returned to campus, the guards were beside themselves. They had agreed to drive the car once or twice a week while I was in the States to make sure the battery didn't die. Considering that the battery appeared to have a mind of its own that, in itself, was a joke. They had done what I asked but had not been able to prevent the inevitable. The CD player had turned itself on and burned itself out. The battery was dead, the headlights had burned themselves out, and someone had hit the car while it was parked in the parking lot. I was going to need a sizeable amount of money to get the car up and running again. This is where my story about John begins.

There was an ATM machine right outside of my apartment. I immediately went to it and tried to withdraw money for my car repairs. When I decided to help Metin open a place of his own, I had withdrawn all of my savings out of my retirement account. I took some of the money back to Turkey with me and left thirty thousand dollars in my checking account in Milwaukee. As a result, I was totally perplexed by the fact that the ATM machine kept telling me that there were insufficient funds in my account. After several attempts to withdraw the money for my car repairs, I finally gave up and decided to call my friends at the bank in Milwaukee to see what the problem was.

The year before I left for Turkey, John discovered he had a life-threatening health condition. He had an aneurism on his carotid artery. The operation he was scheduled to have was extremely dangerous. He was warned that it could just as easily kill as cure him. We discussed the worst-case scenario and decided that in order to avert a financial crisis he would need to give me his power of attorney. While we were in the attorney's office, the lawyer suggested that I do the same. At the time, it seemed like the logical thing to do. How could I have known that trusting him with this power would end up being my financial undoing?

The bank representative I spoke with told me that John had been in the bank early that day and, using his power of attorney, had withdrawn all of the money from my checking account. I could hardly believe my ears! My head was spinning, and I was short of breath. My whole body was shaking, and I was pacing back and forth like a caged animal, tightening my grip on the phone as though it was a lifeline that would somehow pull me out of this quagmire.

How could he have done this? What was he thinking? What was he planning to do with the money? Was he wondering why I was so willing to help Metin when, at the same time, unbeknownst to me, he was in dire financial straits? Did he sense that it was becoming less and less likely that I was going to return to the States? Suddenly, his motivation was of little or no importance to me. Of paramount importance was how I was going to get the money back. Suddenly, as if out of nowhere, my plan crystallized.

I told my friend at the bank not to say anything to John. I was going to call him, and I guaranteed her that he would be in the bank the first thing the next morning to replace the money. She didn't ask how I planned to do this but agreed that mum was the word. I hung up and called John immediately. I told him about all of my car problems and explained that there must be a bank error of some sort, because I couldn't understand why the ATM machine kept telling me that I had insufficient funds since the day before I left for Turkey

I had deposited thirty thousand dollars into my account. I told him I was beside myself and asked him if he would please go to the bank the first thing the next morning and investigate for me. He agreed.

The next day I returned to the ATM machine and learned that the money had been re-deposited. I immediately instructed the officials at the bank in Milwaukee to wire all of the money to Turkey. At the time, I wrote it off as a momentary lapse of good judgment on John's part. Perhaps, I thought, it was motivated by jealousy or insecurity. I probably should have realized that his struggle for financial survival would supersede all his other instincts. My future was no longer of concern to him and neither was our future as a couple. Unbeknownst to me, John was drowning in debt and intended to do whatever was necessary to stay afloat.

Unfortunately, at this point my attention was totally focused on Istanbul and what Metin and I were going to do there. I put this incident out of my mind and assumed that John's sense of integrity would keep him from ever doing anything like that again. This was a very big mistake on my part and the beginning of my financial ruin.

CHAPTER 25

Turkçe Ve Fasil Eve

Cherish your visions and your dreams as they are the children
of your soul; the blueprints of your ultimate achievements.
—Napoleon Hill

By the time I arrived in Istanbul, Metin had already found what he considered to be the perfect spot for our new business venture. It was just off Istiklal Caddesi in Taksim, the hub of all things exciting and decadent in Istanbul. Tourists and Turks alike clog the streets twenty-four hours a day looking for a good time. Whatever kind of action or adventure a person was looking for, it could be found in Taksim. The hustle and bustle camouflages the dark side of a lot of what actually goes on there.

After many trips to this magical city, even I, a naive little ol' school teacher from Racine, Wisconsin, could see that just underneath the exotic veneer, which mesmerizes first-time visitors, there were dark and dangerous elements at work. This was a long way from the charming little café on a quiet residential street that I had envisioned, but Metin assured me there was more money to be made in the bar business in Taksim than in a café anywhere in the world. Okay, I thought. After all, what did I know?

The space Metin found had tremendous potential, but *potential* is the operative word here. It had been vacant for months, perhaps years, and, as a result, was in need of a significant amount of work. Just inside the main door, the floor had collapsed. The kitchen was unsightly, and in order to transform it into the kind of space we imagined, a lot of the interior built-ins and fixtures needed to be removed or replaced. Visions of dollar signs were running through my head.

On the positive side, the space itself was incredible. It reminded me of a loft apartment in New York. The walls were cream city brick, and the windows were almost the height of the ceiling. It was clear that once the renovation was complete, this place was going to be the most inviting one on the street.

Several weeks went by, and at long last, we were ready for the grand opening. New lights had been installed, a stage was built, and the bar was reconfigured. A sound system was purchased, musicians were hired, and we were ready to go. Strobe lights could be seen on the street below and encouraged people to come up and see what we were all about. As a result, a lot of curiosity seekers made their way up the stairs. In order to encourage them to stay, and to return with more of their friends, the price of our drinks was slightly lower than those of the other bars in the area. It wasn't long before our place, The House of Turkish and Gypsy Music, was making a name for itself. Unfortunately, only weeks after we opened, Ramazan began, the period of fasting that precedes the bayram, and all bar and restaurant business suffered. Based on what we had seen up to this point, if we could hang on until Ramazan ended, we were destined to be a legitimate contender on this street of dreams.

Ramazan came and went, and once again, our business was up and running. People who had been there before Ramazan returned and brought new people with them. Metin cajoled them, danced with them, and made sure that when they left they'd had a night they would always remember. We were a rising new star, and apparently, we were shining too brightly in some peoples' eyes.

There was another bar just below us, and by comparison, it was dark, dingy, smoky, and confining. Consequently, more and more people were making their way upstairs to see what the new kid on the block had to offer. Within a very short time, some extremely bad blood was being created with the people downstairs. Suddenly, customers were climbing up to the third floor without giving so much as a passing glance to what was happening on the second. It didn't take long for them to decide they had to do something to turn the tide back in their direction.

In this country, most bars, cafés, and restaurants hire people to stand outside and encourage passersby to come in. They may tout their specialty that day, offer discounts on a meal, or promise a free drink. The bar below us was no exception. However, instead of offering incentives to bring people into their place, they tried to frighten customers who were planning to come up to ours. They claimed that it was a dangerous place because of its mafia connections and warned people that there were frequent fights and shootings, none of which, of course, was true. When word of this reached Metin, he went downstairs to confront the manager and get some answers. Little did he know that this was just a glimpse of things to come.

I loved going to the bar and sitting with Metin. Drama queen that I was, being a regular and having a reserved seat at the manager's table at a popular place like this would have been sufficient in and of itself. I could return home and tell all my friends about my Istanbul connections and life on the wild side in Taksim The fact that there were rumblings of mafia connections, whether true or not, were simply icing on the cake. Being the financial backer was something even I could never have envisioned. I kept pinching myself to make sure I wasn't dreaming and asking myself how in the world this had happened. Istanbul is exotic and exciting, and now I was no longer just a visitor. I belonged there.

I tried to get to Istanbul as often as I could, but my responsibilities in Tarsus kept me busy, and my visits became less frequent. Because of this, I no longer had my finger on the pulse of the business. My conversations with Metin were shorter, and he was reluctant to pass on much information about the bar. Although I wasn't comfortable with this, I had to trust that he knew better than I did about what I did and didn't need to know. Once again, in retrospect, I should have heeded my woman's intuition.

It was Monday morning, and I arrived at school earlier than usual because I had a lot to do before my first class. I was sitting in the English Department staff room when the head of the department handed me the phone and told me Sertaç, Metin's youngest brother, was on the line.

"Sertaç?" I questioned. "Why in the world would he be calling me at this hour of the morning?"

His first words to me were, "Have you heard what happened?" The tone of his voice made my heart beat faster.

"No, I haven't heard anything." I responded.

"Metin's been shot," he said.

At that point, my eyes filled with tears, and I couldn't control the shaking in my voice. "How is he?" was my first question. "Is he alive or dead?" I asked. "How did you find out?" My questions were like machine gun bullets, and I was firing them at Sertaç as though my very life depended on the answers.

"We don't have any information," was his response. "My father wants to fly out in an hour. Do you want to go with him?"

My mind was reeling. There was a clause in my contract that forbid me from engaging in any other kind of work while I was employed by the college. In order to get permission to leave, I was going to have to talk to the director. I would have to admit that I had broken this rule. In addition, I was married. Metin was not my husband, not even a blood relative. How could I justify leaving my responsibilities that day and running off to Istanbul? In the amount of time it took me to walk to the administration building, I decided that nothing mattered but getting to Istanbul to help Metin. If the director wouldn't allow me to go, I would go anyway and resign my position effective immediately.

CHAPTER 26

Becoming Honest

It is your duty to find yourself.

—John C. Maxwell

Metin had stood by my side throughout the court battle, and absolutely nothing had deterred him, not all the drama surrounding it, the threats, the bribes, or the possible repercussions. In return, I had kept my promise to help him follow his dream. It goes without saying that these shared experiences had changed the dynamics of our relationship but to what degree I hadn't admitted to myself until then. Perhaps it was the age difference between us that prevented me from admitting what was actually happening.

Perhaps it was the cultural differences, the educational differences, or the fact that he was such a womanizer that kept me from believing that the two of us could ever have anything evenly remotely resembling a romantic relationship. After all, I rationalized, he was the consummate party animal, and the differences between us were greater than they had been between my mother and father—and look what happened to them. I had no desire to walk in my mother's footsteps. Now, as I sat on the plane next to his father, I came to grips with the fact I had fallen in love with Metin and that, once again, my fear of rejection and abandonment had rendered me immobile. What would have happened if I'd taken any of his many advances seriously and shared my feeling only to have him regard me as simply another one of his conquests? *After all,* I rationalized, *he calls everyone darling, and when he's with you, he makes every woman feel like she truly is the only one.* Why had I been so cautious, so afraid? After all, I was having a great adventure. Was my fear of rejection and abandonment so pervasive that I may have lost my last chance to find true love? Suddenly, I felt compelled to share my feelings with him, as confused as they may be. Silently, I prayed that it wasn't going to be too late.

At this point, neither his father nor I knew if Metin was alive or dead. We had no idea what we would find when we arrived at the hospital, and as a result, we sat next to each other, in silence, prisoners of our individual guilt. The things we didn't do and didn't say were haunting us as we headed for Istanbul. Would we ever have a second chance to say the things we wanted to say and to do the things we should have done? At this point, only God knew the answer to that question.

We landed in Istanbul, caught a cab, and headed for the hospital. We rode in silence as we had done in the plane. Perhaps it was the language barrier that kept us from sharing our feelings, or more likely, we were both lost, once again, in our own thoughts. We arrived at the hospital and catapulted from the cab. We ran, not knowing where we were going. Our only thought was to find Metin, hopefully, before it was too late. As it turned out, he was on the third floor. We bounded up the stairs rather than waiting for the elevator. Time was of the essence. We heard bloodcurdling screams, and the intensity of them made my blood run cold.

On the one hand, we hoped that the screams were Metin's, and he was alive. On the other, we wondered what could have happened to someone that could cause such agony. When we found Metin, he was writhing in pain, and we understood the source of the screams. No one could touch him or get near the examination table. As Metin's father conferred with the doctor on duty, I struggled to understand what was going on. Although my Turkish was getting better all the time, they were using words that were definitely not part of my vocabulary. In addition, I was a woman and a foreigner. I was not technically part of the family, and as a result, no one seemed to feel any obligation to share what was going on with me. The only person I could hope to get any information from was Metin.

I bent down to get closer to his face. I pressed my trembling lips to his ear. In a hushed tone of voice that was barely audible, I told him that I didn't know what had happened, but finally admitted that I had fallen in love with him. My body was shaking, and I was choking in an attempt to hold back my tears. Ever so gently I stroked his temple and whispered that if he lived through this, I would marry him. He looked up, and his eyes met mine. He gave me a faint smile of understanding and passed out from the pain.

I don't know how much time passed before we were in Metin's room and he was semiconscious again. Secretly, I hoped that he didn't remember what I had said. After all, I was still married. Did I really mean what I had said, or was I just looking for something to say that I thought would motivate him to hang on? I really didn't know, and considering what was happening at the moment, this was the least of my worries. His room was filled with male relatives from Istanbul. They were arguing with one another about the best course of action to take. The hospital was undergoing restoration, and there was only one functioning operating room. It was reserved for critical cases that were a matter of life and death. At the moment, two of his cousins who had been with him during the shooting were in there fighting for their lives.

Metin was in excruciating pain, but the hospital reasoned that he could be drugged and sedated until there was an opening in the operating room schedule. They said that depended on what other kinds of cases came in. He could conceivably have to wait two or three weeks before he could be operated on. To me, this was unthinkable. Metin had been shot because he refused to pay protection money. People threatened to close our bar, but as Metin had done with my court case, he took the high road and refused to pay. One night after closing, he was followed and shot in the thigh, fracturing his femur bone. The man could have killed him, but the intent was simply to send a message—cooperate or else. I felt responsible because he was protecting my investment, and I needed to do whatever I could to help.

In general, women have absolutely no clout in a room filled with Turkish men. Therefore, when it came to making an important decision like deciding what was best for Metin, it went without saying that they weren't the least bit interested in my opinion. Metin was the only person I could communicate with, and I was determined to do whatever he wanted in order to try to make up for what had happened to him.

The nurse came in to administer more drugs. The men were arguing among themselves about what to do. Without attracting any attention, I went to Metin's bedside and bent over to get as close to him as I could without attracting any attention. I whispered to him that he may have to wait two or three weeks before they could operate on him. I said, "You're about to pass out because of all of the drugs they've given you. Before that happens, please tell me what you want to do."

In a voice that was barely audible, Metin grabbed my hand and begged, "Please take me home."

I left the room and called Sertaç. I told him what Metin wanted and asked him to please help me, because my Turkish wasn't good enough to pull something like this off on my own. We exchanged several phone calls, and almost before I knew what was happening, four men appeared in the room with a gurney. They loaded Metin onto it, and his screams were so bloodcurdling that they brought tears to my eyes. I looked at his relatives and told them that I was taking control of the situation whether they liked it or not. I asked his father if he wanted to come back to Adana with us, and he declined. The men in the room watched, speechless, as I ran behind the gurney, and we headed for the ambulance waiting for us at the emergency entrance.

Metin and I were in the ambulance and on our way to the airport. I've mentioned the potholes and lack of driving rules here in other parts of the book, so one can only imagine the excruciating pain and bloodcurdling screams as we made our way to Ataturk Airport. I bought nine seats on the airplane for Metin and his stretcher, one for myself, and one for the Turkish man who was required to accompany me. Money was no object. My only concern was getting Metin back home to Adana.

On the flight home, air pockets replaced potholes but elicited the same response from Metin. All of the drugs they had given him were not enough to diminish his pain. He whined and screamed the entire flight. I couldn't help but wonder what the other passengers must have been thinking. I thought about all of the flights I had taken that were ruined by crying babies. Metin's screams couldn't even compare with that.

Much to my surprise, when the plane landed, there was an option to exit from either the front or the rear of it. I assumed that all of the passengers would run, not walk, to the exit at the front of the plane. Having literally shared Metin's pain the entire flight, I assumed they would want to distance themselves as quickly as possible. Once again, Turkish people left me speechless as nearly the entire plane exited from the rear so they could say "*geçmiş olsun*" to Metin, which means get well soon. I am ashamed to admit that, under the same circumstances, I don't think I would have been as gracious.

When we deplaned, there was another ambulance waiting for us. Metin's entire family was waiting with it. I turned Metin over them and returned to Tarsus. I wasn't officially a member of this family, so whatever my connection to Metin, it didn't count for anything at this point. I had brought him home and returned him to them, which, at that point, was the best that I could do.

Later I learned that Metin was transported to three hospitals before his family finally found one that was ready and able to treat him. His mother called me the next day and asked me to please come to the hospital. He was still in excruciating pain and needed surgery immediately. As it turned out, his femur bone was shattered, and the family needed one thousand Turkish liras to pay for the platinum band Metin needed to hold the bone together. It seemed like a small price to pay for what he'd gone through. I gave them the money and, once again, returned to Tarsus.

Metin was eventually released from the hospital and returned home. The doctors said he would be bedridden for at least three months. This may as well have been a death sentence for him. Nightlife as

Metin knew it was finished, at least for the moment. His friends, for the most part, had deserted him. He sank into a depression that no one was sure he would ever recover from. He didn't see or speak to anyone outside of his immediate family. For all practical purposes, he had died. I felt that his family held me responsible. If he hadn't been managing the bar, this would never have happened. As a result, I maintained what I considered to be an appropriate distance.

I was still wondering if he had heard or remembered what I'd said to him as he lay on the gurney in the hospital. If he had, why hadn't he called me? Perhaps he thought he was hallucinating or, worse yet, that I'd said those things not because I meant them but out of a sense of guilt. I tried not to spend too much time dwelling on it. After all, the end of the school year was approaching again, and everyone knows how hectic that is. I would be leaving for the States in a few months, and all of this would be just another memory and an incredible one at that. What would my friends in Milwaukee think about this?

Suddenly, without warning, I received a phone call from Fatma, Metin's mother. Although my Turkish still left a lot to be desired, she and I were able to communicate almost from the start. Perhaps we shared a special bond because we both loved the same man. She was calling to ask me to please come and visit Metin. She was concerned because he refused to eat or speak to anyone. He was so depressed that she wasn't sure he was ever going to be the same again. She said he had been calling my name, and she felt strongly that if anyone could pull him out of this slump, it would be me. I told her that I would be more than happy to come. We made the arrangements, and I agreed to visit the following Saturday.

Saturday arrived, and I was up bright and early. I took extra pains with my makeup and wore what I considered to be appropriate attire, considering that most of the women in his family are covered. I thought a long skirt and a blouse that covered most of my arms would be the best bet. I really didn't know what to expect when I arrived, so I wanted to look my best. It was a beautiful, sunny day, so I opened the sunroof, put on my favorite CD, and headed for Adana. Music always lifts my spirits, so I sang all the way.

I was prepared for anything. I was just minutes from Metin's house when I stopped for a red light. While I waited for the light to change, I decided to change the CD. I was in the process of doing this when the light turned green. Turkish drivers are extremely impatient and merciless if the light changes and traffic doesn't move. Not daring to hold up traffic, without looking up, I put the pedal to the floor and proceeded. Unfortunately, the man in front of me wasn't as quick off the line as I had been. He hadn't moved, and within seconds, I transformed the back of his brand-new car into an accordion. Passersby held their breath, waiting to see how he would react. Turks have a well-deserved reputation of being very emotional people, and it's not uncommon for vicious fist fights to break out after an accident. It didn't take long for the other driver to notice my license plate. It clearly identified me as a *yabanci*, or foreigner. He must have decided he'd rather battle me in court than on the streets, because instead of proffering his fists, he hunched over and clutched his back. *Oh great*, I thought, *another court case.*

The police arrived almost before I knew what happened. They ticketed me, not only for the accident, but for the fact that I wasn't carrying a fire extinguisher and first aid kit. Thank goodness that by this time body bags were no longer de rigueur. They also explained that because I had been in the country for almost three years, my American driver's license was no longer valid. That would result in a fine of eight hundred Turkish liras! I asked myself what else could possibly happen. Fortunately, both cars were still drivable, so after what seemed like an eternity, all of us were free to go. From that point on, it was up to the insurance companies to fight it out.

I eventually arrived at Metin's home. Sleep didn't come easily for him, and because he was sleeping so peacefully when I arrived, I decided I'd leave him alone, chat with his mom, and head back to Tarsus. Instead, she said, "Please don't go. It would mean so much to him to see you."

I went into the room where he was resting and kissed him on the cheek. He slowly opened his eyes, and this is where my story with Metin really begins.

CHAPTER 27

Endings and Beginnings

If at first you do succeed try not to look astonished.
—*Abundance (The Portable 7 Habits)*

After three months, Metin was finally able to walk again with the aid of crutches. We went to Istanbul to see what had happened to the bar. We were devastated to find that the place had been stripped. All of the expensive sound equipment and instruments, as well as the fixtures, had been stolen. Whatever wasn't actually bolted into the floor was gone. Metin was determined to find out who had taken what and to settle the score. I reminded him that he was still on crutches, and as disappointed as I was to see our dream go up in flames, I wasn't willing to throw him into the lion's den to try to recoup my investment.

Reluctantly, he agreed. I tried to hide my disappointment, and we boarded a plane back to Adana. As sad as I was, I took my consolation from the fact that Metin was still alive. Everything people had warned me about going into business in Istanbul turned out to be true. I simply didn't have the moxie or enough money to make it happen.

Spring in Adana is glorious, and Metin and I spent a lot of time together as he recuperated. He still hadn't mentioned what I'd said to him in the hospital. Perhaps he hadn't heard me. Slowly but surely, we were growing closer and closer together. We commiserated over the loss of the bar, entertained one another with funny stories from our pasts, shared our dreams and visions for the future, and, without actually realizing it, laid the foundations for our future together.

Toward the end of the year, the head of the English department where I was working was poached by a private college in Adana. I was crestfallen because I admired him so much. He was one of the most talented people I'd ever met, and he utilized these talents in the classroom like a maestro directing a world-class orchestra. I knew that teaching in Tarsus wouldn't be the same without him. Much to my delight, once he had signed his new contract, he asked me to join him. How could I refuse? I was getting a 10 percent increase in pay and a three-bedroom, two-bath apartment on one of the choicest streets in Adana, and I'd be in the same city as Metin. *Does it get any better than this?* I wondered.

Unfortunately, the director of our school in Tarsus was not willing to let us go without a fight. In his mind, he was losing two of his best foreign teachers, and because it was so late in the year, he knew the chance of finding replacements with the same qualifications was nearly impossible. He realized that the head of the department could not be swayed, but he wasn't sure about me. He offered to make me the new head and sweetened the pot by offering me a complimentary airline ticket to the destination of my choice over spring break. Although I waited until the next day to give him my final decision, I knew in my heart of hearts that wherever my dear friend was going, I was going as well.

The following day we were forced to sign a paper in which we relinquished our rights to our airline tickets home, our insurance benefits, our summer pay, and our moving expenses. The total cost to each of us was about ten thousand dollars. That was the bad news. The good news was that our new employer was going to reimburse us for whatever losses we incurred as a result of leaving Tarsus, so once again, I mused, *It doesn't get any better than this.*

The deed was done. We had both resigned, and before the ink on the paper was dry, we were packing and preparing to move to Adana.

Although I knew I was going to miss my friends terribly, I was off to a new city, a new school, and the promise of new adventures. My new apartment was modern by comparison, and although it lacked the character and old-world charm of my historic home in Tarsus, it had other qualities that more than made up for that. It had three bedrooms, two and a half baths, and a salon with magnificent views of the lake and mountains in the distance. I lived on one of the most posh streets in new Adana, and I would be making more money then I'd ever made in my whole life.

Unfortunately, my red bomb with the sunroof didn't fit into my new lifestyle and neighborhood. After I had settled in, the first thing I did was start making my rounds to car dealerships to see who would be willing to take it in trade on a new model. Obviously, these salesmen were much more astute than I had been when I fell in love with my "boy toy." Although I did my best to try to distract them as they examined it, my efforts were in vain. The question was no longer what kind of car I wanted to buy. It was what fool would be willing to take my car in trade? I finally found a man at the Peugeot dealership near my seaside retreat who must have felt sorry for me. He insisted on driving it. That was a good sign, I thought. No one else had even wanted to get behind the wheel. We went for a test drive, and I was on pins and needles. Will the CD player act up? Will we hit a pothole and blow a 175-lira tire? Will the headlights or horn act up again? Fortunately, the air conditioner was working well that day, and the salesman was impressed.

When we returned to the showroom, I didn't miss a beat. There was a shiny, sporty, brand-new white Peugeot 207 on display. As I had done with my red bomb, without test driving or even sitting behind the wheel, I shouted, "I'll take that one!" The salesman was beaming from ear to ear, thinking that this was the easiest sale he'd ever made. I was smiling too, and I'm sure that, at the time, he was wondering why. What he didn't know was that every other dealership in southeastern Turkey had refused to take my car as a trade-in. When I took my sleek new car in for its first checkup, I learned that the salesman who had sold it to me had been fired. I must admit that I couldn't help wondering whether my trade-in had anything to do with it. I certainly hoped it hadn't.

When I left at the end of June for my monthlong visit to America, I was as happy as a clam. My new apartment was completely furnished and tastefully decorated. It was done in shades of red with gold gilding and had sparkling crystal chandeliers in every room. I had been deeply moved when I first went to Istanbul and learned the story about Pierre Loti. He was a Frenchman who had visited Istanbul in the late nineteenth century. He fell in love with a beautiful young woman who, much to his dismay,was married. He dressed like a Turk, lived like a Turk, and emulated all things Turkish. He eventually returned to France, but as hard as he tried, he couldn't forget his Turkish obsession. Ten years later he returned in order to see her again only to learn that, in his absence, she had died. There are streets, cafés, and hotels in Istanbul that are named after him and that are modern-day testaments to his love of Turkey and this woman. Hopeless romantic that I am, I was deeply affected by his story. I wanted to create the same kind of atmosphere that I imagined he must have had in his home. It necessitated making my surroundings sumptuous, luxurious, and elegant. I must say I was getting pretty close to the mark. Like Pierre Loti, I had fallen in love with all things Turkish, and I was beginning to emulate their lifestyle too. I was determined that my new apartment would be my way of trying to carry on his legacy.

My sporty new car was parked in a secure lot for protection, and I had arranged, as I'd done in Tarsus, to have someone drive it periodically to keep everything running. My dear friend, the former head of the English department in Tarsus, and I lived in the same building and had become closer than ever. In fact, he ended up renting a seaside getaway on the shores of the Mediterranean in the same *sitesi* that I was in, so we were neighbors there as well. He spoke Turkish like a native, so he and I were able to go wherever we wanted and to negotiate for anything we needed without the help of Metin or anyone else.

By this time, Metin was ambulatory again. However, his body had healed, but his spirit hadn't. He was severely depressed not only about the permanent damage to his leg but about the death of his dream. Because of this, we had less and less to do with each other. Although I was saddened by this, it was something that was completely out of my control. I was leaving for the summer and had other things to occupy my mind. What I didn't know at the time was that my normal month long stay would turn out to be six months, and when I finally returned to Turkey, my entire world would be changed forever.

CHAPTER 28

The Summer from Hell

All stressed out and no one to choke.
—Seen on a bumper sticker

My plane for Chicago took off from Istanbul on June 21, and John had made all of my doctor appointments months in advance just as he'd done for the past three years. This insured that I'd have all of my yearly examinations done by the end of my first week in the States. Even my doctors were in the routine now, and all of them knew that if there was any kind of a procedure that needed to be done, it had to be scheduled before the end of my month long visit. July 21 was my departure date.

My first stop, on my first Monday morning in the States, was at the office of my gynecologist, Dr. Nash. He was a delightful man, and I always enjoyed seeing him. This year was no different. As we chatted in his office, I mentioned that I'd seen a gynecologist in Adana, and she had expressed concern about something she'd seen on an ultrasound when I visited her. She asked me to come back in thirty days so she could do a follow-up exam. I told him that I never made the follow-up appointment, because I knew I'd be in the States and would see him. Once again, because of the language barrier between the Turkish doctor and myself, I wasn't able to explain exactly what she'd seen. Dr. Nash thought out loud. "If we do the regular exam, we'll go into this room. On the other hand, doing a more thorough exam will require going into a second room, which is better equipped." He was obviously weighing the pros and cons to determine if it was worth the inconvenience.

I told him not to bother. It probably wasn't anything. "No," he said. "We'll do the entire exam in the second room. It will be a little less comfortable, but I know it will be more thorough."

As it turned out, it was the right thing to do. I had a tumor. He couldn't determine whether it was malignant but decided it must be removed immediately. After consulting with him, it was decided I would have a complete hysterectomy before the end of the week—not exactly what I had expected to hear at nine o'clock on my first Monday morning in the States. When I finally emerged from the examination room, I was oblivious to what was going on around me. I was in a daze. I knew a few women who had gone through this, but I thought I was different and immune to this kind of thing. After all, I was living on the wild side. Other women stayed at home and raised their grandchildren. I was an international jetsetter who simply didn't have time for this kind of thing.

John was waiting for me. "What took you so long?" he asked. "Are you pregnant or something?" His feeble attempt at humor was totally lost on me.

When I got over the shock of his glibness, I composed myself I said, "Thank you for your concern. I've just learned I have a tumor and have to schedule myself for a hysterectomy later this week." *Happy homecoming*, I thought.

Although I'd only been home three days at this point, it was painfully clear that something was bothering John. He was exceptionally quiet and uncharacteristically withdrawn. My homecoming had left a lot to be desired even before I'd seen the gynecologist. My arrival date was not a surprise, and I assumed John would have had everything ready and waiting for me. I am, admittedly, a fanatical neatnick. In our nearly twenty years of marriage, I never went to bed with so much as a dirty glass in the sink. I made the bed every morning and hung up my clothes every night, and no matter what time it was or how tired I might have been, I never went to bed without removing my makeup and brushing my teeth.

When John and I married, I believed I could teach him to hang his clothes up, and he obviously assumed he could train me to throw mine on the floor. After years of heated arguments, we finally reached a mutually agreeable solution. We would have separate closets in separate rooms. In twenty years of marriage, I never opened his closet doors for fear we'd end up in divorce court. If he wanted something washed, it was his responsibility to get it into the clothes hamper. Failure to do that meant no clean clothes.

The year before, I had come home and had been shocked at the deplorable condition in which I found the house. I spent the better part of the month I was there cleaning, and I made it painfully clear that I didn't plan on doing that again the following year. Therefore, I was more than a little surprised to arrive home and find it in worse condition than it had been the previous summer. I couldn't contain my anger, so the first couple of days were tense at best. In fact, I actually considered checking myself into a hotel. However, the fact that I had a major surgery staring me in the face meant that this was not the time to rock the boat.

Later that week I had my hysterectomy. My doctor told me the tumor was benign, and I breathed a sigh of relief. Perhaps to help relieve my distress or perhaps because it was actually true, he also told me that when a woman reaches her sixties it's a good idea for them to have this kind of an operation to help reduce the chances of developing cancer later on. I didn't know if he was telling me the truth or simply trying to cheer me up. I guess it didn't really matter. I hoped the worst was over, so I could get on with my summer.

John continued to be uncharacteristically quiet and withdrawn. It was obvious that he was severely depressed and was hiding something. At this point, I had no idea what was coming, or there's no telling what I would have done. Wells Fargo Bank held the mortgage on our house, and through a clerical error of some sort, every time they sent John an e-mail, they copied me in. The second week I was home I was shaken to my very core when I received a message from them congratulating me on the home equity loan I had just taken. Moments after I read this message, John and I got into the car. I was scheduled to see my general practitioner for my yearly exam, and he was driving me to his office. The checkup would include my yearly mammogram.

As we headed to my appointment, I was reminded about how he had abused his power of attorney the year before to secretly withdraw thirty thousand dollars from my bank account. He still didn't have any idea that I knew what he had done. However, the fact that he was capable of something so devious and underhanded had put me on high alert.

What was this about a home equity loan? Didn't he have to have my signature on something like this? Isn't this something he should have consulted with me about? I could feel my muscles tightening and my body tensing up. We rode in silence until I finally got up the nerve to ask him why Wells Fargo had sent me a message congratulating me on a home equity loan. He looked stunned, and the color left his face. He hemmed and hawed, and then he blew. He started hurtling insults and condemnations at me about Metin. He began to fire questions at me about why I had given Metin money to open a bar.

"What?" I screamed "Did that have to do with the home equity loan?"

John hurled one accusation after another. "You love him more than you love me. You help him, but you don't help me. You care about him, but you don't care about me."

Suddenly, with a voice that sounded like it had originated in the depths of hell, I screamed, "Tell me about the fucking home equity loan!"

He clutched the steering wheel and wrung it between his hands as if he were using it as a substitute for my throat. He was speeding and screaming at the top of his lungs. He kept his eyes focused on the road. He obviously didn't have the courage to look me in the eye. He told me that he was out of money and didn't know what to do. He took a forty thousand-dollar home equity loan in my name, once again, using his power of attorney.

At that point, I lost complete control of all my faculties. I was like a madwoman who had just been stabbed in the heart. I unleashed a tirade at him and started physically attacking him as he drove. As I pounded on his shoulders with my fists, I screamed, "How could you have done something like this? What gave you the right to use your power of attorney to cheat me again? This is exactly what you did last August when you took the thirty thousand dollars out of my checking account. You've ruined our lives. I hate you."

When he felt he couldn't take anymore, he threw the car into park, jumped out, and ran down the road, leaving me alone to go to my doctor's appointment.

By the time I returned home later that afternoon, I was numb. One question haunted me. How could he have done this to us? When I arrived home, I found him sitting in the family room like a stone statue, staring into space. My first words to him were, "We have to talk." And talk we did—for hours! The first thing I told him was that I wanted to cancel my power of attorney. The second thing I insisted on was going to Wells Fargo to see, with my own eyes, what he had done.

The next morning we went to the bank and met with a representative. I was shocked to learn that in addition to the forty-thousand-dollar home equity loan that was in *my* name, there were two others that he had obtained using both of our names. I was speechless. I bought the house after my first divorce and had lived there for more than twenty-three years. Now all of the money and all of the blood, sweat, and tears that had been put into it was gone. The housing market was already beginning to collapse. We were going to end up owing more on the property than we would be able to sell it for. *How in the world had this happened? What else had he done behind my back while I was gone?* I felt totally betrayed and alone in the marriage. Instead of being with the man who was going to take care of me for the rest of my life, I suddenly found myself with someone who would end up being the cause of my financial ruin. What a homecoming this had been.

I was recovering from my unexpected hysterectomy and had discovered I'd lost my house. What else could happen? As it turned out, the worst was yet to come. Later that week, I received a call from St. Mary's hospital informing me that, once again, there were some irregularities on my mammogram. They asked me to come back to the hospital immediately for some additional tests. While I was still reeling from everything that had happened so far, I was diagnosed with stage-three breast cancer. I questioned the results of the biopsy. This couldn't be happening to me. After all, I was a busy person. I had just accepted a new job, moved to a new city, bought a new car, furnished a new apartment, and was ready to start a new chapter in my life. The nurses tried desperately to comfort me. They still didn't understand that I refused to let this stop my forward progress. I was on a new path, and although, admittedly, this was going to slow me down for a while, it didn't change anything. I still planned to go back to Turkey, to start my new job, and to follow my dream. Now, more than ever, I couldn't wait to get back on the plane.

My doctors scheduled the surgery for August 8. I was catapulted into a state of depression because my departure had been delayed, and I wouldn't know until the surgery was over when I could plan to return. A hundred questions plagued me. What will happen to my job? How will I make my car payments? What will happen to my seaside apartment? Who will pay my utility bills? How will the director of my new school react to the news? When will I be able to return? What else could possibly go wrong? Ironically, my concerns didn't revolve around the cancer and how I'd handle that. Instead, they were all about how the delay in my departure would affect my future plans in Adana. This was truly the beginning of the end of my life in Milwaukee.

I had one of the best surgeons in southeastern Wisconsin, so I wasn't worried. I was confident he would remove the cancerous tumor and that before I had time to realize what had happened, I'd be on the plane heading back to my new home. However, much to my surprise, after returning to my hospital room, I learned that the cancer was much more aggressive then they had originally hoped. When I asked how all of this could have happened in the year since my last mammogram, I was told that the cancer was obviously already there and that it just wasn't visible on the mammogram. It had spread into my lymph nodes as well, so thirteen of them had to be removed. Chemotherapy and radiation were absolutely essential, especially because my cancer was not of the type that responds to drug therapy. I staunchly refused to give up my dream. My mind was reeling, and I could hardly believe what I was hearing. All I wanted to do was escape and return to a place far away from John and the financial devastation that he had brought down upon us. My primary goal was to complete all of the treatments as soon as possible so I could return to Adana.

I had to undergo one more surgery before I could begin chemotherapy. It was necessary to install a port in my chest through which the chemo would be administered. The day after the port was installed, I had my first treatment. According to my oncologist, I needed six months of chemo and a month of radiation. The director of the school in Adana had agreed to hold my job for a semester. If

I finished all of my treatments before the end of January, I could return to Adana and pick up my life where I left off. Knowing that I had this chance gave me all the motivation I needed to ensure that I would be back at school for the beginning of the second semester.

Going through chemo was an adventure of a different sort. Everything was new, and I didn't have any idea about what to expect. I knew that I was supposed to lose my hair, but even after several weeks, I still had mine. *Perhaps I will be an exception,* I thought. I always imagined that when it fell out, it would all come out at one time. Every morning when I showered I tugged here and there, trying to speed up the process. I wondered why it wouldn't come out. I checked my pillow every morning and found that I was leaving a little bit here and a little bit there, but these were only strands, not clumps. This allowed me to maintain my fantasy that I was going to be the exception to the rule, and I wasn't going to lose mine. Finally, reality hit, and the actual process of losing my hair strand by strand became so frustrating that I went to my beautician to have my head shaved. It was a great feeling, because, at long last, I had a degree of power, small as it was, over this disease. My beautician cried, but I was smiling from ear to ear. I was relieved to find that my bald head was actually quite attractive. It was smooth and shiny and maintenance free. I began to wonder how bizarre it would be to continue to sport this look once the chemo was over. In the end, I decided that as much of an adventurer as I fancied myself to be, I wasn't quite ready for that.

The second most devastating loss was my eyelashes. I never paid any attention to how much having them enhances a person's looks. It wasn't until they were gone that I really appreciated them. I couldn't help but wonder if they were ever coming back. However, the biggest shock was yet to come. It came in the form of the steroids. That was a word that, for me, already had negative connotations. I'd only heard it used in conjunction with athletes and race horses. *Why would they be giving them to me?* I wondered. I was warned that, yes, there were some negative side effects, but the drugs were supposed to prevent people from vomiting after their treatments. They must have worked, because I never became physically ill as so many other people did. However, the downside of taking them was the weight gain. Every week that passed, I gained another pound or two. During the course of my treatments, I put on thirty pounds. The nurses who were in charge of administering the chemo told me that I was one of the lucky ones. In their experience, they said, it was the people who gained weight who had the best chance of surviving. Those who lost weight usually didn't make it. That probably should have lifted my spirits; however, it didn't provide any consolation for what was happening to my once youthful-looking and curvaceous body.

The days dragged on and on. I felt like I was an inmate marking the passage of each day on my cell wall. John was an excellent caregiver. That was his strength. For years I had asked him why he was always at his best when I was at my worst. He drove me to all of my chemo appointments and picked me up when they were finished. He made sure I was never alone, and he looked after me like a loving parent after a child. His concern for me and my well-being was genuine, but I couldn't get past what he had done to us financially.

I began to think about Metin. I missed Turkey more than I ever imagined possible. The knowledge that my return would be postponed, possibly indefinitely, paralyzed me and made me feel sick to my stomach. It was, in my mind, my last hurrah—the last chance to feel vibrant and alive. Metin, to a great extent, had shaped my life there. I knew that if I talked to him I'd still feel connected, albeit vicariously. We'd weathered more storms in two years than most people do in a lifetime. I had to reconnect with him. I didn't know if I felt this urgency because I was genuinely in love with him, was in love with Turkey, or was simply at my wit's end with John.

When I left Adana, my relationship with Metin was at an all time low. We'd lost the bar, and he would limp for the rest of his life because of the shooting. What, I wondered, would his reaction be if I called him? There was no doubt about it; I was down and out. Within five weeks, I had undergone three surgeries—the hysterectomy, the breast cancer, and the implantation of the port. I had learned that everything I had worked a lifetime to build had been stolen from me. I desperately needed to feel connected to someone, and at that point, I knew it had to be someone other than my husband. After struggling with my demons for several days, I decided to call. After all, what did I have to lose?

When Metin answered the phone, he was surprised and elated to hear my voice. I suddenly felt a sense of calm and reassurance wash over me. He listened intently as I explained what had happened in the weeks since I'd left Turkey. He was supportive and encouraging. When I hung up, I felt rejuvenated and uplifted. How, I wondered, could a man who was half my age be so empathetic and wise for his years?

In the beginning, I only called once or twice a week. As the weeks turned into months, my calls became more frequent and the conversations much more intimate. We were sharing feelings and dreams, and I felt like a schoolgirl again. Suddenly, I was calling every day and relying on Metin to give me the strength I so desperately needed to go on. By this time, I had decided that if I couldn't return to Turkey, life wouldn't be worth living. I felt like a zombie just going through the motions. There was no joy in my life, no laughter, nothing to look forward to except being with Metin again. I kept my eye on the goal, and the goal was to return to Adana.

Metin looked forward to my calls almost as much as I looked forward to making them. I was on pins and needles every morning waiting for John to leave the house. I anxiously awaited my private time with Metin. It became a ritual. John left, and I headed for the sunniest place in the house. I curled up on the couch, fluffed a pillow under my head, and placed my call. We laughed and giggled and told each other how wonderful it would be when I was back in Adana and we could be together again. At the time, I wasn't sure whether Metin was sincere about the plans we were making for the future. However, at that point, all I needed was the promise of something better. My oncologist didn't sugarcoat anything. He told me that my cancer had been extremely aggressive and unemotionally told me what my chances of survival were. They were grim. I desperately needed to believe that after all I'd been through, there would indeed be a pot of gold at the end of the rainbow.

CHAPTER 29

Truth Time

A small leak can sink a great ship.
—Benjamin Franklin

As the days turned into weeks and the weeks turned into months, John and I grew further and further apart. I knew he hadn't been truthful with me, and he knew that I had secrets of my own. As my relationship with Metin continued to develop, I was transported into a world of my own. I counted the minutes until I could call him and hear his voice again. He was the first thing I thought of every morning and the last thing every night.

John continued to be supportive and an incredible caregiver. However, all of his efforts were lost on me. I still couldn't grasp the full significance of what he had done and the long-term impact it would have on both of our lives. We were both simply going through the motions. The only thing that mattered to me was finishing my treatments as soon as possible so I could return to Turkey. There was literally nothing left for me in Milwaukee.

One morning, as if out of nowhere, John confronted me about Metin. He and a friend had hacked into my e-mail account and made copies of all of the messages I'd sent to my friends talking about Metin and my feelings for him. He grilled me unmercifully about what was going on. He also knew about my daily phone calls to him. He was furious and out of control. He raved like a madman and demanded answers. I love football and know as well as John that a good offense is the best defense, so I marched into our bedroom and, from under the mattress, I pulled out a bra that I'd found under the couch pillow in his office. Now it was my turn! I demanded to know where it came from. At first, he tried in vain to convince me it was mine.

"It's not even my size," I screamed, "and don't you think I'd know whether it was mine or not? How stupid do you think I am?"

We argued for hours and hurled brutal accusations at one another. Finally, I didn't have the energy and wasn't interested enough in preserving the marriage to continue the assault. I retreated to the bedroom and decided to let the chips fall where they may.

Because I still had several months of chemo to finish, we continued to exist under the same roof. He drove me to my treatments more out of a sense of duty than anything else. John took up residence in the family room, and I did the same in the bedroom. Our paths seldom crossed. I cried all day and cried myself to sleep at night. I was living in the depths of hell and wondered if I could exist long enough under these conditions to crawl out of it. I likened myself to a prisoner on death row. At that moment in my life, the prisoner and I were kindred spirits.

When I spoke to Metin, I could no longer put on a happy face. Day after day I felt like my life force was being sucked out of me. Chemo became a pleasant diversion. It allowed me to get out of the house and see other people. The rest of my days and nights were spent in solitary confinement. *Will this ever end?* I kept asking myself. I had already decided that if I could possibly finish my chemo in time to get on the plane and back to Adana, I would do my radiation in Turkey. My doctors questioned the wisdom of this. I had to make sure that there was a facility in Adana that could provide the type of treatment I needed. I became a woman with a mission, and that was to get the answers to these questions. Considering that my physical condition was less than optimum and that I had sunk into the depths of depression, I'm not sure how I found the strength to get the job done. But where there's a will, there's a way.

I consulted with a radiologist in Milwaukee to whom I will be forever grateful. He told me all the questions to ask, and I brought the answers to him. Although the treatment would probably not be quite as effective as it would've been if I'd stayed in the States, it would be adequate. It was settled. I was going to finish my chemo by the end of December or the beginning of January to ensure that I was on the plane back to Turkey in time to start the second semester of school.

CHAPTER 30

Financial Ruin

It's been lovely, but I have to scream now.
—Seen on a bumper sticker

My next challenge was working with John to find a solution to our financial problems. It was clear that filing bankruptcy was the only way out. We got in touch with the best bankruptcy attorney in Milwaukee and made an appointment to see him. He needed paperwork to substantiate how much money we had and how much we owed. Neither John nor I were very good at keeping records, so collecting all of this information was a job of gargantuan proportions. It took two or three weeks to get everything together, and time was of the essence. This needed to be settled before I left again.

Both of us were shocked to learn that in spite of hundreds of thousands of dollars worth of debt, we were not eligible to file for bankruptcy. Although John had no job and no source of income, I made too much money for us to qualify. I could hardly believe my ears! I was numb! Bankruptcy seemed like the only viable option, and we were ineligible.

My mind started racing. John had already taken all of the equity out of our house, and now I was going to be the sacrificial lamb. Because Wisconsin was a community property state, I would end up paying off our joint bills as well, as any that he had incurred during the course of our marriage. The whole idea was repugnant to me. I had to come up with another option.

We left the attorney's office and walked back to the car in silence. I wanted to scream. "It's just not fair," I cried over and over through my tears. *I've gotten out of bed every day for thirty years and gone to work while you laid there and then enjoyed your morning coffee with your friends. I've worked my whole life and for what? While you lived off of your inheritance, I made my money the hard way only to have you steal it out from under me. What kind of a man are you? How can you look at yourself in the mirror?*

Suddenly, as if out of nowhere, I said, "John, the only solution is for us to get a divorce so you can file for bankruptcy on your own."

He looked at me dumbfounded and said that he couldn't believe his ears. I argued that this was the only way he could keep me from being sucked into the financial black hole that he had created. All the way home we discussed the pros and cons. He was convinced that this was a ploy. He argued that my real reason for wanting a divorce was so that I could be with Metin. At that moment, I was being completely honest when I said that my main concern was getting out of this mess with what little money I had left. What happened to the two of us after that was, at that particular moment, the last thing on my mind.

John always fancied himself to be quite the expert on everything. He claimed to have known people who had filed bankruptcy and argued that the process wasn't nearly as bad as people thought. Fortunately, the bankruptcy attorney set him straight. The laws had changed. Because economic times were bad, people were using it as a way to wipe their slates clean and start over again, debt free. As a result, the government had clamped down. Under the new law, people were required to let government officials enter their homes and physically remove anything of value. I had visions of our neighbors watching in awe as our beautiful bronze statues, paintings, and objects of art were carried out by an army of government agents. The thought made me sick to my stomach. Our home was like a museum. A lifetime of collecting unique pieces of exquisite beauty was going up in flames.

We had been married for nearly twenty years, so there was a part of me that was crying inside because of what had happened to us. Our relationship was like a beached whale gasping for air. In spite of its best efforts, the whale would die and so, it seemed, would our love. I had to fight the urge to take responsibility for this. I kept wondering what would have happened if I hadn't gone to Turkey. In retrospect, there probably wasn't anything I could have done to prevent the inevitable. John had taken out the first home equity loan a month after I left for Turkey in 2005. In the three years I was gone, he had slowly but surely siphoned off all of the equity in our home. I don't think whether I was in the United States or Turkey would have made any difference. The fact that I was out of the country just made it easier for him to do what he needed to do.

The more we discussed the idea of divorce, the more belligerent John became. After all, he argued, if I had enough money to start a business for Metin in Istanbul, why didn't I have enough money to bail him out of his financial problems? Among other things, he revealed that he owed the IRS a substantial amount of money and that the debt to them had already cost him thousands of dollars in interest. There are many things I could have said in answer to him. However, every time we talked about money, he was quick to remind me that his inheritance was not community property. He was adamant that none of this money be used for joint expenses, because that would change the rules. What was his was his, and that was it. As a child, one of the lessons I learned was that a woman should never, under any circumstances, expect the man in the relationship to share any financial information. I learned the lesson well, and as a result, I had no idea that he had run out of money years ago and had started using the equity in the house to pay for his day-to-day living expenses.

After weeks of discussion, it was settled. He reluctantly agreed that we would file for a divorce, and subsequently, John would file bankruptcy as an individual. It was the only solution that would guarantee I wouldn't be dragged into this financial quagmire with him. It would allow me to keep my pension and the money I was making in Turkey. John seemed confident that he would be left with enough to subsist on. We talked about getting married again once this problem was taken care of and the dust settled. At the time, I seriously considered the possibility. However, as things turned out, that was something that would never happen.

John had absolutely no money, and I was determined I was not going to spend a cent more than I had to in order to file for divorce and put the financial problems behind me. I went online in an attempt to find someone who could help us through the process as cheaply as possible. Bingo! I found a woman in a suburb just outside of Milwaukee. She helped people with uncontested divorces do it as cheaply as possible. She dropped the paperwork off at our home, and I completed it immediately. When I was done, I returned it to her for her approval. Once she was sure that everything had been filled in correctly, she would submit it to the court. I wondered if it could actually be this inexpensive and easy. With the exception of one glitch, the answer was yes.

It was December, and the court was in recess. Most of the judges had left for the Christmas and New Year holiday and weren't expected back until after the first of the year. *Oh my God*, I thought. *That's too late.* I was supposed to fly back to Turkey right after Christmas, and I couldn't possibly think of leaving if this matter wasn't settled. To be honest, I didn't trust that John would go through with it if I were no longer in Milwaukee. Once again, my mind was racing. What could I do? Who could I call to get a suggestion from? Why is everything going wrong? Finally, I decided to call the woman who had helped me with the paperwork and filed it with the court. She suggested that I write a letter to the court explaining the extenuating circumstances. According to her, our case was a piece of cake—an uncontested divorce with no children involved. Perhaps there was a judge who would be willing to hear the case. I did what she suggested, and eureka, she was right. On December 24, 2008, our marriage was ended.

Once again, I boarded the Turkish Airlines plane in Chicago totally consumed by my own thoughts. The past six months had been the most difficult in my life. I had undergone a complete hysterectomy and a lumpectomy to remove breast cancer, had a port inserted to receive chemotherapy, undergone six months of chemo and its side effects, filed for divorce, and watched as my husband began bankruptcy proceedings. I'd lost my house, my car, my husband, and all of my most valued personal possessions. The world that I had spent a lifetime creating was no more.

People always told me that God never gives people more than they can handle. I was beginning to question the validity of this statement. However, my eyes were still on the goal, and that was to return to Turkey. Because of all that had happened, my strength and optimism hung on my daily conversations with Metin. He gave me the courage to believe that, like the phoenix, I too would rise again out of the ashes of what was left of my life.

CHAPTER 31

Coming Home

If you must cry over spilled milk, then please try to condense it.
—Author unknown, "The Road to Success"

When I finally landed in Adana, my friend, who was also the new head of the English department at our school, was waiting for me. At the time, I had so many other things on my mind that I hadn't given much thought to my normally meticulous appearance. His reaction upon seeing me made it painfully obvious that the past few months had taken a real toll on my body as well as my spirit.

As we drove the short distance to our apartments, he couldn't stop staring at me. He was too gracious to ask what in the hell had happened to me, but the expression on his face spoke volumes. I was wearing a wig, and stylish it was, it was nevertheless still a wig. I had gained thirty pounds from the steroids, so my normally crisp and tailored body-skimming suits had given way to a skirt with an elastic waistband and a voluminous blouse. There was no concealing the fact that I no longer had eyebrows or eyelashes, and I squirmed uncomfortably under his scrutiny. As we drove the short distance to our apartments, I tried to summarize everything that had happened. I was clutching for dear life the only remaining thing of great value that I owned. It was a small locked steel box with approximately one hundred thousand dollars' worth of jewelry in it. If all else failed, I thought, I could always sell some of it in order to get my financial feet back on the ground.

When I opened the door to my apartment, a wave of mixed feelings washed over me. I was ecstatic to be back in the place that I now called home. However, in my absence, it was necessary for the school to find a short-term replacement for me. When the first person didn't work out, they hired a second. Both of them had stayed in my apartment, which I had so lovingly furnished and decorated before I left. As a consequence, all of my personal belongings had been haphazardly stuffed into a small room that was supposed to serve as either a guest room or office. Many things were difficult to find because they'd been moved or had disappeared in my absence, and now the apartment definitely had the feeling that it had been lived in. I would liken it to the feeling one has when buying a used car. Even though it was going to serve the purpose for which it was intended, I no longer felt like the original owner. Oh well, I rationalized, it was a small price to pay for guaranteeing that I would still have a job starting the second semester.

The second semester began, and it goes without saying that my students were apprehensive, at best, when I entered the classroom. After all, they had already had two teachers for the first semester, and now a third one appeared in their midst. I guessed that their first thought was probably, *I wonder how long this one will last.* I had anticipated that there may be a period of serious adjustment, and I came prepared. I spoke enough Turkish by this time that I could explain to them why my return had been delayed. They listened intently as I explained about the cancer and chemotherapy. In addition, I brought some very small gifts to give them as atonement for not being with them at the beginning of the term. I assured them that I was not going to be leaving, either the second semester or the second year. That seemed to put them at ease, and the teaching and learning process began.

The school year progressed nicely. The biggest fly in the ointment was my radiotherapy. I was scheduled for thirty to thirty-five appointments, so every day after school, my dear friend Veronica, who had come to Turkey from the States with me in order to fill a position at the same school, and I jumped into my car and headed to the local hospital for my treatment. Perhaps I misunderstood something that was explained to me or perhaps it was indeed true, but I was left with the impression that if I missed a treatment, I would have to start all over again. This was incentive enough for me to make these visits the most important thing in my daily schedule for the next month.

Me, Metin, Veronica Van Dalen, and a friend in an Istanbul carpet shop.

Slowly but surely, my apartment was taking shape again. The chemotherapy and now the radiotherapy were draining me of my energy; as a result, I was moving at a snail's pace. However, at long last, I had learned that everything that needed to be done didn't need to be done before I went to bed at night. My physical condition made it impossible for me to keep up my current pace. I moved more slowly and became content to go to bed with a to-do list for the next day. The goal I was keeping my eye on now was to finish radiotherapy and resume some semblance of a normal life. After my sessions, I went home and, little by little, managed to cross things off my "things-to-do list". Veronica and I still needed to buy a few things for our apartments, and it was after my treatment that we would venture out and about to make our purchases.

There was one thing I hadn't done yet that should have been first on my list—finding a bank that had safe-deposit boxes so I could lock my jewelry up for safekeeping. I really didn't feel a sense of urgency about doing this; after all, I was living in a school lodgment on one of the most prestigious streets in Adana. Because of this, I assumed that it was safe and secure. I should have remembered what people say about making assumptions.

Finally, I decided it was time to find a bank with safe-deposit boxes. Surprisingly, they are few and far between here. I inquired at school and learned that I would have to go into the center of old Adana. The prospect of driving, navigating the narrow, traffic-clogged streets of the old city, and finding the bank were too daunting to even consider, so once again, I called Metin and asked for his help.

There was one day each week that I was allowed to leave school early. That was the day Veronica and I picked Metin up and courageously headed for the city center. Driving in the center of Adana gives new meaning to the phrase "death wish." Metin drove. Parking was a nightmare, and the streets were as jammed with shoppers as they would have been in the States on the night before Christmas.

As we headed for the bank, we were jostled and elbowed. I was hanging on to the strongbox for dear life. Finally, I decided to hand it over to Metin. His presence was much more formidable than mine, and I was tired. When we eventually got to the bank, we found ourselves in the midst of a sea of people. The walls and floor were marble, so the noise was deafening. We couldn't even hear each other. I asked Metin to please find out how long it would be before we could speak to someone who could help us. He looked at me like I was out of my mind and asked, "What's more important, a safe-deposit box or your radiotherapy?" The answer to his question went without saying, so the three of us turned and left the bank.

We arrived in time for my treatment, so I was able to stay on schedule. However, it was clear that, until my radiotherapy was finished, getting to the bank and renting a box before closing time would be impossible. Metin understood this and suggested that I buy a couple of what, for lack of a better word, I would call hope chests. He explained that Turkish people use them as a matter of course to keep important things in. That sounded like a logical alternative, so we were off to the hope chest dealer where I bought three. I knew they'd come in handy, not only to lock up my valuables but to store things in—a wonderful solution, I thought.

I had endeared myself to my students with my explanation of what I'd undergone in the past six months, and life was good. I was thrilled to be with them, and they were thrilled to be with me. I truly believed that I was making a difference, and that energized me. Although I was still suffering from the aftereffects of chemo, I managed to keep this to myself, so no one, teacher or student, was any the wiser. My radiotherapy was coming to an end, and I couldn't have been happier. The material things I'd lost in the States were no longer of any consequence. I had a beautiful apartment and had come to the realization that a lot of the creature comforts I had enjoyed in my former life were of little or no consequence here. Turkish people, even the wealthiest of them, have different priorities. I used to ask my students how a foreigner could tell who was rich here and who was poor. The vast majority of people lived in apartments, and from the outside, they all looked the same. Very few women wear expensive jewelry for fear of being attacked and having it stolen. It was obvious that here, conspicuous consumption was something to be avoided at all costs. In a short time, I was going to understand why.

I have a tendency to repress bad memories. For example, some of my friends who are cancer survivors can tell me the exact date and time their cancer was diagnosed, when they had surgery, and how many days and months it has been since their operation. I, on the other hand, had to search through my hospital records to find that information for this book. Some people would say I'm in denial about having had cancer and I need to get honest. I, on the other hand, would argue that I don't want to be defined by the tragedies in my life. There have been so many, of such consequence, that I've made grown therapists cry. To allow myself to be defined by them would doubtless render me totally incapable of moving ahead. I would rather concentrate on the positive things that have happened. It allows me to be more resilient and to roll with the punches. I had already lost the bulk of my material possessions, divorced for the third time, survived cancer, and returned to Turkey to pick up my dream where I'd left off more than six months earlier. Like the phoenix rising out of the ashes, I was ready to start rebuilding.

I can't tell you the exact date of what happened next. All I remember was that it was a Monday morning. I used to change my jewelry on a regular basis. The watch, bracelet, and earrings I wore one day would be replaced by something different the next. As I got ready to go to school that fateful day, I went to one of the three chests I'd purchased earlier in order to retrieve the silver strongbox and make my jewelry selection for the day. I bent down and opened the chest. I had cleverly concealed the strongbox under a pile of sweaters. I put my hand inside and felt around for the box. It wasn't where I remembered stuffing it. My breathing changed, and my heart started pounding.

"It must have slipped," I said out loud as if to reassure myself. Frantically, I moved my hand farther to the right and then back to the left again. Nothing! I repeated the action once, then twice. Nothing! I stood up, hardly able to believe what was happening. I was walking in circles, wringing my hands and I thought about what to do next. Who should I call? What should I do? I started frantically pulling the sweaters out, one by one at first and then in piles of three or four. I emptied the entire chest. No strongbox!

For a moment, I thought I would vomit. I was bent over in agony, clutching my stomach and fighting back the tears. My hands were trembling. My whole body was shaking. Could this really be happening? My mind was racing a mile a minute. No one else had a key. How could anyone have gotten into my apartment? Suddenly, I remembered that I had purchased two other chests. I had withdrawn eight thousand Turkish liras from the bank in Tarsus. Because I was no longer working in the city, it seemed silly to continue to bank with them. I had intended to open a savings account when I rented my safe-deposit box. Unfortunately, I hadn't done that either because of my radiotherapy. I raced into the guest room as though I was being chased by a mass murderer. This time I didn't bother to remove the sweaters in neat piles of three or four. I flung open the top of the chest and grabbed the biggest bundle of sweaters my hands could hold. I threw them onto the floor and repeated the action until the entire chest was empty. Much to my chagrin, my eight thousand Turkish liras and almost one hundred thousand dollars in jewelry were both gone.

It took me several minutes to compose myself enough to call the school. My voice was shaking, and I was trying to hold back the tears as I explained to the principal what had happened. They called the police and sent a representative from the school to be with me while the police conducted their investigation. As they dusted for fingerprints, they asked me to make a list of everything I could remember that was in the box. I could hardly control my emotions as I listed the items one by one. You see, it was more than a box of jewelry. It was a testament to my life. Every single necklace, watch, bracelet, or pair of earrings was either given to me or purchased by me to commemorate a special occasion. At that point, the dollar value of what was taken was insignificant. These items were irreplaceable. My jewelry collection was one of a kind. Each and every piece was unique, designed especially for me, and had a story or a wonderful memory behind it. These memories were something that no one could ever put a dollar value on.

It took days for the initial shock to wear off. Foolishly, I kept praying and hoping that the police would come up with a lead. I walked past jewelry store windows, night after night, hoping to see one of my pieces. Unfortunately, by this time, the pieces had undoubtedly been melted down and turned into something entirely different and totally unrecognizable.

The school didn't react well either, because the robbery had occurred in a school lodgment. They were shocked that I hadn't changed the locks when I moved in. I was shocked that *they* hadn't changed them if they thought that was a necessary precaution. It wasn't until after the robbery that they explained the prior tenants, as well as school employees, all had keys to the apartment. *How*, I wondered, *could I have known that?* It was a lose-lose situation. Up until this happened, the school had requested keys from all of the teachers in the event that there was a problem in one of the apartments and they needed to send someone to take care of it. After this incident, the school returned all of the keys and explained that the inconvenience that this was going to create was my fault. For days, I heard rumblings about how upset everyone was. Why should they all suffer, they wondered, because of my problem?

As bad as this was, it couldn't compare to the feeling I had when the man in charge of school maintenance decided that Metin was the culprit because we were together when I bought the hope chests. He was convinced that the man who owned the shop was a relative of Metin's and that they had conspired to steal my things. There was no point in trying to reason with this man. Metin wasn't related to the shop owner; in fact, he didn't even know him. Metin didn't have a key to my apartment, and the locks on the chests could have been picked with a bobby pin. However, at this point, the truth was of little or no importance. Metin was poor and uneducated, and the people at the school had acted as judge and jury. Metin was guilty, and there was no point in trying to convince them otherwise.

CHAPTER 32

What Now?

Never give up then, for that is just the place
and time that the tide will turn.
—Harriet Beecher Stow

The ramifications of what had happened had far-reaching consequences. There were rumblings that Metin was not only a gigolo, but a thief. How ridiculous, I thought. If he were truly the culprit, he'd now have more than enough money to start a new business of his own without any help from anybody. To this day, I have no idea who may have taken the jewelry or how they got into my apartment. The only thing I'm sure of is that it wasn't Metin.

I didn't see Metin until a few days after I returned to Turkey. Like my friend who had picked me up from the airport, he cried when he saw me. No longer was I the vibrant adventure-seeker living on the edge. I had slowed down considerably, and it was something I couldn't hide. My close friends could see the toll that the cancer, chemo, and radiation had taken on my body. They tried to hide their concern, but it was written all over their faces.

Veronica was with me every step of the way. She went to every radiotherapy treatment with me and did whatever she could to try to make life easier for me. Veronica, Metin, and I became like the Three Musketeers. We did everything together, and ironically, just like John, Metin was at his best when I was at my worst. He wasn't at all put off by my weight gain or the fact that I was bald. I kept emphasizing the very worst of what had happened to me in an attempt to drive him away. If he was going to end up rejecting me, I wanted him to do it sooner rather than later. I told him, over and over, that I would understand if he no longer wanted to be with me. On the surface, at least, I was no longer the youthful, vibrant woman he had fallen in love with. The bottom line is that he didn't leave, and I began to rely on him more than I ever imagined possible. He was my rock. He was there whenever I need him. It didn't seem like there was anything he wouldn't do for me. Perhaps because of this, when he told me he loved me hair or no hair, extra weight or no extra weight, I finally believed him.

As a result, on May 8, 2009, in front of Metin's entire family and more than a hundred of his friends, I married him in a *hoca* ceremony at Biber Café and Bar. A hoca wedding is a religious ceremony, but it is not legally binding. I was still reeling from the financial devastation that I'd suffered as a result of being legally married to John, so for the moment, a hoca wedding was just what the doctor ordered. To many Kurdish people, it is as binding, if not more so, than a civil ceremony. However, in the event that it didn't work out, I wouldn't have any financial obligation to Metin.

Metin's only request was that I wear a white wedding gown. I patiently explained that he would be my fourth husband, and in my culture, a white dress would be entirely inappropriate. He finally agreed to let me have my way and told me I could choose whatever color dress I wanted. Much to my regret, I chose orange, one of my favorite colors. It would have been lovely for a curvaceous young bride to wear to her engagement party here, but certainly not for a woman in her early sixties who was thirty pounds overweight. It was garish, and because of the weight I had gained, I looked like the great pumpkin. I hid our wedding photo as soon as I saw it, and to this day, I refuse to let anyone see it. It's in the original frame, under an exquisite watercolor of Istanbul. Up until the writing of this book, only I knew where it was, and I swore it would remain my secret forever.

None of my friends, other than Veronica, were invited to the wedding. Both Metin and I were well aware of the animosity the people at my school felt toward him. We married in secret, and we both agreed that because I lived in a school lodgment, he would not stay in my apartment. For the time being, at least, we were content to steal whatever time together that we could. We met for coffee and dinner on a regular basis and spent at least an hour or two together every day. Perhaps because of my physical condition, sex was not uppermost in my mind. Metin understood and, at least for the moment, was okay with that.

Once again, the school year was coming to an end. For years, my friend Veronica and I had dreamed of opening some kind of a business in Turkey. We originally thought of a small café on the sea, perhaps in a place like Side (pronounced "see day"). However, for a variety of reasons, up until this point, we hadn't done anything about it. I had given Metin the bulk of my savings for the bar in Istanbul, so I was no longer in a position to be the sole backer in another venture. Veronica, Metin, and I were like family. We shared everything, including our innermost thoughts, feelings, and aspirations. Therefore, it shouldn't have come as a surprise that Veronica and I both knew that Metin's dream was to open another place. Veronica and I discussed the pros and cons and decided that opening a business in a foreign country was not something we could do on our own. As a result, before leaving for the summer break, we decided to give Metin the money that he needed to do it for us. We agreed we would be equal partners, and Metin would manage the place. Before we left, we told him what we envisioned the place would look like. We crossed our fingers and hoped for the best. This was definitely another leap of faith.

CHAPTER 33

Surprise!

Patience is counting down without blasting off.
—Unknown

My holiday in the States was much shorter than usual that year. Instead of the normal month long visit, I literally ran away after two weeks. My Mercedes had been sold, so I was forced to "rent a wreck." Our house was a basic seventies vintage ranch. However, the addition of thousands of dollars of objects d'arte had transformed it into a veritable treasure trove. In the anticipation of bankruptcy, it had been stripped of all its glory. Once again, when I arrived, it was cluttered and dirty. It broke my heart as I went from room to room searching for familiar objects to remind me of what life there had been like. Sadly, there were no reminders. John and I were legally divorced, and in the months since the final decree, he had become bitter and vindictive. There were daily recriminations that made living under the same roof comparable to a stay in hell. Finally, after two weeks, I could stand it no longer. My good friend Anne helped me plan my escape. I packed my luggage and took it to her house. I returned the rent-a-wreck, and she brought me home. I called Turkish Airlines to inquire about changing my ticket. My friend there did it without a problem. The next day Anne sent a limo to pick me up, and without a word to anyone other than Anne, I was on my way to O'Hare to catch my flight back to Turkey.

When I arrived in Adana, the first thing I did was call Metin. He was surprised and overjoyed to learn that I was back. He could hardly wait to show me what he had done in my absence. We met early the next morning and drove to our new business. However, instead of the upscale café that Veronica and I had envisioned, there was, in its place, a full-fledged nightclub.

It was decorated exquisitely. The drapes were a deep burgundy satin, and the furniture was stained a dark mahogany brown. A raised stage had been built, special lighting installed, and a custom-made bar built. An intricately etched glass panel separated the main room from the restrooms. There were tables on the sidewalk in front and a covered breezeway adjacent to the main building. If the only thing that mattered was presentation, we surely would have won a prize. Unfortunately, Metin didn't do enough research on the neighborhood before deciding to switch gears and open a nightclub. There was a *dershane* upstairs and one next door. These are businesses that offer day care, as well as after school programs. Unless there was a way of shutting them down, we would never be able to get a liquor license. When Veronica returned, she was as shocked as I was to see the direction things had gone. However, Metin kept reassuring us not to worry. The situation was in his hands, and he was going to take care of it.

Once again, I was able to enjoy the rush that comes from sitting at the manager's table and watching him run the business. Only this time things were different. I was his wife. I admired the way he greeted the customers, made sure they were having a good time, and handled the potential troublemakers. Yes, I could see his point. This place had potential, and within a very short time, there would be standing room only. I was as proud as a peacock.

We never talked about the business. That was Metin's responsibility, and we trusted him. Veronica and I simply functioned as honored guests. We could hardly contain our enthusiasm as we watched the number of customers grow by leaps and bounds. We had customers every day of the week, and by the weekend, every table was filled. On New Year's Eve there was standing room only. Metin had hired the best singer in the area, and people came in droves to listen to him. Business was booming. There was only one problem. Veronica and I didn't have any idea how much profit, if any, the bar was generating. The bar was never fully stocked, and it wasn't unusual for Metin to send one of the waiters to the market across the street to buy more liquor. We wondered why he wasn't ordering it from a liquor distributor so he could get better prices. Before we had time to ask that question and get a response, we started to hear rumblings that some of the staff weren't being paid on time. It was clear that there were some financial issues here, and it was time to get to the bottom of them.

Unfortunately, it wasn't until Metin was buried alive under police penalties that we finally learned what was going on. He had accumulated, literally, thousands of liras in penalties. There were penalties because people had been caught smoking in the bar, penalties for having tables on the sidewalk in front of the bar, and penalties for serving liquor without a license. Not a week went by that he wasn't served with at least one, and in some cases two or three. He kept as much of this as he could from us by paying the fines with the profits each week. Eventually, there were so many that he couldn't cover them with the profits from the bar, and he had to take a loan from some very unsavory characters. As long as business was good, he was able to make the payments on this loan, so Veronica and I were never the wiser. It wasn't until he was no longer able to keep up with the payments that we learned how bad things were.

Veronica and I wanted to know what was going on. First of all, several of our regular customers were policemen. Why weren't they doing something to fend off the incredible number of penalties we were being served? Secondly, it was common knowledge that some of the largest and most popular bars in Adana were serving liquor without liquor licenses. That's just the way things go in Turkey. Why was our bar being singled out? Metin was told that we were being targeted, but he didn't know why or by whom. Eventually, the police actually set up a surveillance camera in an empty apartment across the street in order to film all of the activity every night. It would have been laughable had it not cost thousands of liras in additional penalties.

Metin, Veronica, and I knew that history was repeating itself. There were bars in the area that were losing customers to us just like there had been in Istanbul. Could one of them be so vindictive that they kept calling the police and demanding some kind of action be taken against us? The music didn't start until nine at night, so we didn't suspect anyone from the dershane. We were all at a loss. All we knew was that we were dying under the weight of the penalties. If something didn't change, and quickly, we would have to close our doors.

CHAPTER 34

The Other Woman

"Heaven has no rage like love to hatred turned /
Nor hell a fury like a woman scorned."
—William Congreve, *The Mourning Bride*

For five years before I met Metin, he had an on-again, off-again relationship with a woman whose "professional name" was Deniz. She was a belly dancer who moonlighted as a prostitute and, as such, fit perfectly into Metin's postdivorce lifestyle. During that dark period in his life, day after day was the same for him. Drinking, gambling, womanizing, and trying to assuage the guilt he felt over the failure of his first marriage. However, since he and I had met, he tried repeatedly to distance himself from Deniz and everything she stood for. He wasn't a part of her world anymore, but that, apparently, was not something she'd come to grips with yet.

Although at this point I had never actually met Deniz, I was well-acquainted with who she was. Since my first year in Tarsus, she had been calling me and trying to stir up trouble between Metin and me. The first few years she didn't make much headway because my Turkish wasn't good enough to understand what she was trying to say, and she wasn't bright enough to enlist a friend who spoke English to help her with her insidious game. All I knew was that she was trouble and was determined to do everything she could to come between Metin and me.

She knew that Metin and I had gotten married, and this had apparently driven her over the edge. She was infuriated. She had known him for five years before I had even met him, and she not only couldn't understand why he had never married her, but why he had chosen to marry a woman who was older than his mother! I wondered the same thing, and he told me it was simple. He didn't love her. However, she also knew that the conditions of our marriage left something to be desired. I still lived in a school lodgment where Metin was not welcome.

He owned an apartment, and we originally thought that perhaps I would move into his place. In anticipation of this, we spent a small fortune transforming it from a bachelor pad into a sumptuous and elegant retreat. However, upon further inspection, I realized it didn't have nearly enough closet space to accommodate my extensive collection of clothes, shoes, and accessories. Even more important, however, was the difference in our lifestyles. Metin's definitely wasn't conducive to living with a teacher who got up early in the morning for school. Our routines were, quite literally, upside down. I was getting up when Metin was going to bed. In addition, there was always a musician or waiter who needed someplace to stay on a temporary basis, so they inevitably ended up crashing at Metin's. When all was said and done, we decided that as long as I worked at the college, the best place for me to be was in the school lodgment. Neither one of us took this as any kind of comment on the state of our marriage. Apparently, Deniz did because she was launching an all-out attack to ruin him financially in the hope of ultimately getting him back.

She was angry and vindictive about our marriage, and to add insult to injury, Metin had given strict instructions to all of the security at the bar that she was never to be allowed inside. Her curiosity was killing her, but the best she could do was to send one of her sisters or friends in her place to see what was going on inside. She was a woman scorned and determined to administer her own type of justice.

Deniz maintained close ties with her friends on the police force to make sure that, when and if she was arrested, she'd have friends on the inside. She supplied entire police stations with rice, cigarettes, and coffee as her private insurance policy in the event things went south. She used these connections to her own advantage and, in the case of our bar, to destroy us. Every night she and twelve or thirteen of her best friends would start calling the police to complain that the music was too loud, people were drinking in the street, or there was smoking inside the bar. Like the bar owner below us in Istanbul, Deniz was determined to do whatever was necessary to guarantee that our business failed. She had decided that if she couldn't have Metin, no one would.

By the time Metin, Veronica, and I finally met to talk about the problems, it was too late. He had already accumulated more than twenty-five thousand Turkish liras in penalties and had borrowed money to try to pay them off. Metin was at his wit's end. He was struggling just to pay the monthly interest on the loan he'd taken. He didn't know which way to turn or what to do. He admitted to us that he had borrowed money from the mafia to pay some of the earlier penalties. However, at this point, he knew couldn't borrow anymore from them until he started paying off the principal that he already owed. He asked Veronica and me if we could help. As much as we empathized with him, we were tapped out. There simply wasn't anywhere from which we could pull more money. We apologized and told him he was going to have to find another solution. He started to speak in riddles. Neither Veronica nor I were exactly sure what he meant.

He said, "If a person is drowning and they see a snake swimming by, even if they know the snake is bad, they have to grab it."

Okay, Veronica and I thought, *but what does that mean?* It wouldn't be long before we found out.

Two or three days later, Metin called and asked me to meet with him privately. This, in itself, was unusual. After all, we were the Three Musketeers. Why wasn't Veronica invited? Metin refused to explain, and in a tone of voice that couldn't mask his distress, he asked me to come to the bar immediately. Over coffee, he asked me for the last time if there was any way I could help him pay off all of the penalties he owed. By this time, I was also at my wit's end.

I was angry, and I screamed. I told him that I'd already given him the bulk of my savings for the bar in Istanbul. If Veronica hadn't agreed to share the expenses for the bar in Adana, there was no way that I would have had enough money to finance another business venture. In fact, the scales were already tipping. Veronica was covering for both of us when I didn't have the money to give. What else did he expect me to do?

He grasped my hands in his, and he was fighting to hold back his tears. He looked me straight in the eyes and in a voice that was barely audible said, "Then we have to divorce. The only way out is for me to marry Deniz. She keeps calling me and she told me that if I divorced you and married her, she would pay off all the penalties at the bar." With that, he bowed his head, closed his eyes, and said the words, "*Boş ol, boş ol, boş ol.*" Those words are enough to nullify a hoca wedding. Metin and I were now divorced.

Chapter 35

Never Say Never

Faced with crisis the man of character falls back on himself.
—Charles de Gaulle

It took weeks for me to come to grips with the reality of what had happened. Metin had insisted over and over that Deniz was nothing more than an uneducated street girl, and he didn't want anything to do with her. He sincerely enjoyed being with my friends, and slowly but surely, he was distancing himself from the people he had associated with when he and Deniz were together. I questioned him relentlessly about his sincerity. I was determined to do whatever I could to ensure that I wouldn't be abandoned again. After all, there was the age difference, the cultural difference, the educational difference, and the socioeconomic difference. Anyone in their right mind would have bet this relationship couldn't last. However, Metin assured me that none of this mattered. He would never, under any circumstances, leave me.

All my childhood memories of being left alone came flooding back like a raging river filling my mind with uncertainty and self-doubt. My self-esteem was at an all-time low. I suffered, and I suffered deeply. Veronica was the only person at the college who knew I had married Metin. As a result, day after day I had to put on a happy face at school. I was like a jet pilot flying his plane on automatic. I went through the motions, not daring to let myself retreat into my private thoughts. That would surely result in a flood of tears I wouldn't be able to explain. I watched and waited impatiently for the day to end, so I could rush home to the comfort of my apartment and bury myself in my grief. I felt as though Metin had died, and the grieving process I went through wasn't much different from how it would have been if he had. No one but Veronica knew the depth of my sadness and despair. I had finally let go of my fear of rejection and married him only to have my dreams dashed months later.

Veronica did her best to get me out of the house and back into circulation. If it hadn't been for her, I probably would've spent the next few months locked in my apartment, in my pajamas, watching reruns on TV. There was a lovely restaurant within walking distance of our apartments, and we became regulars there. It was a Friday night, and we decided to go there to watch a soccer game. We were seated at our table and prepared to place our orders when suddenly we noticed that our waiter had disappeared. We wondered why but didn't stop to ask any questions. We were hungry, and getting some food on the table was paramount in our minds. Suddenly, a tall, breathtakingly handsome and athletic waiter appeared in his place. I was smiling from ear to ear as he tried to communicate with us in English. We learned his name was Feyzullah. I could hardly take my eyes off of him. He looked like a model in the midst of a photo shoot impersonating a waiter. He was definitely top-shelf eye candy!

After the appetizers arrived and he opened our bottle of wine, he got up the courage to ask me if I was single. I told him I was and then asked the same question of him. Bingo! He was single too. Before the meal was over, we had exchanged phone numbers, and he promised to call. I was floating on cloud nine. I remembered my mother's words: "Men are like streetcars. There's always another one coming." If this was going to be the next man in my life, bring it on, I thought! Suddenly, things were beginning to look up.

The next day my phone rang, and it was him. That day was the beginning of what turned out to be a torrid love affair. We saw each other every night, and he proved to be one of the best lovers I'd ever had. He worked across the street, so he came to my apartment every night after he finished work. We'd curl up on the couch wrapped around each other like vines around a tree. I'd lie between his legs with my head on his chest while he encircled me with his long, slender, and athletic legs. He was gentle and thoughtful and always put my needs first. He stroked my cheeks and hair and told me how beautiful I was. Those words, coming from my Adonis, were music to my ears.

After a glass of wine or two, he'd cup my chin in his hands and rub his lips against mine until eventually he slowly parted them with his tongue. Once our tongues were together, they danced a special dance of their own, a preview of what was to come. As my breathing became faster and the breaths shorter, he would pick me up in his muscular arms and carry me into the bedroom. After gently placing me on the bed, he would slowly and sensuously start to remove my clothes. Once I was naked and longing to feel him inside of me, he would begin to remove his. I watched in awe as he revealed his perfect body. Tall, tan, and muscular, he was my Greek god. Before taking his place next to me on the bed, he would shower me with soft, gentle kisses from my head to the bottom of my toes. This man loved my body, and I was his for the taking. His kisses were sweet and succulent and made me squeal with joy. His primary concern was pleasuring me, and he filled me with rapture. Every night I waited breathlessly for his return. I hadn't experienced sexual bliss like this since my trysts with Terry. I couldn't believe I was fortunate enough to have found another man who could take me to such heights night after night after night.

Once again, my feelings of insecurity started to wash over me. What was someone as good looking as him doing with me? This man could have any woman he wanted. Once again, there was a significant age difference between us, but like Metin, it didn't matter to him at all. I felt like Mrs. Robinson but eventually managed to convince myself that if the age difference didn't matter to any of these men, why should it matter to me?

Feyzullah had a friend who thought Veronica was quite good looking, and both he and Feyzo were hoping that they could come over some evening and chat. It sounded like a good idea to me, so we agreed that they would both come for dinner the following night. Unfortunately, Feyzullah's friend didn't speak a word of English, and Feyzo's was limited at best. We definitely needed a translator. Our mutual friend Peter was alone for the week because his wife had gone to Ankara to visit her sister. It was settled. We'd invite Peter, and the five of us would have dinner together.

Turkish people are notorious for not being adventuresome eaters. They stick to the dishes their mothers made. There is no room for experimentation. As a result, my culinary skills were totally lost on our guests, so we finished the meal early and sat in the salon chatting and sipping wine. The conversation was grueling. Only one person could speak at a time, because Peter needed to translate. It was exhausting, so by ten o'clock everyone was ready to call it a night. We bid each other adieu, and I headed for bed.

The next morning I was absolutely dumbfounded to learn that the school was conducting an investigation into the "wild party" that I had hosted the evening before. According to one source, the party went into the wee hours of the morning, approximately three o'clock, I was told. In addition, Metin was supposedly there and purportedly got angry and broke several things in my apartment before destroying the mailboxes and security camera in the lobby on his way out. Veronica and Peter arrived at school before I did that day, and they were both called into the office and grilled. They both maintained that there must be a huge misunderstanding. They explained exactly what went on and added that perhaps the "wild party" was given by someone else in the building. When I arrived at school, I was also questioned. Once again, I repeated exactly what Veronica and Peter had said and, in addition, adamantly denied that Metin was even there. *What are they trying to do?* I thought. The people at school were obviously so out of touch with things that they didn't even realize Metin and I were no longer seeing each other. Why was this happening now?

Even though Metin and I were no longer together, I was appalled at the accusations that were being made about him. I hadn't had any contact with him since we'd last spoken at the bar. At this point, I didn't know if he was married or not, but I decided that the right thing to do was to call him and let him know how his reputation was being further maligned at the college. I felt that if the tables were turned, he would have done the same for me. Our conversation was short and to the point. After I explained what had happened and told him that he was being falsely accused of doing all kinds of damage in my apartment as well as in the lobby, he asked me what I thought he should do. After my experience in the courtroom I should have remembered that people in this country are not encumbered by the truth, and right is definitely not might. However, by now my memory of that travesty had faded, so I told him that if I were him, I'd call the school and set them straight. That piece of advice was the beginning of my undoing at the college.

Metin called my department head, but he refused to answer either his cell or his house phone. Instead, he called the director of the school to complain that my boyfriend was harassing him and placing threatening phone calls. The next day the director called me. I couldn't contain my anger at this, for lack of a better term, witch hunt. I explained that Metin and I were no longer seeing each other and that I thought it was grossly unfair that people were making these kinds of unfounded accusations about him. My anger got the better of me, and I didn't mince any words about the injustice of the whole thing. I had been under scrutiny for several days, and my dinner guests had been unnecessarily interrogated. The whole situation was absolutely absurd, and I was furious.

After a week, I was finally cleared of all accusations. Indeed, they admitted a mistake had been made. Unfortunately for me, by this time, the party was no longer the main issue. The focus now was on my conversation with the director. No foreign teacher was going to talk to him the way I had done and continue to work at the college. I was about to pay a hefty price for defending Metin's honor.

A few days later, I received a letter from the head of the English department rescinding the contract offer they'd given me for the following year. They acknowledged that I was a professional of the highest caliber but added that because of the complaints that they'd received from members of the administration they were forced to let me go. They recognized that it was probably too late in the year for me to find another job and apologized if their actions would, in any way, affect the course of my career. I had been fired.

I walked home from school that day as if in a trance. My feet were moving, but I barely felt them touch the ground. I was on automatic pilot and, as such, gave no thought to which street I was on or my ultimate destination. I had taken the same route to and from school for the past year and a half. I knew every pothole in the sidewalk, and navigating my way around them was second nature to me now. I was totally consumed in thought.

I thought about how my relationship with the head of the English department had changed since our days together at Tarsus and our beachfront hideaways outside of Mersin. He had gone from being my best friend and confidante to an adversary. There had been a time when I swore I'd never work with anyone else. Wherever he was going, I was going too. We'd spent long days and many lonely nights together sharing our thoughts and feelings with one another. I knew his weaknesses, and he knew mine. I didn't think that anything could ever come between us. I loved him as much as a woman could love a man she knew she'd never have as a sexual partner or lover. As long as we were both in Turkey, I never imagined that there would be anything that could come between us. Now I understood why people say, never say never.

CHAPTER 36

What Now?

Experiences that will strengthen your character:

Getting audited.

Getting fired.

Waitressing.

Vacationing with your three best friends.

—Lesley Dormen

If it's true that these are the criteria for strengthening a person's character, mine should have been pretty strong by now. I'd experienced all of the above, and the burning question was, "What now?" I could stay in my apartment until August, but I didn't have a job for the following year. Feyzullah and I were still together, but I didn't look at him as a long-term partner of any sort. He provided a much-needed distraction, but he was even younger than Metin, which made any kind of long-term commitment out of the question. Now that I was no longer an employee of the college, I had lost my health insurance and, more importantly, all the services that I was entitled to as a teacher there. Any and every sort of problem one could imagine could be solved by one of the people at the school. The carpenters, plumbers, electricians, translators, doctors, and so on were all at our disposal. My Turkish was getting better all the time, but I was in no position to venture out into the real world here without help. In addition, my social network was pulled out from under me. At that point, I wasn't even sure that I was going to stay in Turkey, but if I left, where would I go? My home and my car in the States were gone, and John and I were divorced. There was no reason to go back to Milwaukee. My home now was, quite literally, wherever I was. I began to pack my things in the anticipation of moving, but at the time, I had no idea to where.

I've always believed that when God closes a door, He opens a window, and once again, the Universe conspired to provide me with a little bit more than I actually needed. While I was still working in Tarsus, I met a very interesting woman named Patrice. She lived in Adana. While I lived in Tarsus, it was unrealistic for us to try to get together on a regular basis. It was just too inconvenient. However, once I moved to Adana, it was a different story. Patrice lived in a magnificent villa on the shores of Seyhan Lake. Her apartment was huge. She had three large bedrooms, two baths, an enormous salon, and an open kitchen. In addition, she had a natural fireplace, quite a luxury in a city where it never drops below freezing. The villa had a balcony that wrapped around three sides of the building and a fabulous yard in which her five dogs romped and played to their heart's content. She was literally the only person I knew in Turkey who had a yard and owned a lawnmower. She didn't actually cut the grass, her gardener did, but I was impressed.

Patrice had met her Turkish husband in Arizona while she was teaching sixth-grade bilingual education there. They married and in a short time moved back to Adana, his hometown. Patrice had inherited a large sum of money, and because they were married, her husband didn't feel any guilt about going through it like a duck through water. They wanted desperately to have a child, but that was not to be. Instead, they adopted a baby. Patrice was the Martha Stewart of Adana. She cooked fabulous meals, baked from scratch, and decorated with the imagination and skills of a seasoned professional. She was determined to be the best wife she could be.

Unfortunately, her husband wanted more and eventually ended up having an affair with his secretary. The secretary became pregnant, and in an attempt to save her marriage, Patrice offered to forgive him if he agreed to stop seeing her. He agreed, but it wasn't long before his secretary was pregnant for the second time. It would take another book the size of *War and Peace* to describe the heart-wrenching drama and details of the legal battle that followed. It took Patrice eight years to get a divorce. She was finally victorious, and the court ordered that her ex-husband pay back all the money that he had taken from her and used to build his financial empire. Patrice freely admits that she still loves him and always will. She understood the cultural mandate that a successful man often has more than one woman in his life. Patrice had assimilated and adapted to many of the cultural differences. This, however, was not one of them.

When I received the letter informing me that the college was rescinding my contract, I called Patrice immediately. We agreed to meet later that week to talk about my options. We went to my favorite restaurant for dinner. As we lingered over coffee and dessert, Patrice said that it was a shame she didn't know sooner that I was going to be looking for an apartment. The doctor who lived on the third floor of her villa was getting married and moving to another house at the end of the street. Unfortunately, he had promised his apartment to one of his friends who was also a doctor. He hadn't signed a contract yet, but it appeared as though it was a done deal. I was crestfallen.

The views of the lake and the mountains in the distance were spectacular. The salon was big enough to skate in, and the portion of the yard that went with the apartment was almost an acre. Perhaps the best part of all was that Mustafa, my attorney, lived on the second floor. With Patrice and Mustafa in the same building, I'd have a new social network. What a shame that I'd missed this chance by just a few days. I went back to my school lodgment that night and continued to pack.

Every night after school Veronica and I walked the streets looking for for-rent signs. We had a list of ten, but we were eliminating them at an alarmingly fast rate. Sometimes we didn't need to go any farther than the foyer before we knew it wasn't an option. Most Turkish apartments are designed exactly the same way. There's a central hallway, and all the rooms have doors that lead off of it. This allows them to close off most of the rooms in the winter to conserve heat and to close them off in the summer to conserve on the air conditioning. Fortunately, all of the places I'd lived in so far were atypical and, as a result, infinitely more interesting. As Veronica and I were strolling down the street heading to another showing, my phone rang. It was Patrice. She was ecstatic! Mustafa had worked his magic and convinced the doctor that he didn't want the apartment after all. It could be mine if I wanted it. I made plans to meet Patrice immediately after school the next day.

There was absolutely no comparison between Patrice's sumptuous and tastefully decorated apartment and what the doctor left behind. There was no real furniture to speak of, only a rattan patio set off the salon. The toilets and showers in both bathrooms had problems. Every room was painted a different pastel color, and the darker colors underneath were bleeding through. The kitchen was a total disaster, and the stone fireplace and island screamed "paint me." A small puppy was the only resident, and it was obvious that he was not house trained yet. There were urine-spattered papers everywhere, and the little piles of dog poop were too numerous to count. I began to seriously question whether I had the money, time, and energy necessary to restore the place. Every time I turned around, another problem reared its ugly head. I knew I couldn't tackle a project this big by myself.

Veronica and Patrice assured me that it would be a group project. Even Feyzullah volunteered to help. I went home and slept on it, and the first thing the next morning I called Mustafa. I told him how much work there was to be done, and he agreed to let me and my crew have an entire month rent free to do what we had to do.

"Then it's settled," I said. "I'll take it."

My friend and neighbor Patrice.

CHAPTER 37

It's Not Over Until the Fat Lady Sings

Experience is how life catches up with us and
teaches us to love and forgive each other.
—Louise Nevelson

The school had agreed to let me stay in my lodgment until August. This was great news, because it meant I could pack at my leisure, get the new place up to snuff before moving in, and still have time to squeeze in yet another foot surgery. I hadn't heard a word from Metin, so I wasn't sure whether he had married Deniz. Feyzullah was still my main man, and I appreciated all the work that he did to help with my new home. I couldn't help but wonder how he could be so good looking and know so much about electricity at the same time. No, he wasn't just a pretty face.

Veronica, Patrice, and I worked day and night. We cleaned. We painted. We scrubbed. We painted. We hauled furniture, and then we painted some more! It was an endless cycle, but the apartment was coming together beautifully. Veronica and I made several trips to the secondhand furniture stores in Mersin. They were veritable treasure troves! I bought an antique brass canopy bed that came out of a *paşa's* (nobleman's) house. It was too tall to move into my bedroom, so I had to have more than a foot of it sawed off. Patrice and I went to the fabric store and bought meters and meters of cream-colored chiffon festooned with gold sequins to drape over the canopy. It was fit for a princess. On the next trip, I bought an exquisitely hand-carved wooden bed for the guestroom. Chandeliers were sparkling in every room. Soon, I could see, my Pierre Loti theme would be carried out in this apartment as well.

In the midst of all of this chaos, I had another foot surgery. Once again, it was a simple procedure, and I was in and out of the hospital in one night. Granted, I had a pin sticking out of my big toe, but I was ambulatory and that was all that mattered. Veronica could drive my car, so we were still able to go back and forth between my new and old homes. Things were really starting to take shape, so we began to move some of the fragile things a little bit at a time.

Feyzullah continued to help, and I was extremely grateful for the loyalty he was showing in these truly stressful times. It goes without saying that we were both rendered speechless when, out of the clear blue sky, Metin came banging on my door one afternoon. He covered the lens on the security camera so neither Feyzullah nor I knew who was coming up in the elevator. When I opened the door, Metin stormed in with three of his friends following on his heels. Feyzullah was in the salon and moved to the farthest side of the dining room table in order to avoid what appeared to be a pending physical altercation. Metin and his friends surrounded him and told him that if he knew what was good for him, he had two minutes to get out of my apartment. Metin went nose to nose with him and said if he ever found him in my apartment again, he was a dead man. I was speechless when I saw Feyzullah pick up his things and leave. As far as I was concerned, Metin's bark was a lot worse than his bite, so I didn't understand why Feyzullah had gone. It wasn't until later that I learned that Feyzullah's brother was part of the mafia in Izmir. He was in prison, at the time, for shooting the man who had killed his wife and daughter. As a result, death threats were something Feyzullah took very seriously.

After he left, I lost control. I shouted and screamed and asked Metin what in the hell he thought he was he doing and who in the hell he thought he was.? We were divorced, and he had no business interfering in my life. I could see whoever I chose to see, and there wasn't a thing he could do about it.

263

"You sold yourself to the highest bidder," I screamed, "so get out and go back to your bitch. You crawled out of the gutter to be with me, and now, as far as I'm concerned, you need to go back to the streets, which is where you belong!"

By this time, my fists were raised, and I was pounding on his chests as I pushed him toward the door. My adrenaline was pumping, and I was suddenly emboldened with a strength I never knew I had. I put my whole body into it as I thrust my shoulder into his chest and moved him, albeit very slowly, toward the door. Although he wasn't intimidated by my strength, he was in awe of my anger. He'd never seen me like this before, and I don't think he believed that the depth of my animosity and hatred for him could ever run this deep.

He grabbed me by the shoulders and looked right into my eyes as he screamed, "Once a Kurdish man marries, his wife [or ex-wife, as was the case in this instance] is cheating if she sees another man."

I could hardly believe my ears. I was raging now as I continued to push him, albeit ever so slowly, toward the door. "You have absolutely no business interfering in my affairs," I countered. "I am not a Kurdish woman, and I have no intentions of being bound by some antiquated cultural rules of behavior."

Metin was holding my wrists and trying to control me as I squirmed and tried to wiggle free.

"I am a free agent now, and I am going to date whenever I want and whomever I choose," I bellowed. With that, I shoved him and his friends out the door, and they left.

It was several days before I heard from Feyzullah again. Unbeknownst to me, he had spoken with his brother in Izmir and told him what had happened. His brother was understandably upset that someone had threatened his younger brother. He was ready to send a contingency of his associates to Adana to support and protect Feyzullah. Thankfully, Feyzullah realized that no one would win if that happened. He was intent on keeping a low profile. He didn't want to do anything that would escalate the tension between him and Metin, and for that, I would ultimately be extremely grateful.

In the meantime, I was moving right along, blissfully unaware of what Feyzullah and his brother had discussed. Feyzullah had put some of his photos on my computer. I made prints of three of my favorites, framed them, and put them on display in my apartment. There was a part of me that wished he had stood his ground with Metin and called his bluff. However, he was obviously outnumbered, so in retrospect, it was prudent to choose the route of least resistance. However, drama queen that I was, I would have loved it if he'd held his ground and fought for me. I didn't like seeing my main man scared off by my ex-husband.

A little more than a week later, Feyzullah finally found the courage to come to my apartment again. I suspected that Metin may have planted spies outside to watch and report back to him about my comings and goings. He always seemed to know who went in and out of my apartment and when. It was extremely unnerving. This particular day was no exception.

Metin called and announced that he knew Feyzullah was in my apartment, and he would be over in less than five minutes to deal with him. "If Feyzullah doesn't want to die," he said threateningly," he better leave now."

Once again, within seconds, Feyzullah had collected his belongings and fled. Metin appeared only moments later and wanted to know why Feyzullah was such a coward. "If he was a man, and if he really loved you," Metin said menacingly, "he would have stayed and fought for you."

I sat in an easy chair with my arms folded in front of me and watched as Metin paced around the apartment like a caged lion, desperately looking for anything that Feyzullah may have left behind as well as clues to what we might have been doing before he arrived. I clenched my fists and bit my tongue as Metin picked up the first of Feyzullah's photos. He gave it a cursory glance before throwing it on the floor and smashing it into a hundred different pieces. As he prowled from room to room, he found the other two photos, and they suffered the same fate.

I crossed my arms defiantly and sat in silence as Metin vented his rage. Finally, with a strong, steady, and controlled voice, I faced him and asked, "Are you done?"

He grunted once or twice and stormed out of the apartment.

It shouldn't have come as any surprise that Feyzullah called several days later and said that he couldn't deal with Metin, his anger, and his threats. He was certain that his brother would eventually get involved if Metin didn't back off, and he definitely didn't want that. He told me that he was sorry, but this was good-bye.

CHAPTER 38

The Dilemma

The heart has its reasons of which reason knows nothing.
—Blaise Pascal

Moving day was quickly approaching, and I was in a serious bind. Feyzullah had made all the arrangements with the movers, and he was gone. He had left the city shortly after breaking off our relationship, and I had no idea where he was or which movers he had made the arrangements with. I called several different companies, but it was moving season in Adana and everyone was booked solid. During their busy times, the companies routinely booked two or three customers on the same day. They were literally working 24/7. I was frantic. I had given the school my notice, and they fully expected to have access to the apartment by the end of the week. Everything was packed, and I was living on takeout food from a nearby restaurant and drinking water out of disposable paper cups. The only things that weren't already in sealed boxes were the broom, dustpan, and cleaning rags that I intended to use as the last box was carried out the door. What to do?

My mind was racing. All of my friends who were foreign teachers were gone for their summer holiday. While I was with Feyzullah, I had burned my bridges with all of my other male friends. The only one from my past who I'd had any contact with while I was with Feyzullah was Metin, and everyone knew how that had gone. However, the end of the week was rapidly approaching, and Metin had always said that no matter what happened between us he would always be there to help me if I needed him. I swallowed my pride and dialed his number.

Metin was notorious for either closing his phone completely or making the line busy if he didn't want to talk to someone. Our relationship had its ups and downs from the beginning, and there were times when he would close his phone for days at a time to punish me or to teach me a lesson. Consequently, I was shocked to have gotten through at all, much less on the second ring. When he answered, he seemed genuinely surprised and pleased to hear from me. I explained my problem and let him know that I felt he was responsible for putting me in this predicament.

"If Feyzullah were still here," I argued, "my movers would have been lined up, and I wouldn't be wringing my hands and losing sleep over what to do."

While Metin wasn't prepared to take responsibility for scaring Feyzullah away, he readily agreed to help. We hung up, and he told me he would come over right away so we could talk and figure out the best course of action.

When he appeared at my door, he was smiling the familiar smile I knew so well. He pulled me close to him and kissed me on both cheeks. We lingered with our arms around each other, and I could feel our hearts beating almost in unison. He told me how much he had missed me and how glad he was to see me. I admitted that I had missed him too. We walked hand in hand into the salon and sat down. We reminisced about the good old days and talked until the wee hours of the morning. Although we were both struggling to keep our eyes open, neither one of us wanted to call it a night. Now that we were together again, it felt as if we'd never been apart. I snuggled up in the crook of his arm, and I was home again.

All the old feelings were bubbling to the surface, and there, in the comfort of his arms, I remembered why I had fallen in love with him. However, morning was just around the corner, and there was much that still needed to be done. It was time for bed, and much to my surprise, Metin asked if he could spend the night.

"No problem," I said. "I'm finished at the school, so no one is going to object at this point."

First thing in the morning we could start calling movers. I had to be out of the apartment in three days, so there was no time to waste.

I was so exhausted that I don't even remember my head hitting the pillow, but suddenly, as if it was part of a dream, I heard frantic pounding on the apartment door. The pounding alternated with a frenetic ringing of the bell. Both started slowly but rapidly gained momentum. I sat up in bed, lowered my feet to the floor, and headed to the door still in a daze. *Who could it be?* I wondered. All of my friends were gone for the summer. Who was this who had broken my sleep and was now trying to invade my sanctuary? Cautiously, I opened the door, still wondering who or what was the source of this intrusion.

Without so much as a warning, a woman pushed the door wide open and stood with her hands on her hips, glaring at me defiantly. The commotion had awakened Metin as well, and he came running into the foyer. He took me completely by surprise when he yelled, in Turkish, "What in the hell are you doing here, bitch?"

For a moment, I was stunned. Metin recognized the intruder. I looked at him, and a thousand questions were running through my mind. I wanted to ask, "Who is this woman? How do you know her? What is she doing here? What does she want?"

Then suddenly, without warning, all of my questions were answered. The woman produced a piece of paper and threw it at me.

"What's this Metin?" I screamed.

"It's our marriage paper," he yelled before picking it up and tearing it into shreds.

Now there was no time for my questions and certainly no time for the answers. Metin grabbed the woman by the shoulders and pushed her into the hallway. She pulled out a knife and tried to stab him. They were exchanging insults in Turkish, and my heart was pounding a mile a minute. He had overpowered her, but she continued to fight. It was clear that she wanted to hurt him, and I stood in the doorway watching the two of them struggling, powerless to do anything. Metin finally managed to take the knife from her. He opened the elevator door and pushed her in before the elevator door closed. He returned to the apartment out of breath, struggling to control his rage. I was mute. I could hardly believe what I had just witnessed. When I was finally able to speak, I asked him what in the world was going on. We sat in the salon, and the story began to unfold.

Two weeks ago he had married Deniz, just as he had forewarned me he must. However, it was a match made in hell. He needed her financial help, and she needed a husband. Her father was terminally ill and wanted to be sure that, before he died, she would be married. Because of her profession, it was highly unlikely that any man would ever want to marry her, much less a man from a good family. Metin and his family were well known and respected in Adana, and as a result, he would be quite a catch for her. She and Metin had negotiated, and if Metin agreed to marry her legally, not in a hoca wedding, she would give him the money he needed to pay the penalties from the bar.

Metin never professed to love Deniz, and she accepted that. This was definitely nothing but a business proposition. They were both getting what they needed. However, Deniz was still hanging on to the hope that she could love him enough for the both of them. She believed that, in time, she could make him understand the depth of her feelings, and eventually, he would begin to return them. In an attempt to encourage him and to make it worth his while, she withheld a portion of the money she had promised to give him. He was on probation, so to speak. If he proved to be a good companion and a faithful husband, she would give him the rest of the money at a later date. She made of list of her expectations, and if he hoped to get the rest of the money, he was going to have to comply with them.

This was not what he had agreed to, and two days after their marriage, they had such a violent disagreement that Metin threw his wedding ring into the lake. After eleven days of marriage, he moved out. It was after all of this had happened that I had called him. I had no idea that they had actually gotten married. To be honest, if I had known, I would never have contacted him.

I listened to his story, and my heart went out to him. I knew he still loved me, but I no longer had the resources to help him. With the loss of my job, my monthly income had been cut in half, and I was now responsible for all of my living expenses, not the least of which were my rent and utilities. My days of working at a private college with all of its benefits were over. I knew he didn't love Deniz, but the fact was she had enough money to take care of the both of them, pay off all of the penalties, and still have enough left to travel and enjoy a luxurious lifestyle. I couldn't compete, I couldn't even run on the same track, so if he was looking for someone to solve his financial crisis, he would be barking up the wrong tree if he chose me.

I apologized profusely for having called him for help. I explained that if I'd known he'd gotten married, I would never have imposed on him. Deniz had been insanely jealous of me since I arrived in Turkey and met Metin. If I were no longer in the picture, I reasoned, perhaps they may be able to work things out. I told him that I still needed his help to move, but after that, I would never again call him or do anything that would interfere in his marriage.

The next day I was on pins and needles waiting for Metin to find a mover. Unfortunately, every professional moving company that he called told him the same thing they'd told me. They were fully booked and didn't have an opening until the middle of the month. Metin told me that he knew some men who had a truck. Granted, they were not professionals, so they didn't have a lot of the extras, as Metin called them, that the pros had. That meant they didn't have the large blue plastic containers that were used to haul all the things that didn't fit anywhere else, they didn't have the padded blankets to protect the wooden furniture, and, perhaps most importantly, they didn't have the cherry picker that the professionals used to lower large pieces of furniture down the outsides of high-rises.

I lived on the thirteenth floor of the apartment building and was moving into the third floor of a villa. I had huge pieces of furniture that wouldn't fit into the elevator. That meant that instead of moving them to the balcony and lowering them down to the ground with the cherry picker, they were going to have to be physically carried down thirteen floors. "Allah hallah," I said. All of this was devastating information, but the worst was yet to come. Even they were double booking because of all the people who were moving, so they couldn't start moving my things until ten o'clock at night.

Oh my God, I thought. *Could things get any worse?* By now I should have known better than to invite trouble by asking myself this question.

CHAPTER 39

The Move

Count your rainbows, not your thunderstorms.
—Alyssa Knight, age 12

By the time the movers, and I use the term *movers* loosely, finally arrived at 10:45 p.m., it was clear that they were already exhausted. *How in the world*, I asked myself, *were they going to muster up enough energy to move the contents of my apartment?* No sooner had I processed this thought than I looked out the window and saw that it had started to rain. *Wonderful*, I thought.

The truck was an open-air flatbed, so there was no protection there. In addition, the contents of my apartment were slowly but surely being moved to the pavement in front of the building—once again, no protection there. The movers didn't have anything to use to cover my upholstered pieces or the wooden dining room set and armoire, so I just closed my eyes and hoped for the best. When they saw the size of some of my pieces, they tried to negotiate a higher price. I was literally over a barrel now and truly thankful that Metin was there. He told them a deal was a deal and that was all there was to it. Perhaps because they were tired, or perhaps because they were getting even, they moved at a snail's pace. By three o'clock in the morning, I was beginning to wonder whether they were going to be able to finish the job. They were hungry, they were thirsty, and they were exhausted. We took coffee breaks, water breaks, snack breaks, bathroom breaks, and smoking breaks. By breakfast time, we were all ready to throw in the towel. The later it got, the more careless they became until I'd finally had enough. I paid them and told them to be on their way. I was ready to take care of whatever they hadn't finished. They were doing more harm than good and, at that point, were virtually useless.

It wasn't until they were gone and I had a chance to take stock of things that I realized there were some things missing. There were things that I definitely saw them bring in, and now they were gone. There were also some things that I didn't see come up the stairs, and I wondered where they were. I hopped in my car and drove back to my old apartment. I was speechless when I opened the door to the guest bathroom and found all of the things that they had decided they were too tired to move. They didn't fit on the last truckload, and the movers were bound and determined that they were not going to make another run. When I drove back to my new home, I was so angry that I was sputtering.

"Who in the hell were those jokers?" I screamed. "You won't believe all of the things they left behind." In my mind, it was bad enough that they hadn't moved everything but to have hidden them to cover up their incompetence was unforgiveable. Not only were they incompetent, they were thieves.

Later that day Metin called them to lodge my complaint. While he was on the phone with them, I asked him to find out where the missing items were. It turned out that one of the moving men liked some of the things he saw, and he assumed that because I had so many beautiful things, I'd never miss one or two items. I could hardly believe my ears. I told him that I wanted them to know I was going to tell all of my friends about what they'd done and warn them against ever using anyone from this crew. They were sloppy, incompetent, unprofessional, and dishonest, and I was furious. They'd gotten their money, and that was all that mattered to them. I could complain until I was blue in the face, but nothing was going to change. It was an expensive lesson, but I learned it well. It was a cinch; I was going to do things differently next time.

CHAPTER 40

On My Own

It is your duty to find yourself.
—John C. Maxwell

For the first time since I'd arrived in Turkey, I found myself, quite literally, on my own. I was no longer living in a school lodgment and, as a result, had forfeited the sense of security that is a natural byproduct of being an employee of an established institution here. Metin and I were no longer a couple. As frustrated and disillusioned as he was, he was still legally married. This was his problem and he was going to have to deal with it. Because I was no longer teaching, I had also lost the network of friends that I had cultivated. We were no longer able to meet during the tea breaks to share our problems and collectively work out the solutions.

Yes, indeed, I was alone, and the many problems that I would encounter, and the accompanying frustration, would eventually prove to be character-building experiences. I was beginning to realize that for my entire life, I had always looked outside of myself for the solutions to my problems. The new situation in which I found myself was going to force me to change my perspective and my modus operandi. This was to be the beginning of my journey of self-discovery.

The next few months were spent arranging and rearranging furniture, closets, and drawers. My new place was not the typical Turkish apartment, and as such, it took some getting used to. It had been built when Incirlik, the NATO base nearby, was in its heyday and was designed with Americans in mind. There were no walls separating the salon, dining area, and kitchen. To a Turkish family, this was unthinkable. It would make heating the apartment in the winter and cooling it in the summer prohibitively expensive. As I would find out later, this proved to be true. However, I was more than willing to pay the price for the amazing unobstructed view this gave me of the lake below and the snowcapped mountains in the distance.

There were still a lot of small repairs that needed to be done, and it seemed at the time as though every day a new one reared its ugly head. *Is there no end to this?* I thought. Because I no longer had the school's army of repairmen at my disposal, there were days when these little irritations seemed insurmountable. Granted, I had a toolbox and tons of tools. Unfortunately, I lacked the skills to do anything more than the smallest kind of repair. Fortunately, my downstairs neighbor Patrice and my friend Veronica continued to help me through the first few difficult months. As a result, it wasn't long before my new home was starting to look even more sumptuous and elegant than even I had imagined it could be.

Much to my surprise, Metin continued to seek refuge with me. He was trying to obtain a divorce from Deniz, but this proved to be a monumental task. Turkish courts are very reluctant to grant a divorce if a couple hasn't been married for at least a year, and to further complicate matters, both parties must agree, or the process can drag on for years. I know one person who waited for ten years, and my friend Patrice waited for eight years before her divorce was finalized. Metin clearly didn't have the temperament to deal within this time frame. He and Deniz continued to torment each other, each one in an attempt to get their own way. Metin is easily angered and, when he's frustrated, can become extremely aggressive. He would frequently arrive at my apartment spitting and sputtering about their latest battle. There was nothing that could be said or done to assuage him, so more often than not, he ended up storming out on me as well.

In addition to having to adjust to a new apartment and new living conditions, and perhaps even more significantly, I had to come to terms with the fact that I was no longer working. I started working part-time when I was fourteen, and until I was fifty-five, I never stopped. I learned at an early age that if there was something I wanted or needed, I was going to have to work to earn the money to buy it. At age fifty-five, I retired after thirty years of teaching. However, I didn't adjust well, and before I knew it, I found myself with three part-time jobs.

Once again, history was repeating itself. I didn't have a clue what to do with all the time I had on my hands. Out of sheer boredom, I found myself becoming a couch potato. In the past, I had unmercifully berated John, my ex-husband, for the hours he spent mindlessly channel surfing. Much to my dismay, I now found myself doing exactly the same thing. I'd stay up well into the wee hours of the morning, because that would guarantee that I'd be tired and would sleep until almost noon the next day. That meant I'd only have to fill half of a day, rather than a whole one, with something meaningful to do.

I usually lunched with *Oprah* reruns, which kept me busy until one o'clock in the afternoon. I'd do a little channel surfing before turning on my computer to check and see if I had any messages and from whom. The days dragged on, and I was beginning to feel, once again, as if my life was slipping away. I was losing my energy and my zest for life. I was still watching paint dry and the grass grow, only now I was doing it on the other side of the world.

Clearly, something had to change. I asked myself what gave me the greatest pleasure in life, and the answer was, as it had always been, travel. That settled it. I would plan to take a trip or two, and that would keep me productively occupied, as well as giving me something to look forward to.

CHAPTER 41

Serendipity

Expect nothing; live frugally on surprise.
—Alice Walker

Now that I had decided to plan a trip, the question of the hour became where would I go, and who would I go with? Ten years ago, I discovered that I had some long-lost relatives on my mother's side of the family who were living in the former East Germany. I knew that we had family somewhere in Europe, because, as a child, I could remember my mother sending boxes of food and clothing to them. Unfortunately, when my mother was still alive, I wasn't interested in hearing anything about some people I didn't know and probably would never meet. It wasn't until after she died that my quest to find them began. I don't want to bore the reader with the details of everything I did to try to find these lost relatives. Suffice it to say that I did everything from prowling through local cemeteries to going to Ellis Island to search for them on the computers there.

It's clear to me that I was meant to find them, because the story of how I eventually got their contact information is almost too bizarre to believe. My mother had a younger brother who became seriously ill while they were both in high school. She left school to nurse him back to health, and she never went back. Perhaps because she felt cheated out of her education or perhaps because she was overly protective of her brother, the relationship between my mother and the woman he eventually married was always strained. My mother's brother passed away at a very young age, and his widow began to date a man who was much younger than she was. My mother was irate, perhaps because of her loyalty to her brother or perhaps because her own marriage was in shambles. At any rate, she cut off all communication with her sister-in-law and her children, and I never saw my aunt or my cousin after that.

More than forty years later, I found myself driving near my aunt's old house. I wondered if she was still alive and if she still lived there. For some unknown reason, I very impetuously decided to knock on the door to see for myself. After all, I reasoned, I didn't have any problem with her. The bad feelings were between her and my mother, and my mother had been dead for years.

When my aunt opened the door, she recognized me immediately, as I did her, in spite of the years that had passed. She invited me in, and we chatted for a while, desperately trying to fill in the blanks that the past forty years had created. Suddenly, as if an afterthought, I asked her if she had any idea how to get in touch with the relatives I knew we had somewhere in Europe. Amazingly, she told me that she still had a letter she had received from them more than twenty-five years earlier. She hadn't answered because she was busy, and she didn't speak or write German or Hungarian. Her husband was dead, and she no longer felt any affinity for these people. However, she thought she may have kept the letter anyway. She told me she would look and see if she could find it and invited me back the following Saturday.

Saturday came, and I could hardly contain my enthusiasm. My aunt had called and said she found the letter. If I stopped by, I could pick it up. I returned to her house, thanked her profusely, and told her I would let her know if I found anything out about these mysterious relatives on the other side of the world. I immediately wrote a letter to them, had it translated, and sent it off to Neideroderwitz, Germany, a small village six kilometers from the Polish and Czech Republic borders.

Less than two weeks later, much to my surprise, I received a box from them. They were absolutely ecstatic to have received a letter from a relative in the States. They sent photos, a copy of a family tree (my family's side of it was blank), and a letter summarizing everything that had happened to them and their relatives since the war. I was ecstatic. I immediately called my aunt to give her the news. A strange voice on the other end of the line informed me that my aunt had passed away suddenly that week. I stood for a moment, with the phone in my hand, unable to speak. The most incredible thoughts were running through my head. How, after more than forty years, was I able to find this window of opportunity? It had been less than a month since that fateful day I rang my aunt's doorbell. In that time, she had provided me with the information I needed to reconnect with all of the relatives on my mother's side of the family. Had I not stopped in to see her that day, these people would have been lost to me forever. This was nothing short of a miracle!

I won't go into detail about our first reunion in Vienna, Austria, or the many times we've been together since then. Nor will I go into detail about the incredible stories they shared with me about their life during and after the war, their many failed attempts to escape from East Germany, and what happened to other members of the family as a result of the war. Those are stories that are best reserved for another time. However, it was necessary for me to introduce these people into this story, because they are the ones who convinced me to get up off of the couch and to meet them for a skiing holiday in Italy the following February. They ski in Italy every year during the semester break. It was settled. This year, I would join them. I would fly out of Istanbul on February 12 and meet them for a week in the Italian Alps. At long last, another adventure was looming on the horizon.

After changing planes three times and boarding a train for the last leg of the journey, I finally arrived at my destination. My cousin Anett and her husband, Egbert, were overjoyed. Ever since our first meeting, we had tried to get together every year or two, but being able to meet them for their annual skiing holiday was truly a special treat. All together, there were seven of us, and of the seven, there were six expert skiers. Even the children could tackle the most difficult of the runs. It was as though they had emerged from their mother's womb wearing skis. I, on the other hand, hadn't skied for more than forty years. To say I was a little apprehensive would have been putting it mildly. However, the first order of business was checking me into the hotel. We would worry about my skiing ability, or lack thereof, the following day.

The hotel was small and quaint and situated right at the foot of the mountain. My relatives were regulars and, as a result, received the royal treatment. Because I was their esteemed guest from the States, I received it as well. The rooms were cozy and immaculate. Mine had a spectacular view of the mountain. The temperatures were mild enough that it was possible to sleep with an open window and enjoy the cool, fresh, and invigorating mountain air. I was in heaven!

The next day we were up early, and after an amazing breakfast fit for a queen, we headed off to the slopes. I was dumbfounded by how much things had changed in the past forty years. Obviously, the equipment itself was dramatically different. However, over and above that, everything else was now automated and utilized state-of-the-art technology. I marveled at how efficiently people were outfitted with their gear, transported to the bottom of the mountain, and carried up to the summit. *Wow*, I mused, *times really have changed.*

As I mentioned earlier, everyone in the family was an expert skier. I knew it would be foolhardy for me to try to keep up with them. I decided that the smartest thing to do would be to take a few lessons before heading to the summit. I found an instructor who spoke English, and we headed to the beginner's slope. After only five or six minutes, he said, "It's obvious that you've skied before. We need to go farther up the mountain."

Before I knew it, we were quickly approaching the area where my cousins were skiing. I really wasn't sure I was ready for this, and when my lesson ended, I suggested that the next day the instructor and I should meet again for another hour. "Nonsense," was the response. "You're ready to tackle any of the runs on this mountain. Ski today and tomorrow, and if after that you still feel the need, we'll schedule another lesson." I felt very apprehensive but decided that he was the expert and knew what he was doing. I headed up the mountain to meet my cousins.

Holger, Anett's brother, was the best skier in the group, and he very patiently guided me down the mountain over and over again. There were several restaurants located on the mountain, but the very best one was at the summit. My goal was to become confident enough that I could join everyone for lunch at the top.

The following day was Valentine's Day, and although I was a little stiff, I was prepared to tackle the summit that day. We headed off for the slopes, and it was heartwarming to see how my two littlest cousins watched out for me. They didn't mind lagging behind their parents to make sure that their "aunt" didn't get separated from the group. They were precious. We all met for lunch at the restaurant on the summit, and based on what Holger had said, I already knew what I was going to order. He had described their specialty, and my mouth was watering before I had removed my skis. The sun was shining, and the sky was a magnificent shade of blue. It was warm enough that people had removed their jackets, hats, and gloves. It felt like we were, literally, on top of the world.

Holger left to place our orders, and we searched for a place to sit in the sun. Within moments, Holger returned looking crestfallen. Unfortunately, we were too late. The lunchtime crowd was larger than usual that day, and the restaurant was completely out of the special. I tried to hide my disappointment. I had taken my life in my hands by riding the gondola up there, and now I was going to have to try to make my way back down. It was definitely too far to walk, and as I surveyed the trail in front of me, my heart began to beat wildly. What in the world was I thinking? The vertical drop was daunting, and the trail was too narrow for me to traverse successfully. I imagined myself, totally out of control, plummeting down the mountain full speed ahead, screaming at the other skiers to get out of my way. I was fighting to hold back the tears. This was a long way from the bunny hill I started out on yesterday. My cousins could see the panic in my eyes, and they tried to reassure me that everything was going to be all right. For a fleeting moment, I thought about coming clean and telling them that I was terrified at the thought of having to ski back down. Perhaps they could call one of the ski patrol and have him bring a snowmobile to take me down. *Too embarrassing*, I thought. *I'm going to bite the bullet and pray for the best.*

The next twenty minutes were twenty minutes from hell. I skied and stopped, and skied and stopped, and skied and stopped again. My heart was in my throat, and I was praying. I couldn't remember what had possessed me to do something as foolhardy as this. I was on the summit of one of the highest mountains in the Italian Alps and trying to get down. I would have been scared if I'd been in a snowmobile. The fact that I was trying to ski down was nothing short of insanity. I zigged and zagged and zigged and zagged again. My cousins kept shouting words of encouragement, but they fell on deaf ears. I prayed that I would make it to a lift station in one piece. I was going to hop on and ride down the mountain in the gondola in spite of the embarrassment it would cause.

After what seemed like an eternity, I spotted the lift. It wasn't going to be easy to get to it, because it was intended to take skiers up, not down, the mountain. *No matter*, I thought. My goal was in sight. Finally, I reached a flat stretch where it was possible to stop and collect myself. I relaxed for a moment, caught my breath, and turned to see where I had come from. The sight of the mountain behind me, reaching directly up to the sky, made me weak in the knees. *Surely, I must be insane*, I thought.

Once again, I tried to appear calm as I put my gloves back on and prepared to continue my descent. Suddenly, without warning, my skis flew out from under me! I saw stars and gasped for breath.

Holger was the first one on the scene. He wanted to know what had happened. I was at a loss to explain. I had skied halfway down the mountain without incident only to fall as I stood completely still contemplating my next move. I struggled to get up. The pain was excruciating. At the time, no one could have suspected the extent of my injuries. My fall was completely uneventful. There were no stunts, nothing exciting or out of the ordinary. I was standing completely still and literally just fell over.

I struggled to get down to the lift station. I couldn't turn my left ski. I tried to explain this to Holger, but because neither of us spoke the other's language, communication was difficult. I felt nauseous. I looked at the distance I had to go to get to the lift. I removed my skis and began to walk. My ski boots were like huge lead weights, and every step was painful. There were times I just wanted to sit down and cry. *Perhaps if I do that,* I thought, *the ski patrol will come and get me. On the other hand, the longer I procrastinate, the longer it's going to take me to get down the mountain.* It was a long and unbelievably arduous walk to the lift. When the gondola arrived, I could barely lift my legs to get into it. *Something is really wrong,* I thought.

I tried to put on a happy face when I went down to dinner. However, even navigating the stairs to the dining room was painful. Everyone was convinced that I had a pulled muscle, so they gave me some ointment and sent me to bed early. "By tomorrow morning," everyone said, "you'll be back to normal."

God smiled on me the next morning, because when I awoke, I could see we were in the middle of a blinding snowstorm. I was still in a lot of pain, so when everyone else decided to head back to the mountain to try to ski, I took the bus into town. In Italy everything closes from noon until three in the afternoon, so I was relegated to window-shopping. However, I congratulated myself for not simply lying in bed. At least I'd gotten up and done something. When I returned, I found that everyone had called it a day early because of the snow. It was impossible to ski safely because of it, so they'd returned to the chalet early in the afternoon. I was still hobbling, so after an early dinner, once again, I went straight to bed.

Anett and Egbert Renger in the background, Annett Scheibe
on the ground, and her daughters, Vanessa and Emilie, on
either side of me. Her husband, Holger, took the photo.

When the next morning dawned, the sun was, once again, shining brilliantly. The sky was bright blue, and the air was crisp. I couldn't resist the urge to put my skis back on and give it another try.

Unfortunately, the pain was so intense that I wasn't able to put my boots on without help. Anett fastened my boots, and Egbert carried my skis. *If only I can get to the lift,* I thought, *I can get back on the mountain and work out the cramps in my muscles.* I rode up with Anett and Egbert but got off the lift before they did. I decided it would be better to start out easy and work my way back up to the summit again.

As I pushed off and started to ski down, it was painfully evident that I was going to be out of commission for the rest of the trip. I still couldn't lift my left ski at all, and my right one wasn't responding the way it should have either. I found a lounge chair at the bottom of the slopes and spent the rest of the day relaxing in it as I watched everyone else ski up and down the mountain. Fortunately, I only had two more days left before I would be heading back to Turkey. Although I didn't get to ski as much as I would have liked to, I thoroughly enjoyed being able to spend time with my relatives. Every cloud has a silver lining, and that was mine.

When I returned to Adana, I resumed my normal day-to-day routine and tried to ignore the pain, which, by now, had become even more debilitating. After a week and a half, I finally decided I should visit the local clinic and see if there was anything I could do to quicken the recovery process. The doctor took one look at me and sent me to the orthopedic hospital where I had X-rays and an MRI taken. Much to my surprise, the doctor who treated me was the one who had previously lived in my apartment. *What a coincidence!* I thought. I was thrilled. He spoke perfect English and still lived in the same sitesi (housing development), so he told me I could call him any time of the day or night, and he'd help me. *What more could a girl ask for?* I thought. I learned that I had fractured my pelvis in two places, sprained my thumb, and damaged a spinal disc. *No wonder it hurt*, I thought. Genghis, the doctor, was in awe. He wondered, out loud, how in the world I was able to tolerate such incredible pain for so long. It would take fourteen months for my bones to mend. I will have to think twice before I decide to book another skiing holiday.

CHAPTER 42

From the Sublime to the Ridiculous

Things will likely get worse before they get better.
—Ian Shepherdson

The next few months would prove to be no less exciting and challenging than those that had preceded them. There would be good times and bad, laughter and tears. At times, it seemed as if I was simply going from the frying pan into fire. Perhaps because I came from such a dysfunctional family, I was used to a life filled with drama. Events that would shake a normal person to the core were par for the course for me. My friends used to marvel at the calm way in which I accepted adversity. They credited me with superhuman attributes that rendered me unflappable in the face of a crisis.

Little did they know, nor did I suspect, that I had simply become numb to most of the forces outside of me. It was a survival technique that I had unconsciously developed to insulate me from the pain associated with day-to-day living. I was as sensitive as a newborn babe, and I wrapped myself in this blanket of numbness to protect me from the fear I would have felt if I were actually in touch with my feelings. I was an orphan in every sense of the word, literally and figuratively. I was alone in a strange country trying to manage to live and to do the right thing in the face of what often seemed to be insurmountable obstacles. Before I managed to extinguish the first fire, another one would break out behind me. I often wondered if it would ever end.

There were more court cases. The electric company sued me for supposedly using *kaçak* electricity. *Kaçak* means stolen, or literally "smuggled." The case had been going on for more than two years, and finally, as this book goes to press, it has finally been settled.

I underwent eight unsuccessful surgeries in an attempt to reconstruct my right breast after my lumpectomy. I spent two years in and out of the hospital fighting infection after infection and a series of other complications. In the end, I was left with a gaping hole in my chest where my breast used to be and a permanently deformed midsection. I filed a lawsuit against the doctor who performed all of the surgeries, and shortly thereafter, he left Turkey to practice in the United States. As I write, my case against him is also still in the courts, and it looks as though it may be years before it's finally settled. I have also filed lawsuits against the two schools I had worked for in order to get the severance pay that I am entitled to.

Up until I arrived in Turkey, my only trips to the courthouse were to appear in divorce court. I used to think that perhaps there was something in my DNA that made me more susceptible to drama than other people. However, I no longer believe that this is true. I believe these things have happened to me in order to provide me with an opportunity to learn a lesson. The people involved have been my teachers, and I think I'm being given another chance to get things right. My dearest forever friend, the late Caroline Loose, told me that God will send a teacher to help you learn your lessons. If you refuse to learn them the first time, He will send another teacher and a stronger message. This will go on and on until a person finally gets it. Each teacher will be stronger and more direct than the last so that, eventually, it becomes impossible to ignore what's happening. It's at that point that a person must decide whether to learn the lesson or not. I am beginning to see and to understand that perhaps the reason I now find myself in Turkey is because this is where the most difficult lessons and teachers are to be found.

297

On the bright side, I did manage to make one more trip to Syria before my life suddenly changed dramatically. Veronica and I took a trip to Syria, Lebanon, and Jordon. The highlights were a visit to the Dead Sea, a day trip to Petra, and the nightlife in Beirut. I have always been interested in helping to preserve ancient historical sites. In fact, while I was still in the States, I joined the World Monuments Fund. They worked in conjunction with American Express to preserve endangered historical sites. Every year they choose one hundred of the world's most endangered sites and allocate funds to help restore them. Every year I anxiously awaited the publication of their list. I'd look it over and put check marks next to the places that I felt should be included on my list of places I must see. Petra was at the top of my list.

When we arrived at Petra, I was overwhelmed at the sheer size of it. It was extremely hot that day, and the locals surmised that there would be a significant number of tourists who either couldn't, or wouldn't, want to do their sightseeing on foot. They were more than willing to oblige by offering to lead them through the site on horseback. Veronica and I decided not only that we needed the exercise, but that we were entirely too young and physically fit to join the army of elderly overweight people who were opting to go on horseback. However, by the time we had reached the end of the tour and were on our way back, we were beginning to wonder where the young men with the horses were. We walked and walked, and much to our chagrin, there wasn't a rider less horse in sight.

Finally, when our final destination was almost within our reach, out of nowhere galloped a handsome young man on horseback. He came to a sudden stop, his horse reared up on its hind legs, and I couldn't help but think that the whole thing looked remarkably like a scene out of a B-class movie set in the desert of some far-off land. He dismounted with the grace and agility of someone who had ridden for years. He bowed and introduced himself and asked whether he could be of service. At the time, the only service we thought he was offering had to do with renting his horse. Once again, our assumption proved to be flawed. Veronica, being much more astute than me, immediately recognized him for the charlatan he was. I, on the other hand, being the consummate drama queen, couldn't extricate myself from this B movie. I envisioned myself as a desert princess being whisked off the ground by a handsome young desert prince and galloping off into the sunset with him, my hair flowing in the wind behind me.

Veronica and I continued to walk while the desert prince continued to try to convince us how much more comfortable we'd be riding his handsome steed. The more persistent he was, the more determined Veronica became to walk. It didn't take him long to surmise that I was the more malleable one, and he concentrated all of his efforts on me. Eventually, I gave in, and before I knew it, he had mounted his faithful steed and was trying his best to help me do the same. Unfortunately, gravity was not my friend, and the horse was a lot taller than it looked from a distance. After several failed attempts, it became obvious that there was no way I could hoist myself up without a significant amount of assistance from behind. The handsome prince dismounted and gave it his best effort. Because I was wearing a skirt, I was more concerned about not flashing him than I was about mounting the horse. As a result, on the first attempt, I ended up completely missing the saddle. Instead, I found myself lying flat on my stomach across the backend of the horse.

I started to giggle, and my prince looked puzzled. I'm sure he was asking himself what was so funny. Little did he know that in my mind, I pictured myself continuing to slide on the horse's silken coat until I'd picked up enough momentum to catapult me to the other side where I would end up landing on the top of my head—not a pretty picture but perfectly plausible the way things were going. I slid back off the horse, and we mounted our second attempt (pun intended) to get me up into the saddle. I missed it again, but at least this time I was sitting erect. I ended up riding on the back of the horse rather than in the saddle, while my prince, once again, mounted gracefully, and off we went. By now, Veronica was so far ahead of us that I could barely make her out in the distance.

"No problem," said the handsome prince. "Do you really have to meet her? If not, we could go to my village. I would love to show you my manhood."

"No thank you," I countered. "We came together, and we're going to leave together."

The journey back became more and more uncomfortable with every passing minute. His constant references to his manhood and his insistence on showing it to me was wearing thin on my nerves. I had gotten on the horse in order to fulfill my fantasy of galloping off into the sunset. Almost as soon as I was actually on the horse, my fantasy was complete. All I wanted to do now was catch up to Veronica and get back on the bus. After what seemed like an eternity, Veronica and the bus were both in sight.

"There they are," I yelled. "This is where I get off."

My handsome, dejected prince dismounted and attempted to help me do the same. He didn't even try to hide his disappointment at not being able to display his manhood. Mounting the horse was a piece of cake compared to trying to get off. There was no wall to stand on and nothing to grab hold of. My prince did everything in his power to help me do it gracefully, but alas, my foot got caught in the stirrup, and I plummeted to the ground. That, in and of itself, was bad enough, and my pride was mortally wounded. However, as I fell, I knocked my prince backward and onto the ground and, without even a moment's warning, landed squarely on top of his manhood. Macho man that he was, he didn't scream. However, he was writhing in pain as I lay on top of him. I couldn't stop giggling, because no matter where I tried to grab him in order to get some leverage, I ended up slipping again. I was laughing hysterically. The harder I tried to get off of him, the more difficult it became, and the harder I laughed. My eyes were filling with tears, and because I was laughing so hard, I was snorting louder than his horse.

From a distance, it appeared to all the onlookers that we were indeed enjoying a little afternoon delight. Veronica watched in horror, assuming the worst. She knew I was the consummate adventure seeker, but she couldn't imagine that I would have succumbed to the wiles of someone as shady as this character. I finally stopped laughing long enough to stand up and give my prince some much-needed relief. I tipped him twice as much as the cost of the ride and told him he had made my day. I was left with a memory that brings a smile to my face every time I think about it. This is something that money can't buy, and I rewarded him handsomely for this special gift he gave me.

Chapter 43

Lessons I Still Need to Learn

". . . I've come to believe that there exists in the universe something
I call "The Physics of The Quest"—a force of nature governed
by laws as real as the laws gravity or momentum. And the rule
of Quest Physics maybe goes like this: "If you are brave enough
to leave behind everything familiar and comforting (which can be
anything from your house to your bitter old resentments) and set
out on a truth-seeking journey (either externally or internally), and
if you are truly willing to regard everything that happens to you on
that journey as a clue, and if you accept everyone you meet along
the way as a teacher, and if you are prepared—most of all—to face
(and forgive) some very difficult realities about yourself . . . . then
truth will not be withheld from you." Or so I've come to believe."

—Said by Liz at the end of the movie *Eat, Pray, Love*

Metin eventually managed to get a divorce from Deniz. He tricked her into granting it to him by telling her that he had incurred an eighty thousand-lira gambling debt that, as his wife, she was legally responsible for. Although his story wasn't actually true, considering some of the things he had done in the past, it was certainly believable. After consulting with her attorney and finding out that he was right about her liability, she reluctantly agreed to the divorce. Metin still considered me to be his wife and, as such, eagerly looked forward to finally being able to live with me under the same roof. I was well aware of the fact that although he didn't have an eighty thousand-lira gambling debt, he still had monumental financial problems. However, since we had never actually lived together as man and wife, I put my apprehensions about that behind me and welcomed him with open arms.

Initially, things went well. It was like the honeymoon phase of a normal marriage. However, as the days turned into weeks and the weeks into months, it became increasingly obvious to me that, once again, I had managed to find a man just like my father. He was financially irresponsible, had problems with alcohol and later drugs, and was emotionally unavailable. As he became increasingly more depressed and withdrawn, he lost interest in me, in sex, in life in general. He became verbally and emotionally abusive. From all that I'd read about personality disorders, I should have known that it wouldn't be long before he became physically abusive. At the time, I had no idea how things would eventually play out. Perhaps, if I had known, I wouldn't have allowed him into my house in the first place. On the other hand, if I hadn't, I wouldn't have learned the lessons I needed to learn in order to move on into a calmer and healthier phase of my life.

For the first time, I began to see that the way Metin was treating me was completely unacceptable. I began to realize that my childhood issues, particularly my fear of abandonment, had become so pervasive that they distorted my reality. I couldn't see things for what they were. I rearranged events to fit into my version of reality. My emotional baggage paralyzed me and kept me from doing what was necessary to effect a positive change in my life. I was beginning to understand that the reasons I used to explain why I didn't leave him weren't really reasons. They were simply rationalizations used in a desperate attempt to justify my inability to take the necessary action. The universe had sent people to be my teachers. Unfortunately, it would take many more months of insanity before I would be ready to learn my lessons.

CHAPTER 44

The Darkest Hours

No matter how confused, self-doubting or ambivalent we are about what's happening in our interactions with other people, we can never entirely silence the inner voice that always tells us the truth. We may not like the sound of the truth, and we often let it murmur just outside our consciousness, not stopping long enough to listen. But when we pay attention to it, it leads us toward wisdom, health and clarity. That voice is the guardian of our integrity.
—Susan Forward, PhD

Since my first days in Tarsus, my friends had questioned Metin's motives and my sanity for being involved with him. They couldn't understand what attracted me to him. "Surely," they said, "you can't find him attractive. He has no visible means of support, and he's uneducated, uncultured, and uncouth."

Although I knew they were right on many counts, there was something about him that drew me to him like a moth to a flame. Even before my court case against the hospital, there was something dark and mysterious about him that I eventually found irresistible. He didn't make any pretenses. He openly admitted to being poor, which is why, he said, he didn't have proper clothes. He dropped out of school to help support his family, which was why he couldn't find a decent job and was forced to use his wits and his charisma to make a living. While my friends saw a gigolo, I saw someone who was doing his best with what he had to work with. This, combined with the fact that I had mounted a one-woman crusade to help the Kurdish people because of the discrimination they faced, made me a perfect target.

By the time Metin and I actually began to live together on a permanent basis, I had known him for more than six years. During that time, he had been involved in fights, had numerous brushes with the law, and had become dependent on me to provide him with whatever it was he needed to solve his many problems. At first, I followed him like a lemming to the sea. However, after the first few years, I began to ask him what he felt he was giving me in return that would make me want to continue to do this. He never had an answer. Instead, he changed the subject by telling me that I was truly an angel sent from God. He admitted that he would never be able to repay me for all the kindness that I had shown him and told me that he would be forever grateful to me. Before we lived together, I wasn't exposed to his chicanery on a daily basis, and I wasn't aware of how selfish, inconsiderate, and emotionally unavailable he could be. As long as our time together was limited, he could charm me and talk his way out of any situation. Now that we were actually living under the same roof, it was a new game with a new set of rules.

On a day-to-day basis, life with him was difficult at best. As a Kurdish man, he naturally assumed that the woman in his life would be in charge of, literally, everything in the house. She would shop, cook, clean, pick up his dirty clothes, wash and iron, and tend to his every need. Initially, I carried out these duties with the same enthusiasm with which I approached all of my responsibilities. After all, I was an adult child of an alcoholic, and as such, I was filled with a sense of shame. I needed to do everything as well or better than the next person to prove that I was okay. However, it didn't take long for me to rebel.

"I didn't go to school for nineteen years to become a housekeeper and a maid," I screamed. "Something has to change." I pleaded, cajoled, and screamed again. I tried to explain that living together connoted some sort of a partnership. Having him in the house with me was supposed to cut my responsibilities in half, not double them. Eventually, he succumbed and agreed to water the plants on the balcony and carry the garbage out—not exactly a fifty-fifty proposition.

The disagreements over the household responsibilities were nothing compared to the war we waged over the car and Metin's "job." My sporty white Peugeot was my baby. I had it washed every week and didn't allow anyone to smoke, eat, or drink anything but water in it. After four years, it only had sixty thousand kilometers on the odometer, which is about thirty-six thousand miles. To me, it was a serious investment, because cars that are well cared for in Turkey retain their value. There isn't any ice or snow in this part of Turkey and, therefore, no salt on the roads. Cars that are seven or eight years old can still look brand-new. This is something that Metin either didn't understand or adamantly refused to accept.

Now that the bar was closed, he worked at a gaming house, and his hours were erratic. He went to work between six and seven o'clock in the evening and didn't return until four, five, or six the following morning. He provided car service for the club, which meant that he went to nearby cities and either picked up or dropped off players. As a result, he drove anywhere from three hundred to six hundred kilometers (180 to 360 miles) a night. In eight months, he put more than fifty thousand kilometers (30,000 miles) on the car. Metin, as well as the people he was driving, burned holes in the carpet and the seats and spilled drinks that stained the upholstery. In addition, he had several minor accidents that resulted in hundreds of liras' worth of damage that he promised he would take care of and never did. Every morning when he returned, I checked the mileage, and we had violent arguments about where he'd been and what he was doing.

"If the police stopped you," I screamed, "I'm the one they'll hold responsible, because the car is registered to me."

He argued that because we were "married," he was legally entitled to drive it anytime he wanted.

I countered, "If our marriage was legal and recognized by the government, you'd have a legal right to drive it. The marriage isn't legal and, therefore, neither is letting you drive the car!" I was furious! I couldn't believe that he didn't understand the severity of the consequences if there were to be a problem.

However, his Achilles' heel was that he never paid any attention to consequences. He was somehow, magically, always able to avoid them. I eventually told him he couldn't take the car anymore, and rather than agreeing that this was in my best interest, he began to take it without asking, like a thief in the night.

The little voice inside of me kept urging me to end the relationship. What kind of a hold, I wondered, did this man have over me that prevented me from seeing him for what he was? The arguments escalated and became physical. Both of us were out of control, and my life was unmanageable. I was suffering from an addiction that was no less damaging and frightening than alcohol or drugs. Why was I so gullible that even when I knew he was lying, I continued to take him back? Why didn't I believe that I deserved to be with a man who respected me and my things? *What in the hell is wrong with me?* I questioned. The little voice inside of me responded, "You're afraid of being alone."

CHAPTER 45

Angels to the Rescue

When the student is ready, the teacher will appear.
—Buddha

Cary, my late forever friend and spiritual mentor, knew all about my skiing accident in Italy and the fact that my bones weren't healing as quickly as they should have been. She sent me an e-mail with the name of a long-distance healer in California named Robert. Her thought was that he could do something to hasten the mending of my broken bones. I contacted him immediately, thinking that this would be our focus. How could I have known that my physical injuries would end up taking a backseat to what was happening to me emotionally and spiritually as a result of being together with Metin?

One of the first things Robert told me was that the angels were sorry for causing my skiing accident. However, they knew that I needed Robert's help, and they believed that the accident was the easiest way to get me into contact with him.

Our first conversation was in November 2011. We spoke only briefly about my physical problems before he sent divine blessings to Cary for bringing us together and sending me into to the next phase of my life. He told me it was time to unfold my next destiny and that Metin was sent as a dark angel to rid me of past-life karma. Robert told me that through forgiveness I could heal Metin and that I, in return, would also be healed. He sounded a little like Harville Hendrix, I thought.

He said that Metin's name was proof that there was karma to deal with. He told me to look closely at it. Metin breaks down to "met in," which, according to Robert, meant "met in order" to heal. Robert maintained that in order to clear certain things out of my life, I would have to learn to love myself for letting Metin hurt me.

He suggested that Metin may not actually be the source of my anger and that he may simply be acting as a catalyst to bring to the surface the issues about my father with which I needed to deal. Believe it or not, that made real sense to me. In fact, as I thought about it, there were numerous times that I actually told Metin that he was doing exactly the same kinds of things to me that my father had done. *Eureka*, I thought, *a breakthrough.*

By December, I was ready to invite Metin to participate in the next session. A month earlier, I had finally reached my limit and sent him packing, so it required a leap of faith on my part to call him and tell him what Robert had said. Although we weren't speaking at the time, if it was true that the only way I could be healed was to help heal Metin, I needed to talk to him. Metin had told me again and again that whether we were together or not, he would always be there for me, and I shouldn't hesitate to ask for his help. I didn't know what his response would be when I told him that I was consulting with a long-distance healer from California. Surprisingly, he was uncharacteristically interested in what I had to say. I told him there was no pressure on him to do anything but come to my house and listen to what Robert had to say.

On December 6, 2011, Metin was sitting next me when Robert told me that I was now cleansed of the need to suffer a terrible death through cancer. He also told me that I had carried the damnation and anger of my bloodline and that that prophecy was now also fulfilled. Of greatest significance from that conversation, however, was what Robert said about Metin and me. He told us that we had been together in four different lifetimes over a period of several hundred years and that there was a divine purpose for us to be together in this lifetime. He explained that I had treated Metin very cruelly in a past life and that I had a karmic debt to repay. At last, a plausible explanation. Perhaps this karmic cycle is what prevented me from ending what had obviously become an abusive relationship. If I had to stick it out a little longer to pay my karmic debt, so be it. I certainly didn't want to have to reincarnate again in order to complete this unfinished business.

The impact these sessions had on Metin was nothing short of miraculous. He hung on Robert's every word and sang his praises to everyone he knew. Metin was a new person. His attitude improved, and his behavior changed. He learned about karma and vowed that he was going to give up his old ways in favor of creating a better life. Unfortunately, as with everything else, his enthusiasm waned, and in January, he cancelled two appointments. Robert took that as a sign of his lack of commitment and decided there was no point in continuing to work with him.

By this time, Metin had moved back in with me. The effect that Robert had on him continued to keep him on the straight and narrow for a few weeks. However, after that, things began to deteriorate again, and I was back to asking myself what it was about this relationship that was keeping me stuck. My friends were tired of the drama. Metin and I had broken up so many times that it had become a joke. People who knew us both questioned my sanity. His mood changed from day to day, and sometimes from hour to hour. One minute he was planning our wedding, and the next he was packing his bags. It was like trying to maintain some kind of balance while sinking in a pool of quicksand. As he became more desperate, he became more cunning. He lied even when he didn't have to and eventually found it just as easy, if not easier, to lie than to tell the truth.

I did what I always do when I'm in a quandary. I prayed for guidance and lost myself in one of my self-help books. Among my favorites are *How to Break Your Addiction to a Person* by Howard M. Halpern, PhD; *Excuse Me Your Life is Waiting* by Lynn Grabhorn; and *Stop Walking on Eggshells* by Paul T. Mason, MS, and Randi Kreger. However, once again, it was one of my guardian angels who brought me precisely what I needed to have at that moment in time. My friend and neighbor Patrice was close friends with a woman who had decided to leave Turkey and return to the United States. As a result, she was getting rid of a lot of things to make her move easier. She gave Patrice her books, and as Patrice went through them, she came across one that she thought was a must-read for me. It was titled, *The Journey from Abandonment to Healing* by Susan Anderson, and it was exactly what the doctor ordered.

Anderson wrote about the causes, signs, and symptoms of post-traumatic stress disorder of abandonment. Years ago, one of the health-care professionals I had seen told me I was suffering from PTSD. I had heard the term before but only in conjunction with soldiers who were returning home from the battlefield. At the time, I didn't have a clue that, years later, it would turn out to be the key that would unlock the mystery surrounding my inexplicable attachment to Metin.

As I read the book, I identified with the causes, signs, and symptoms of the syndrome. As an adult, I had desperately tried to convince myself that my parents did the best that they could when it came to raising me. However, when I was finally old enough to leave my family of origin, I knew in my heart of hearts that I was damaged. I couldn't have explained, at the time, how the disappointments, shame, and broken promises I endured as a child would prevent me from developing and sustaining healthy relationships later on in life. I couldn't have known at the time that these same events would eventually be responsible for the hole in my soul, my obsessive-compulsive behaviors, my problems with addictive behaviors of all kinds, or the feelings of despair and hopelessness that were my constant companions. I credit Susan Anderson's book for finally helping me put these things into perspective so that I could forgive myself, as well as my parents, and begin to heal.

The most important thing that I gleaned from Anderson's book was the fact that it wasn't simply a lack of self-control or resolve on my part that prevented me from moving forward. I lost many friends because of my inability to draw a line in the sand with Metin and stick to it. Over and over again, we fought, and he left. Over and over again, we fought, and I told him to leave. But over and over again, after a short period of time, we were back together again. Robert attributed this to karma, and I would never be presumptuous enough to discount what he said. However, after reading Anderson's book, I understand that there are also some other forces at work.

One of these, according to Anderson, is symbiotic feelings. She writes:

Symbiotic feelings are the ones you experienced prenatally and during early infancy when you were in a state of oneness with your mother. You were inseparable, in fact, incapable of surviving without a caretaker. These feelings of dependency . . . place abandonment survivors in a painful emotional paradox: The more you experience the impact of your loss, the more you are compelled to seek your lost partner . . .

Your friends and family may wonder how you could want someone so badly who has treated you so poorly. What they don't understand is that your partner's leaving automatically aroused symbiotic feelings that had been stored deep in your emotional memory. You are left to cope with feelings that stem from psychobiological processes that operate independently of your conscious thought and beyond your immediate control.

Susan Anderson, *The Journey from Abandonment to Healing*. (New York, New York, The Berkley Publishing Group, a division of Penguin Putnam Inc., 2000). page 29.

Anderson goes into great detail about these and other issues that explain, to a great extent, an individual's inability to extricate herself from an abusive relationship. The fear of abandonment cuts right through to the heart of our primordial core and keeps us stuck. Her book has helped me to understand that it wasn't simply a lack of willpower that was preventing me from moving forward. The problem goes much deeper than that and, as a result, is something that will require time and a lot of hard work to overcome.

Perhaps I'll never fully recover from the damage to my inner child. However, the knowledge that there are many forces at work, struggling to keep me from forming and sustaining healthy relationships, will, hopefully, allow me to be less and less critical of myself when I lapse back into an old pattern. As Robert had said, I must learn to love myself. I must let go of the shame, regret, and recriminations and move forward. I will not abandon the idea of having a loving relationship. However, there will be ground rules this time, and I will adhere to them.

CHAPTER 46

Metin and Me

Things do not change, we change.
—Henry David Thoreau

Metin and me in the summer of 2012.

Change has never been my friend. As we all know, it's difficult and uncomfortable, and because of this, it takes time. However, in the case of Metin and me, a radical change of some kind was imperative, and time was of the essence. Neither of us was happy with the status quo, but neither one of us seemed to know what to do to alter the course of the relationship. As the saying goes, if you always do what you always did, you'll always get what you always got. Quite simply, if nothing changes, nothing changes.

In our case, it would be me who would be responsible for sounding the wake-up call. Robert's advice to me was to handle Metin with the force of God. "Don't tolerate any of his Hitlerian tactics," he admonished. Surprisingly, once I was fortified with Robert's advice and the information in Anderson's book, changing the course of events seemed to be within my grasp for the first time.

319

In spite of Robert's influence, Metin gradually slipped back into his old ways. Once again, we argued about his use, and abuse, of the car and his job. His reaction was, as it had always been, to raise his voice, become verbally abusive, and storm out of the house. This was his modus operandi. He would take a self-imposed time-out only to return calmly and apologetically as if nothing had happened. However, things were different now. Armed with the knowledge that I was trapped in an addictive, codependent relationship, I had new options. Granted, we had a shared history, but I no longer saw us as being inextricably tied together through karma or anything else. In addition, I had come to grips with the fact that as a cancer survivor I had to choose my destiny carefully. I vowed that I was going to spend the rest of my life doing the things that gave me pleasure.

For the first time, I recognized that there wasn't enough time or energy left to waste being unhappy or struggling to transform a relationship that was doomed into one that would be mutually fulfilling. Admittedly, I still loved him. However, I now felt a kinship with his first wife who had said to him, "I will always love you, but I love myself more and, because of that, I must leave you." I had reached my saturation point. If he was going to continue on the same path, I was ready to deal with the gut-wrenching pain that's a natural by-product of swearing off an addictive substance or relationship. I had an inner strength and resolve that gave me the courage to move forward into the next phase of my life. Whether or not Metin would be a part of that would be entirely up to him.

On September 1, 2012, Metin's father, son, and two friends came to the house for a visit. Metin had worked late the night before, so he was still sleeping when they arrived. I made something for everyone to eat, and we were all sitting on the balcony chatting when Metin finally appeared. I could tell from the expression on his face and the way that he spoke to his father that he was feeling surly and argumentative. I went into the kitchen and realized that before he came out onto the balcony to join us, he had gone into my purse and taken ten liras from my wallet. Granted, ten liras is not a lot of money. However, I had told him over and over and over again that there were certain things that were off-limits to him, and one of them was my purse. In seven years, I never went into his wallet, and I expected that he extend the same courtesy to me. If he needed something, the solution was simple, *ask*.

I went back out onto the balcony and whispered into his ear. I asked him to please come into the kitchen, because I had something to say to him. Suddenly, he leapt from his chair, picked it up, and threatened to throw it at me. I retreated into the kitchen while our guests watched, awestruck. He followed me and knocked me onto the floor. I got up and headed for the bedroom. He intercepted me in the foyer and knocked me down again. Finally, he went into the kitchen and grabbed a butcher knife. By this time, his father, son, and best friend were in the kitchen, watching in horror as Metin ran toward me. They tried to restrain him as he cursed and threatened to kill me. After what seemed like an eternity, his son was able to reason with him and convince him to put the knife down. Suddenly, and without warning, his father, son, and friend left, leaving me alone to deal with the aftershock. Frantically, I threw all of Metin's things into a suitcase and drove him to his family's house. I drove off and told him we were finished. For the first time in seven years, I really meant it.

Days passed, and I refused to answer his calls or text messages. He had friends and family members call, but I remained resolute, and ironically, the pain of separation that I felt was lessened by the sense of peace and calm that I enjoyed in his absence. I knew where my car was and who was driving it. I wasn't being awakened at five or six o'clock in the morning when he finally came home. I wasn't lying awake at night trying to determine whether or not what he was telling me was the truth. Granted, there was a void in my life, but the serenity that I was experiencing for the first time in a long time was more than enough to compensate for the emptiness that I felt. Yes, I was alone in a foreign country, but I had friends to help me with the things that I couldn't handle on my own. To be honest, we had been down this road so many times before that the separation was far less painful than I thought it would be. Yes, there would be life after Metin.

After this incident, I was prepared to accept the fact that we would never see each other again. I was numb. In the past, I used to remark about having butterflies in my stomach whenever we were together. At the moment, as far as I could discern, the butterflies had died. I wasn't sure what that meant as far as my feelings for him were concerned. All I knew for sure was that I was ready to move into the next phase of my life, and at least at the moment, it didn't appear as though Metin would be part of it.

CHAPTER 47

Forgiveness

Everything that happens along the way is part of the journey. Everything can be incorporated into our healing process. All roads lead to growth.
—Melodie Beattie, *Journey of the Heart*

Once again, slowly but surely, Metin found a way to talk his way back into my life, and once again, slowly but surely, I succumbed to his charms. This time, however, the process was more gradual than before. I was shell-shocked at the way he had behaved in front of his family and friends and at the cavalier way in which he threatened me. As a result, my guard was up. If he intended to try to reconcile, it was going to be on my terms this time.

For several days we met and shared our feelings about what had happened at the house, as well as our feelings about the prospect of a *bariş*, or reconciliation. I opted to meet in public places to avoid the possibility of another outburst. For at least two years, Metin and I, as well as his family, had been discussing the fact that he was out of control and needed professional help of some kind. His treatment of me on September 1, made it impossible for them to continue to turn a blind eye. Metin was severely troubled, and if there wasn't an immediate intervention of some kind, it was only a matter of time before he seriously hurt someone or himself.

Metin, once again, was sincerely penitent and freely admitted that he couldn't control himself. He knew he was fighting his demons, but he didn't know what to do about it. He continued to profess his love for me and maintained that his dream was to build a secure and happy future for himself, Yilmaz, and me. I told him that unless he agreed to get professional help this simply wasn't an option.

Metin was no stranger to health-care professionals. A year earlier we had sought help for him. Unfortunately, because we chose to see a psychiatrist in a government hospital, Metin didn't have a chance to talk about what was troubling him. After a five-minute interview, the doctor prescribed some medication and sent us on our way. The medication seemed, for a time, to relieve him of some of his anxiety and depression. However, it didn't get to the root of the problem, so it wasn't long before his demons reared their ugly heads and he acted them out. This time, he said, he wanted things to be different. He said that he would like to go to a private facility where he would have a chance to talk about the things that were bothering him. I was thrilled that he made the suggestion, and I agreed with it wholeheartedly. We set about making an appointment for the next day.

When I agreed to take Metin back, I told him there were two conditions with which he would have to agree. The first was that he would stop lying to me. The second was that he would seek professional help. I told him that nothing he could say or do would be so bad that lying would improve the situation. I insisted on complete transparency. If he couldn't do that, I wasn't interested in reconciling. At this point, we had an appointment with a psychiatrist, and Metin vowed that he would be completely honest moving forward. I knew that expecting a complete transformation overnight would be unrealistic. After all, he'd spent a lifetime cultivating these bad habits. There would be setbacks. However, as long as I could see forward movement, I would be satisfied.

We'd been together in varying capacities for the better part of seven years. I had invested time, energy, and love in this relationship. If there was even a remote possibility that we could turn things around, I felt that I had to give it a chance. In my heart of hearts, I had to admit that it takes two to make or break a relationship. I hadn't been completely blameless, and I was willing to accept a good share of the responsibility for what had or hadn't happened. We were both optimistic that we could turn things around, so armed with the courage of our convictions; we looked forward to happier times.

It was only a few days later that I decided to take the car to the body shop to have the damage from all of Metin's fender benders repaired. In order to do this, I needed a copy of my insurance papers. I always kept them in the glove compartment, which I assumed was a safe place. I couldn't imagine why anyone, other than Metin or me, would have had any reason for going in there. Wrong again! The papers were gone. It took days to finally get a copy of the original. However, the following Monday, with insurance papers in hand, I drove to the auto body repair shop. Because Metin wasn't with me, making the arrangements to drop the car off was arduous. I had an appointment at six o'clock that evening. After that, I agreed to drive back to the repair shop, pick up Adem, the owner, and have him take me home before he returned to his shop with the car. It took an entire day to finalize all of these arrangements, and Adem would need the car for four or five days. Therefore, I was hell-bent that nothing and nobody would interfere with the plan.

When we arrived at the house later that evening, Metin shouted something down at us from the balcony. At first I couldn't hear him. However, as I got closer, I understood that he wanted me to stop Adem from driving away with the car. I pretended not to hear him. He was pacing back and forth on the balcony like a caged tiger and screaming like a madman. *What now?* I wondered.

When I opened the door to the apartment, Metin was there to meet me. He was seething. He was holding his arm and yelling that he had broken it and needed to go to the hospital. He had lied to me so many times before that I didn't believe him. I thought it was a ruse to stop me from sending the car off for repairs so he could take it to work again that night. He ranted and raved like a lunatic. At one point, he picked up a plate and threatened to throw it. However, for the first time, he controlled himself. I told him that I'd be more than happy to call him a cab. He refused. He asked for forty liras, which I gave him, and he left.

Once again, after he was safely out the door, I packed his bags. I vowed I wouldn't take any further abuse from him, verbal or otherwise, and I was determined to make my point. Shortly thereafter, he returned. He banged and pounded on the door. I refused to open it. He shouted and hollered at the top of his lungs. I told him he was insane if he expected me to open the door and let a raging madman into my apartment. He left. Within the next three days, he called dozens of times. His sisters called, and he called from his friend's phone. I refused to answer. He called my house phone, and I refused to answer. He sent text messages, and I refused to answer. He told me he had great news to share. I wasn't interested. I was resolute. Five days passed, and his suitcase was still outside the door.

On the fifth day, he sent me a message asking me to please bring his suitcase to his mother's house. His arm actually was broken, and he desperately wanted some clean clothes to wear. When I arrived, his mother motioned for me to come up. I refused. She persisted, and eventually, I gave in.

My determination not to weaken and give in this time finally made a difference. Metin was distraught over the breakup, and his mother said he was inconsolable. She couldn't stand to see him cry. The mafia continued to threaten him, and now his brother-in-law as well, about the balance of the money he still owed them. Fatma, Metin's mother, had several health issues, including high blood pressure and diabetes. The stress that she was experiencing because of his problems was severely affecting her physically, and as a result, she was finally moved into action.

Metin's depression and aggressive outbursts resulted, to a great extent, from the fact that he knew his parents had the means to help him but stalwartly refused to get involved. He had bought an apartment when he and his first wife married. After they divorced, Metin's mother had put the apartment in her name to guarantee that the family would still own it when Metin's son, Yilmaz, became of age. Repeatedly, Metin begged them to sell it so he could pay off his debt. There would still be enough money left to buy another apartment for Yilmaz. Up until this point, neither of his parents would even entertain the idea. In fact, it had driven a wedge between his father and mother that nearly ended their marriage. However, the stress finally became too great to ignore, and his mother came to the realization that this was the only way out. She could see the toll it had taken on Metin and everyone who loved him. In the past few months, he had lost more than twenty pounds and, because of his state of mind, had hurt all of the people closest to him. He was, in every respect, only a shadow of his former self. If something wasn't done, and done quickly, it would only be a matter of time before he was finished, either by the people to whom he owed the money or by his own hand. At long last, she agreed to put his apartment on the market.

CHAPTER 48

The Aftermath

All the art of living lies in a fine mingling
of letting go and holding on.
—Henry Ellis

Metin's mother met with the people to whom Metin owed money, and together they went to a real estate agent and listed the property. She assured them that as soon as the house was sold they would receive their money. They agreed that in the interim their only contact would be with her. Metin was out of the equation. He felt like the weight of the world had been lifted off of his shoulders, and for the first time in a long time, he was optimistic about the future. He had a smile back on his face and a spring back in his step. He began to eat again and started to regain some of his weight. Life was good.

In addition, the two of us seemed to have found our rhythm. I became less fanatical about the car, and Metin, in turn, tried to be more considerate of me and of my things. Both of us made a concerted effort to communicate more openly and honestly about our feelings. We dropped all the pretenses and our defense systems. We learned to cry together. We were beginning to function as a unit as opposed to two separate individuals whose primary concern was meeting their own needs.

Perhaps, however, the greatest change that I experienced was in my heart of hearts. As a result of all that had transpired in the past few months, I was forced to come face-to-face, not only with my demons but with the fact that my relationship with Metin may have run its course. If it ended, it would be the first time in fifty years that I wouldn't be involved in a relationship. I used to joke that I didn't date, I married. However, the painful truth was I really didn't marry either. I took hostages.

Although I was saddened by that thought that our love affair might be over, that reality no longer paralyzed me. In the past, I had been completely immobilized by our separations. I spent days pouring my heart out to anyone who would listen and ruminating over the "if onlys" and the "should haves." I wandered aimlessly around my apartment, trying to quiet my mind and find some kind of consolation. I asked my angels to help lessen the pain of the breakup. I read my tarot cards and my Angelic Messenger cards; I consulted fortune-tellers and asked my pendulum for advice. I surfed the Internet looking for articles about what to do when the love of your life has left you. Ultimately, I usually ended up buying a pack of cigarettes and a bottle of wine and trying to lose myself in an alternative addiction.

These last few times, however, were different. There wasn't anyone with whom I shared my tale of woe. I didn't spend hours surfing the 'net for advice or looking for free online tarot readings. Miraculously, I continued to function. I lost myself, for hours, reading books and writing. I met with friends. I cleaned my apartment. I pampered my inner child and told her that I was going to be taking care of her from now on and that she had absolutely nothing to worry about. I was no longer the pathetic, weak, sniffling woman incapacitated by a broken heart and wearing it on her sleeve for the whole world to see. I had a new inner strength that could only have come from the realization that I do have choices and that I don't have to suffer any kind of abuse from anyone. Slowly, but ever so surely, I understood that I don't need to look outside of myself to feel complete. I was enough.

The hole in my soul was beginning to fill itself in, and every new step toward independence that I took made it that much smaller. I no longer sat in silence when my feelings or my rights were being abused. I spoke up and explained in a clear and succinct way why I could no longer tolerate that kind of treatment.

Ironically, as I changed, so did Metin. He began to realize that his macho facade was just that—a facade. He learned to be vulnerable and to share his feelings. He learned to cry. He started sharing with me the things I did that made him feel like he was being used. Admittedly, I was shocked at some of the revelations. There were clearly some cultural differences that he simply couldn't ignore, and if we ever hoped to have a mutually satisfying relationship, I was going to have to come to terms with that.

He pointed out that although my financial condition had changed drastically, he was still with me. Instead of dining out in fabulous restaurants three or four nights a week, we were eating in small family-run diners or enjoying a frozen pizza at home. Clearly, I hadn't taken the time to view the state of our relationship through his eyes. I had begun to change, and this, in turn, had resulted in changes in him. For all intents and purposes, it appeared that Robert was right. In order for me to heal, I had to help Metin, and in return, he would continue to help me. We seemed to be on the right track.

CHAPTER 49

A New Beginning

I've always heard every ending is also a new beginning; you just don't know it at the time. I'd like to believe that's true.
—Said by character Emily Prentiss in *Criminal Minds*

A sense of peace and calm had settled over our home. Metin continued to point out all of the things that he did for me, and did around the house, that most men in his country wouldn't be caught dead doing. Although many of them were things that I just took for granted, it was painfully clear that he felt he was moving mountains. I continued to try to understand more about the culture so that I could be more appreciative of the efforts he was making. Deniz, his ex-wife, had told him years ago that a relationship with me would never work. She told him that because I was an American, I was going to expect him to share equally in the duties around the house. Actually, she was right. I just assumed that even though I lived in Turkey, I could superimpose my cultural mores on the people around me. Little did I know or understand how difficult it would be to find a happy medium. However, I am pleased to report that, although we are a work in progress, we are continuing to move forward with a level of intensity and honesty that, heretofore, we hadn't known. This, in itself, is enough to make me ask: Why is it that just when a person thinks they've learned the rules of the game, someone changes the game?

Early in the morning on October 1, 2012, I opened my computer to check my messages. There was one in particular that jumped out at me. It was from a volunteer organization I had registered with when I retired from teaching. Their mission was to provide auxiliary staff to hospitals and schools around the world. Since the economic crisis, the number and amount of donations they were receiving had dramatically decreased. As a result, there were few placements being made. In the two years that I was registered, I only received one other notice regarding a position. It was in China, and I definitely wasn't interested in going there. The second was in

Tripoli, Libya, which piqued my interest, but because of my age, I didn't think I'd be considered a serious contender. You can only imagine my surprise when I opened the message and learned that I had the option of going to there!

I raced into the bedroom and awakened Metin to share the news. He opened his eyes and tried to make sense out of my ramblings. I never told him that I had registered with this organization, so he had a difficult time trying to figure out why in the world someone had sent me an e-mail asking me if I was interested in going to volunteer at a school in Libya. As he struggled to understand exactly what was happening, the magnitude of what I was saying began to register with me.

Metin and I were not legally married. Although we spent hours dreaming about and planning a "real" wedding, so far, for a variety of different reasons, it hadn't happened, and this would have devastating results for Metin once I left the country. Metin was completely dependent on me for a place to live and a car to drive. His apartment had been rented the previous June and was now on the market to be sold. He adamantly refused to live with his parents because of the stormy relationship with his father. Occasionally, he had stayed with one of his sisters and her husband, but that wasn't a viable long-term solution. Deniz, his ex-wife, was always waiting in the wings, hoping that he would return, but that certainly wasn't an option if he wanted to continue his relationship with me. Because of the number and intensity of our arguments, my neighbors would not agree to let Metin stay in the apartment if I wasn't there. They were tired of his outbursts and eagerly looked forward to his departure and the subsequent return to normalcy. If I left, so must Metin.

In addition, the potential loss of the car was a major problem. My car had a foreigner's license plate, which meant that, technically, it was illegal for anyone other than me to drive it. If Metin and I were legally married, there wouldn't have been a problem, and he could easily have been covered under the insurance policy. However, because we weren't married in the eyes of the law, I would have to put the car into storage while I was out of the country. This would mean that Metin could no longer provide car service for the club, which would result in a substantial loss in income for him.

Months earlier, Robert had suggested that Metin and I spend three or four months apart. He felt that we both needed some time and space to find ourselves and to decide what each of us really wanted. As long as we were living under the same roof, we couldn't put the distance between us that would be necessary to do this effectively, and as long as we were both living in Turkey, it looked like we would be living under the same roof. There was absolutely no way, other than leaving the country, that I could separate myself from Metin. As a result, I looked upon the opportunity as a gift from God. I needed to go and let the chips fall where they may.

CHAPTER 50

The Awakening

It's no big deal they say
It's just the kind of madness you get used to
But where do you run when fear stalks your dreams
How do you measure the weight of those things?
—Carrie Newcomer, "The Madness You Get
Used To" from *My Father's Only Son*

As I prepared to leave for Libya, something incredible happened. I experienced a state of euphoria that I hadn't felt since I first moved to Turkey. Yes, once again, I was leaving literally everything behind. Considering how much I enjoyed my life, my apartment, my students, and my friends, it should have resulted in some sense of loss or angst. After all, there was still a war being waged in Libya and the US Ambassador had been killed just a few weeks earlier. Why, my friends desperately wanted to know, would I voluntarily leave everything behind and move to a place where my very life might be in danger? The answer was simple: I needed to put some distance between me and Metin.

Something inside of me had changed. I had reached the end of my rope. I no longer felt compelled to stay with him in order to pay off my karmic debt. I no longer felt compelled to solve all of his problems. I no longer felt compelled to put his needs first. I no longer felt compelled to settle for a relationship that wasn't all that I had hoped it could be.

Suddenly, I no longer felt trapped. I no longer felt that I had to make concessions in order to keep the peace. I no longer had to try to convince myself that given enough time this relationship would ultimately be all that I wanted it to be. I no longer had to sublimate my needs because I was with a man who was either uninterested or unable to meet them. However, this time I wasn't running away. I was making a conscious decision to strike out on my own in an attempt to build a life that would finally fulfill my needs, with or without Metin.

This was uncharacteristic behavior for me. The old me would have stayed the course. I would have continued to try to be a better wife. I would have continued to try to be a better sexual partner. I would have continued to do whatever I could to look younger and sexier for him. I would have continued to take the blame for whatever went wrong in the relationship. I would have continued to let him abuse me emotionally, financially, and physically. I would have continued to rationalize and justify his inappropriate, and often criminal, behavior in order to keep us together. I am reminded of the song "Stand by Your Man," and stand by my man I did, until I finally realized there was absolutely nothing more I could do to create a relationship that would be mutually satisfying. I had given my all, and it wasn't enough. It was time to leave.

I'm not exactly sure when or how I came to this realization. Perhaps it was my fear of being alone that kept me trapped. Perhaps it was my love for Metin that kept me trapped. I guess I'll never know. All I was certain of, at that point in time, was that I was going to Libya and Metin wasn't. I had cast our fate to the wind, and I was willing to deal with whatever fate held in store for us. If we were destined to be together, things would have to change. If this was the end, I would have to be content with the knowledge that there was absolutely nothing more I could have done to prove my love for him. I was no longer content with the status quo.

Yes, he had told me I was an angel, he had told me that he would never be able to repay me for all that I'd done for him, he had told me he would pray for me. I was grateful for all of this; however, it was time for me to accept the fact that I also have needs that must be met. For the first time in my life, I was willing to accept the responsibility for my own happiness. This was a frightening prospect for a woman who, for her entire life, had looked outside of herself for someone to complete her. The Universe always sends us teachers, and if we refuse to learn our lesson the first time the teacher appears, the Universe will send another one whose methods are much more painful. In my case, I believe I have had three teachers before I met Metin. When God sent the first one, he tapped me on the shoulder, and I didn't respond. The second teacher hit me with a stick, and I didn't respond. The third teacher hit me with a sapling, and I still didn't respond. Metin hit me with the entire tree, and perhaps, at long last, I had seen the message and responded.

As I said before, I'm not sure when or how this happened. Growth is a gradual process, not a destination. All I know for certain is that, at long last, I was ready to face the future alone and undaunted. I am an incredible human being, and it's my God-given right to be happy. I am more than willing to compromise to make a relationship work. However, in the case of Metin and me, I had subverted all of my needs in order to please him. This was not the kind of a relationship I want, and it wasn't the kind of relationship for which I was willing to settle. For the first time in my life, I had come to the realization that my relationship with myself is the most important one I will ever have. If I've done everything I need to do to nurture this relationship, all will be well.

CHAPTER 51

Surprise!

To keep your character intact, you cannot stoop to filthy
acts. It makes it easier to stoop the next time.
—Katharine Hepburn

At long last, it was time to leave. I was to board the plane for Istanbul in Adana on October 19, 2012, at 3:35 in the morning. I would have a short wait in Istanbul before boarding the Turkish Airlines flight to Tripoli. Metin was still using the car, so he took me to the airport and helped me check in. I was glad to have him with me, because the airline employees were very concerned about the document that was supposed to serve as my visa. My Turkish still left a lot to be desired, so Metin acted as the translator, and at least for the moment, my problem seemed to be solved. He accompanied me to the security check-in. We kissed good-bye and promised to stay in touch.

After much discussion, Metin had finally agreed that it would be in the best interest of everyone involved for him to leave the apartment. The other two families in the villa were at the end of their ropes. Metin's erratic hours and unsavory associates had worn everyone's patience thin. It was, in their words, a "family house," and these kinds of activities and people were not welcome. As a result, by the time I left, Metin had removed all of his clothes and had given me his key. We agreed that he would finish his last-minute business and return the car to the *otopark* of my apartment by three thirty that afternoon. Once the car was back in the parking lot Mustafa, my attorney, would take care of it.

I boarded the plane to Istanbul, relieved that all of the problems seemed to be behind me. I was off to a new city, in a new country, on a new continent, and I was ready for whatever would follow. After a light breakfast and a short flight, we landed. I had three hours to kill until my plane left for Tripoli, so I wandered around the airport, window-shopping in the duty-free section and drinking coffee at Starbucks.

Finally, they announced it was time to board my flight to Tripoli. I got into the line with the rest of the passengers. I couldn't help but notice that I was the only woman who was not wearing a head scarf. I lowered my eyes and concentrated on my feet in order to avoid making eye contact that would be considered inappropriate. The boarding process took forever. Everyone's documents were thoroughly checked. Finally, it was my turn. I waited impatiently to be processed and waived on. One can hardly imagine my embarrassment and confusion when I was asked to step aside while the rest of the plane boarded. I felt like a convicted criminal as all of the passengers filed passed me, casting inquisitive glances, clearly wondering what my transgression might have been.

After what seemed like an eternity, a supervisor arrived. It seemed that the problem was with my "visa." There hadn't been enough time to formally complete the process; so instead, I was carrying a photocopy of a visa that hadn't been signed by the immigration officials in Tripoli. The agreement was that the visa would be stamped when I arrived. Unfortunately, the school administrator wasn't aware that the airline had to be notified in advance of my boarding. The airline supervisor called the Libyan immigration officials to try to verify my story. Unfortunately, whoever was on duty that morning wasn't aware of what had transpired, so I was politely ushered out of the boarding area.

What now? I thought. I didn't have enough minutes on my cell phone to call anyone. I don't have any credit cards, and the amount of cash I was carrying wasn't enough to solve any of the impending problems. The supervisor suggested that I stay in Istanbul for a couple of nights and complete the visa process there before attempting to board another flight. I mentally calculated the cost of this option and immediately disregarded it. There was only one thing I could do, and that was to go back to Adana. Questions, questions, and more questions. Would the airline charge me for a return ticket to Adana? Would I have to repurchase the ticket to Libya? If this was any indication of what my new adventure was going to entail, did I really want to go?

After several cups of coffee and what seemed like an interminable amount of time, another airline official approached me to give me the news. The good news was that they were going to put me on a return flight to Adana, and there would be no charge. The bad news was that it didn't leave for another four hours. The good news was that they had taken my baggage off of the plane to Tripoli. The bad news was that they weren't exactly sure where the bags were. No one was able to tell me what was going to happen regarding the ticket I had already purchased. I would have to wait until I got to Adana to sort that out. I found a comfortable place to sit and waited for the plane home to depart, asking myself whether the decision to leave was actually in my best interest.

Once I arrived in Adana, I immediately headed for the ticket counter. I explained what had happened, and the gentleman behind the counter told me not to worry. As soon as the visa problem was sorted out, I could rebook my flight at no additional cost. I wanted to leap over the counter and kiss him, but I got a grip on my emotions, thanked him profusely, and headed out the door to find a taxi back to my apartment.

As the taxi turned the corner and drove into the parking lot, I was astounded to see my car was already there. *Oh my goodness*, I thought. *Metin kept his promise. He brought the car back without any argument. In fact, he brought it back early! Perhaps I had judged too quickly. Perhaps I hadn't given credit where credit was due.*

As I climbed the stairs to my apartment, I was puzzled when I saw a pair of Metin's shoes in the hallway. My first thought was that perhaps he'd forgotten to pack them. However, as I unlocked the door and walked in, I'm not sure who was more surprised, Metin or I. I opened the door and found him sleeping soundly in the guest bedroom. He bolted upright as I walked into the room and stared at me in wide-eyed wonderment.

"What in the world are you doing here?" he asked.

"I'd like to ask you the same question," I responded.

I opened the closet door only to find that he had brought back all of his clothes. He had taken the spare key that I thought was lost and hid it away until I left. He hadn't argued about returning the car, because he had had no intentions of turning it over to Mustafa. He thought that once I left, he could return to the apartment, live there and entertain his guests, drive my car, and live the life of Riley while I was in Libya. After all, what could I have done from there?

Patrice, my neighbor on the first floor, was beside herself. She knew that Metin had come back to the apartment and that I was supposedly on the plane to Libya. She had visions of late-night parties and unsavory characters coming and going at all hours of the day and night. When she saw me, she hugged me and nearly broke into tears. We both agreed that there are no coincidences. This was definitely another case of divine intervention.

What were the chances that after boarding the plane in Adana, I would return to the apartment the same afternoon? What were the chances that after all the preparation the school administration in Libya had done, my visa would be rejected? Clearly, this was the Universe at work. I was supposed to come back and find that Metin had broken his promise to leave the apartment and go quietly. It was now obvious that I was going to have to stay there long enough to make sure that he was gone once and for all. If I ever doubted that everything happens for a reason, this surely had made a believer out of me.

CHAPTER 52

The Final Deception

Hell hath no rage like a borderline (personality) scorned.
—From the non-BP Internet Support Group

By this time, it had become clear to Metin that things had changed. The very foundation of his existence had been pulled out from underneath him. He was losing his home, his car, and his ATM machine. He must also have seen that my feelings toward him and the relationship had changed. I no longer needed his validation that I was okay. I was angry about what he had done and the promises he had broken. I was scheduled to leave again on October 24, and all I had to do was hold it together until then. I told him he could stay in the apartment until I left but that I would personally help him pack and deliver his suitcases to his mother.

I should have known that he was not going to accept what he perceived as my abandonment of him without a fight. My attorney warned me repeatedly about letting Metin drive the car, especially in the days immediately preceding my departure. He was sure that Metin was going to make a last-ditch effort to salvage something out of the relationship. "Surely," Mustafa warned, "he isn't going to agree to give up the right to stay in your apartment and relinquish the car as well. Given the chance, he will take your car."

Unfortunately, I had no idea how the thought of no longer having a car at his disposal would shake Metin to his very core and force him to come up with a plan that would drastically alter the course of events.

Two days before I was scheduled to leave, Metin told me that he wanted to buy my car. He said he loved it like his own son, and he wanted to be sure that it would be taken care of in my absence. After all, he argued, I had told him that I would give him the car as soon as I was financially able to buy a new one for myself. He offered to give me ten thousand Turkish liras, which wasn't even close to the car's actual value. However, he reasoned, it was a lot more than I would have gotten if I simply gave it to him as a gift. I told him that I didn't want to sell the car and that, if I was planning to sell it, I certainly wouldn't do it for ten thousand Turkish liras. My protestations fell on deaf ears, and we spent the next two days running from one government agency to another trying to complete the sale.

The longer it took, the less enthusiastic I was about the plan. The fact that I was a foreigner in Turkey complicated the process, and after nearly sixteen hours of rushing from one office to the next, we learned that it would be impossible for me to sell the car that day because my residency permit had expired a week earlier. If we had had more time, I could have reapplied for a new permit. However, the clock was ticking, and I was boarding the plane in less than twelve hours. I took my visa problem and subsequent return to Adana as a sign that Metin was supposed to be discovered and that he was not supposed to stay in the apartment. Similarly, I took this as a sign that, for whatever reason, I wasn't supposed to sell him the car. Over the years, I've learned to pay attention to the signs that we're given. To me, it's the Universe communicating directly with us and showing us the way.

After trying, but failing, to sort this out, we returned to the car, and Metin and his friend Murat were arguing heatedly. My mind was reeling with all of the things I still had to do, so I didn't pay any attention to what they were arguing about. Metin and I had already taken care of several things that were on my to-do list for that day.

However, there were still two important stops to make. One was the bank, and the other was the pharmacy.

We got into the car and headed for the bank. Metin and Murat continued to argue. Turkish people are very emotional and have a tendency to speak loudly, so I couldn't accurately ascertain if this was a real argument or just a heated discussion. Metin and I went into the bank. There was standing room only. I got my number from the machine, and it was clear that there was going to be a long wait. Metin said that he wanted to smoke, so he excused himself and went outside.

After nearly thirty minutes, I completed my transaction and headed for the car. When I opened the door of the bank, I looked in the direction where the car was supposed to be parked. *Perhaps they had to move it,* I thought. I looked up and down both sides of the street, and there was no sign of a car. Finally, I called Metin and asked what was going on. He told me he needed money, and because I couldn't give it to him, he had taken the car and was going to turn it over to a car rental agency. I was speechless. I called him again and again, begging him not to do this.

"There's no other alternative," he said and closed his phone.

When he refused to answer, I called Murat and asked if they were still together. He told me they weren't and hung up.

I took a taxi back to my apartment and was embarrassed to tell my neighbor Patrice what had happened. She and Mustafa warned me over and over, and in spite of this, I fell for Metin's tricks again.

I borrowed Patrice's car and picked up our mutual friend Hatice. Together, we went to the police station and filed a stolen car report. Because Metin and I shared a house and were considered to be married, the offense was listed as a breach of trust rather than an actual theft. This carries a lighter penalty. Just when I thought things couldn't get any worse, they did.

The police asked me if there was anything of value in the car. It wasn't until that point that I stopped to realize that my two TV satellite receivers, two remote controls, two smart cards, my residence permit, and the car registration were all still in the car. Hatice and I went back to the apartment. Patrice was waiting for us and invited us in. I explained that I could only stay for a short time because I was leaving in three hours and still hadn't finished packing.

My good friend and sometime translator, Hatice Gezer.

A little while later, my phone rang; it was Murat. He wanted to come over and talk. I told him it was out of the question, because I still had to finish packing. He said that he really needed to talk face-to-face. I grew very impatient with his persistence and told him, once again, that it was out of the question. However, he persevered. Minutes later, he called again, said he was in the parking lot, and wanted to know if he could please come in. Patrice opened the door to let him in and she, her son, Hatice, and I sat down to listen to what he had to say.

He told us that he knew where Metin had taken the car and that he could get it back for me. He told all of us how dishonest Metin had been with him and guaranteed us that when he found him, he was going to teach him a lesson. He even promised to show us pictures of what Metin would look like when he finished with him. He said that he was a charlatan and not to be trusted. Murat couldn't understand how I could have been so naive that I believed all of his lies. Before he left, Murat asked me to please write a document giving him permission to drive the car. He said that once he located it, he would have to drive it back to his house to store it. He didn't want to have any problems with the traffic police if he got caught driving my car. It sounded reasonable enough to me. Once again, I should have stopped to consider the kind of man I was dealing with.

Murat took me to the airport in a taxi and helped me check in. I was off to Libya feeling confident that, once again, an angel had appeared out of nowhere who was going to solve my problem for me.

CHAPTER 53

Things Aren't Always as They Seem to Be

The cause is hidden but the result is known.
—Ovid

I arrived safely in Tripoli and spent my first few days settling into my new apartment and getting to know my neighbors and the people with whom I would be working. Although I tried to concentrate on the things at hand, I constantly found my mind wandering back to Adana and wondering what had happened to my car. Murat didn't speak any English, so when I communicated with him, it was through my friend Hatice. Occasionally, I would write him a text message just to let him know that I was still counting on him to find my car and put it safely in storage.

Each time I wrote to him and each time Hatice called him, we emphasized the fact that when he found the car, absolutely no one was to drive it. If Metin couldn't drive it while I was out of the country, I certainly wasn't going to authorize anyone else to drive it.

Eventually, word came from Hatice that Murat had found the car. According to him, he took it to a body shop and had some repair work done so that it would be in perfect condition when I returned in the summer. He assured her that I would be thrilled.

A week or two later, I started receiving messages from friends in Adana who had seen my car on the street. When I asked who was driving it, they said Murat. I was shocked. I immediately called Hatice and asked her to contact him and reiterate that absolutely no one was to be driving the car. Hatice told me she spoke to him and delivered the message; however, the reports that he was driving it continued to come.

By now, it was December, and I had a three-week holiday coming up. I had originally intended to stay in Libya. I had no plans to return to Turkey, especially since I'd been gone less than two months. However, the news that I was getting from Adana about the car and some problems in my apartment there resulted in a change of heart. I decided to fly back. I flew out of Libya on December 15 and landed in Istanbul. I planned to spend three days there. Shortly after I left Adana, Metin had moved to Istanbul. My dear friend Hatice also lived there, and occasionally she and Metin would meet and talk. He told her that he had heard I was coming and wanted to know if that was true. Before she answered, she asked me what to say. I told her it was perfectly fine to tell him, because I had no intention of falling into his trap again. All I wanted was information about what had happened to my car. When I arrived in Istanbul and met with Metin, I finally got the truth.

He knew that he would fall on hard times when I left and went to Libya. He was trying desperately to figure out how he could come up with some seed money to start a small business. He and Murat had worked out a plan whereby Metin would buy the car from me using ten thousand Turkish liras that he borrowed from Murat. As soon as the car was in his name, he and Murat were going to turn around and sell it to a car gallery for nineteen thousand Turkish liras. Metin would give me my ten thousand, which he believed I would be thrilled to get since I was planning to give him the car as a gift the following June. Murat would get three thousand Turkish liras for providing the money to buy the car and arranging the sale of it, and Metin would get six thousand Turkish liras to start a business in Istanbul. However, when the sale of the car couldn't be finalized, the deal went south.

Murat insisted that he was owed three thousand Turkish liras regardless of whether the car sold or not and he was determined to get it one way or the other. Metin never took the car to a rental agency. In fact, Metin never even took possession of the car. Murat had it all along. Metin was furious with me because I had signed a paper giving Murat permission to drive it, and he wondered why I hadn't done the same thing for him. I explained that the permission was intended to be for one night, and one night only. If Murat was using it to drive the car on a daily basis, he wasn't honoring the agreement we had made.

Before I left for Adana, I sent several messages to Murat asking him to pick me up at the airport, in *my* car, at 3:45 on Monday afternoon. At 3:45 Murat was there and waiting, but instead of picking me up in my car, he picked me up in a taxi. My first question, obviously, was, "Where is my car?"

Murat began to tell an almost unbelievable tale of what had happened to it. He said it had been in several accidents that had resulted in significant damage to the front end, all four tires were flat, and, at the moment, it couldn't be driven. He maintained that it would take several days to repair, and he didn't know how much it would cost. He obviously didn't know that I had spoken to Metin in Istanbul, so he blamed all of the damage on him. I insisted on at least seeing the car, but he said that it was too late. The body shop where the work was being done would be closed. He told me that it would take two or three days to finish the repairs. I told him that I hadn't authorized any repairs and that if the car couldn't be driven, I would hire a tow truck and have it towed to my apartment.

Every suggestion I made was met with resistance, and it wasn't long before we were screaming at each other, in Turkish, at the top of our lungs. I told him I wanted to go to the police department and that I was going to file another police report, but that this time it would be against him! I finally admitted that I'd spoken with Metin and knew that it was him who had the car all along. In the middle of this fiasco, Metin's mother called me and asked me how I was. I asked to speak to Metin's father and told him what was happening. He asked me to put Murat on the phone and told us both to come to his house.

I sat and listened patiently while Murat gave his version of what had happened. Metin's father tried to mediate, which aggravated me even further. The truth was that there was nothing to mediate. Murat and Metin had tried to convince me to sell the car under false pretenses. I had no intentions of selling it. I had agreed simply so that Metin could drive it legally while I was in Libya. If I had known about the arrangements that Metin and Murat had made, I would never have agreed to the sale. Now Murat maintained that he had sustained a loss of three thousand Turkish liras because he sold his wife's jewelry in order to come up with the ten thousand Turkish liras to loan Metin, and in the interim, the price of gold had skyrocketed. The truth was that he was desperately trying to get the three thousand Turkish liras that he planned to get from the sale of the car whether it was sold or not! We continued to scream and shout for hours, and in the end, nothing was resolved. Murat finally drove me home and agreed to pick me up at eleven o'clock the next day to go and look at the car.

Eleven o'clock came and went, and no Murat. Noon came and went, and no Murat. One o'clock came and went, and still no Murat.

Finally, I called and asked when, and if, he was planning to come to pick me up. He assured me that he would be there shortly. It was almost three o'clock before he finally arrived. We rode in silence to the auto body shop, and when we arrived, I was absolutely flabbergasted at the condition of my car.

Although he had told Hatice that he had the original damage repaired, that wasn't the case. In addition, there was damage to the right front, as well as the left, and damage to the rear left side. All four tires were flat, and the wheel covers were gone. The spare tire and jack were gone, and two rims were damaged beyond repair. My Digiturk boxes, remotes, smart cards, the car registration, and my residence permit were no longer in the car. He said that he forgot to bring them. The truth was that he had taken everything out of the car and had sold it for whatever he could get. He blamed Metin for all of the damage and said that what Metin didn't do, the rental company did. Because I already knew that the car was never rented and that Metin had been in Istanbul since I left for Libya, I knew everything Murat said was a lie.

I told him to have the worker put the front end back on the car. I was taking it "as is," regardless of what he said. I would drive it with four flat tires to the nearest tire repair shop. Murat protested loudly, but I stood my ground. As I prepared to leave, Murat handed me a bill for seven hundred Turkish liras for the work that had been done. I threw it back at him and told him to take care of it. Because nothing had actually been repaired, I knew it was a "dummy" receipt intended to help him recoup some of the three thousand Turkish liras he felt he was entitled to. I had already sustained a huge financial loss because of the additional damage that had been done to the car, the equipment that had been stolen from it, and the electronic equipment that had been stolen and sold. I didn't have any intention of giving him another cent.

As I limped along to the nearest tire store, I realized that the time I had waited for Murat to arrive must have been spent stripping everything of value off of the car. Since he was driving it every day, one has to wonder how suddenly all four tires were flat and it became "undrivable." It was simply another ruse to try to get a portion of the money he still felt he was entitled to.

CHAPTER 54

The Bottom Line

Unless I accept my virtues, I will certainly
be overwhelmed by my faults.
—Robert G. Coleman

Replacing all of the items that had been damaged or stolen was a very costly proposition. It cost 1,000 Turkish liras to replace the tires, damaged rims, and missing wheel covers. It was 135 Turkish liras to replace the car registration and 172 Turkish liras to replace my "lost" residence permit. The day after I left for Libya, Murat hooked up my two Digiturk boxes and reconnected the service in my name, using the information from my residence permit. As a result, I had a bill for 230 Turkish liras from Digiturk. In addition, the fact that I couldn't return the two receivers to them would cost another 370 Turkish liras.

Murat called me regularly, and I refused to answer. Perhaps he wanted to negotiate a settlement. I wasn't interested. I would rather pay the excessive cost of replacing these items than continue to deal with a charlatan like him. Unfortunately, the car no longer felt like mine. It had been savagely ravaged by the unsavory characters who stole it. I made arrangements with a car gallery in Adana to sell it when I returned to Libya at the end of the week. The people at the car gallery told me that it was unfortunate that the car had been beaten to death. If it had been in better condition, it would have been worth three thousand Turkish liras more than I was actually going to get.

Earlier in the book, I wrote that there are no coincidences. Everything happens for a reason. Although Metin wasn't directly responsible for the damage sustained to the car while Murat was driving it, Murat would not have been driving it if it hadn't been for the plan that he and Metin conjured up. They were both equally culpable, and without knowing it, by giving Murat written permission to drive it, I had been an unwilling accomplice.

For seven years, I have rationalized my choices in a desperate attempt to give credibility to my relationship with Metin. I was blinded by my fear of being alone. I knew we came from two different worlds, but instead of acknowledging this and accepting him for who he was, I tried to erase all of the cultural, educational, and socioeconomic differences between us. Instead of seeing him for who he was and accepting that, I attempted to mold him into my idea of a perfect partner. If I looked at our relationship with an objective pair of eyes, I would have seen, as my friends did, how insurmountable the obstacles were. Instead, I was like the doting old man with a younger wife. I was willing to jump through hoops and do whatever was necessary to keep the relationship together, even when it meant demeaning myself.

I subjugated all of my needs—financial, sexual, emotional, and physical. I longed for a warm embrace, but I was with a man who didn't like to hug. I begged for kisses from a man who didn't like to kiss. I longed for passionate moments from a man who wasn't passionate. I'd like to believe that there were moments during our time together that he felt true love for me on some level. However, when I'm honest about how easily and how often he walked away from the relationship, perhaps I'm still deluding myself.

Having said all of this, I have to thank Metin. What he demanded from me was so excessive and so out of the realm of reality that it finally shook me to my very core. If I were to sit back and do a tally sheet on what I gave as opposed to what I received, it would be heart wrenching. I was never sexy enough, young enough, unselfish enough, or loving enough to satisfy him. However, in retrospect, what I have come to realize is that I am loving enough and sexy enough for most of the men on the planet. I just happened, as I usually do, to pick one who wasn't emotionally available. His only interest in me was what I could do for him. This was an extremely hard lesson to learn, but the Universe couldn't have sent me a better teacher. Fortunately, the realization came over a long period of time. If it hadn't, and if it had instead come all at once, it would have been too devastating for me to handle. There were literally thousands of signs that I should have picked up on if only I'd been willing to see them for what they were.

As I complete this chapter, I am preparing to head back to Libya in a few days. I have decided to keep my apartment in Adana until I decide whether I want to stay in Turkey. Perhaps it's time for me to move on, but only time will tell. Metin is still in Istanbul, undoubtedly chatting up another older foreign woman with some money to spend. I will miss him and the good times that we had together. However, as I move forward into the next phase of my life, I realize that there's absolutely nothing wrong with me or with being alone. I don't have to apologize to anyone for who I am, what I look like, what I've done, or what I want in this very precious life of mine.

This is the first time in my life that I have been without a significant other. I will admit that there are still times when I feel a little afraid, a little uncomfortable, and very much alone. However, all of the significant relationships that I have had with men in this life have been detrimental to my emotional and spiritual health. There may have been someone sharing my life and my bed; however, I still felt very much alone. Now, at long last, although I am alone, I have complete freedom. I can spend my money on whatever I want, and

I don't have to justify why I haven't shared it. I can watch TV in my underwear or spend an entire weekend without makeup and not have to explain my reasons to anyone. I can eat popcorn for dinner and watch all of the chick flicks that my little heart desires. I don't have to pretend that I like football, and if I worry about gaining five pounds, it's because I want to look my best for *me* and not for someone else. I am becoming my own best friend, and I will nurture this new relationship with myself with the same intensity that I did all of my dysfunctional ones. If I do this, I know I don't have to be afraid, because I will never be alone again.

I used to ask myself what my greatest fear was. What was it that kept me attached to men who I knew weren't good for me? What did they have that I didn't have? What could they do that I couldn't do? As I struggled to find an answer to these questions, I realized that my greatest fear used to be what I would do if the toilet overflowed and my significant other wasn't there. This happened to me while I was living with my third husband. I watched in horror as the dirty toilet water overflowed and gushed out of the bathroom onto the pristine white carpeting in the living room and dining area. After forty years of seriously pondering this perennial question, I have, at long last, come up with the answer. Call a plumber.

CHAPTER 55

Finding My Bliss

We all live with the objective of being happy; our
lives are all different and yet the same.
—Anne Frank

As I reclined in my seat, I took a deep breath and looked out of the airplane window at the brilliant blue, cloud-filled sky. I realized that for the first time in months, perhaps even years, I was completely and thoroughly relaxed. For the first time that I could remember, there was absolutely nothing for me to worry about. My apartment in Adana was empty, and Mustafa, my neighbor and trusted attorney, was taking care of selling my car. I had made all the necessary arrangements to make sure that my monthly bills were paid, the plants watered, and the apartment was cleaned periodically. Metin was no longer an albatross around my neck. I was returning to pick up my life in Libya, and I was feeling optimistic that better days were just over the horizon.

My lodgment in Libya fell far short of the mark when I compared it with my apartment in Adana and with what the private schools in Turkey provide guest teachers. I had, nonetheless, worked my special brand of magic and had turned it into a place that was quite remarkable by anyone's standards. While most of the foreign teachers were content to live as minimally as possible, I spared no expense when it came to creating my personal sanctuary. I bought lamps, expensive paintings and posters, and yards of gold lamé to turn my nondescript, beige apartment into something that looked like it could have come out of *One Thousand and One Arabian Nights*. I had created my own little slice of paradise right in the middle of the desert, and I was content.

The majority of the foreign teachers at the school lived in a compound, and because of the constant threat of kidnappings and terrorist attacks, we had a curfew. There was a small market at the end of the road, but it wasn't even safe to walk alone the short distance down the road to it. Therefore, unless someone else, preferably a man, was interested in going, we were, in essence, marooned. Most of the people living there were loners, so I spent my evenings watching television or surfing the Internet—when it was up and running, that is. Service was intermittent at best, and the government was in the habit of shutting it down completely when they suspected that terrorist organizations might be using it to lay the groundwork for another covert operation.

There were several terrorist camps close to our compound, so the distinct hum of drones was our constant companion. I couldn't help but be a little amused by the uproar in the States regarding the use of drones for civilian surveillance. In my current situation, I couldn't have been happier to know that they were watching us 24/7. There was also a military base near the compound, so there was gunfire every night. We learned quickly to distinguish between the sound of practice rounds and actual combat. It's surprising what a person can get used to. Eventually, the threat level increased, and armed guards were hired to actually live in the compound. Considering how young and inexperienced they looked, I couldn't help but wonder how much use they'd actually be in the event of a real attack. However, the fact that they had automatic weapons, missile launchers, and hand grenades, at least for the moment, was comforting. They were also responsible for escorting our bus back and forth to school. At one point, they were even instructed to stand outside the corner market, AK-47s in hand, while we picked up our few essentials. Car bombings were a constant threat, but because none of us had a car and because most of them occurred in the city center, at least for the moment, those weren't an issue.

I thoroughly enjoyed being at the school and working with the children, so it was easy for me to minimize the potential dangers. After all, I reasoned, most of these people had lived here during the actual war and survived. Because of the incredible circumstances under which I had ended up being sent there in the first place, I believed that it was another case of divine intervention, and as such, I was going to be protected no matter what. Perhaps if I'd been a little more astute, I would've been more cautious, but I never felt afraid.

During the forty-two years that Muammar al-Gaddafi ruled Libya, the teaching of English was banned, so I was more than a little surprised at how well my students were able to communicate. Unfortunately, the same couldn't be said for many of their parents. However, in spite of the language barriers, the reception I received from them and from their parents was heartwarming.

Libyans realize that in order to compensate for the forty-two years of isolation imposed upon them, they are going to need help from the outside world. The terrorist groups who are intent on keeping Libya isolated realize this as well and do everything in their power to frighten foreigners away. Every foreigner who arrives and is determined to help is treated as an honored and respected guest. In all my years of teaching, I never felt so valuable or so appreciated by a group of students. I received gifts and cards on a daily basis, thanking me for coming to help them and professing their undying love and appreciation. This was just what I needed to help fill the hole in my soul. I was learning that it doesn't take romantic love to make a person feel whole. The hugs and the kisses that I had longed to get from Metin were now coming from a different source but were no less fulfilling. I had found my bliss.

CHAPTER 56

Cultural Differences

I wake each morning with the thrill of expectation and the
joy of being truly alive. And I'm thankful for this day.
—Angela L. Wozniak

Each and every day brought with it an array of new experiences. The school was different, the culture in the school was different, and daily life was full of surprises.

One of the first, and perhaps most astounding, differences I noticed was the fact that the students had no textbooks, and there was no library to speak of. A small area adjacent to the main staircase had three bookcases with a few very well-worn copies of Oxford readers, but that was the extent of it. This was the largest and, by far, the best private school in the city, and yet there were no books! Most of the teachers had teaching assistants who spent their days in the copy machine room photocopying pages out of old textbooks and gluing them into notebooks. Instead of actual textbooks, students had loose-leaf notebooks for each class, and their workbook pages were glued into them. It was time-consuming and a grossly ineffective use of manpower.

I was told the textbooks had arrived months earlier. However, they were supposedly sitting on a ship in the harbor waiting to be unloaded. When Gaddafi's government was overthrown and he was eliminated, so were all of the people who had been in charge of keeping the wheels of government rolling smoothly. As a result, there was supposedly no one who knew exactly what needed to be done to release the books. Books that should have arrived before school started in September didn't arrive until well into the second semester. The manner in which the students, teachers, and parents dealt with the situation was commendable. They all adjusted to this unorthodox situation without missing a beat. In fact, even after the books arrived, most of the teachers continued to use the notebooks for a large portion of their assignments. They decided it was too late in the year to hope to finish the books and, as a result, opted to keep them to use, in their entirety, the following year rather than using just a portion of them during the current year. I couldn't help but wonder if parents at expensive private schools in other countries would have reacted as graciously.

In addition, I had never been in a school that had its own mosque on the school grounds. Islamic Studies was a required subject, and even the youngest students were taken there regularly to learn the proper way to pray. The fact that I went with them several times touched their hearts, and before I knew it, I had received another gift—the proper garment necessary for a woman to wear when she enters a mosque. As I struggled to put it on properly, a dozen little hands jumped to my rescue, pulling here and tugging there to make sure that I was the pinnacle of propriety. The first time I wore it and accompanied them into the mosque, the entire class was smiling from ear to ear. I was one of them, and their Islamic teacher couldn't disguise her delight as the students lovingly guided me through the proper motions and recitation of the prayers. I was the student now, and the students were my teachers.

What the children learn in their Islamic Studies class extends into all areas of their lives. They tried extremely hard not to do things that were considered *haram* (forbidden), and they were enthusiastic to help educate me. I learned that, at the top of the list of no-no's are tattoos and Valentine's Day. Considering how many of my Turkish friends have tattoos and how important a celebration Love Day is, I couldn't help but wonder how many of them had ever taken an Islamic Studies course! It's also considered haram to throw a piece of bread into the garbage. My students explained that it's forbidden because there are so many people who don't have enough to eat. In the city, it was very common to see plastic bags with leftover bread hanging from lampposts and fences. They were put there for poor people to collect.

There was a lot of food that was being wasted every day at our school, so after a class discussion about this problem, my students decided to jump into action. After every break and at the end of the lunch hour, they collected all the food and drinks that had been left behind. As long as the things hadn't been opened or partially eaten, they collected them and gave them to the cleaners who worked at the school. They were all men from Bangladesh who lived in a single room in a small building on the campus. They slept on the concrete floor without so much as a pillow or blanket, and because of the prejudice against them, they never left the school grounds. They were at the very bottom of the social pecking order. No one greeted them or showed any appreciation for the work that they did, and as a result, they were overwhelmed by the kindness and generosity that the children in my class, who came from extremely wealthy families, displayed toward them. This level of caring and respect toward workers was clearly not something the children had been taught at home as was evidenced by the fact that most of them didn't even know the first names of their drivers, the men who brought them to school in the morning and picked them up again after school. Something good was happening in our classroom, and now it extended beyond the confines of our room and into other areas of the school.

The students, in turn, were amazed that the cleaners were so grateful for such small gestures of kindness, and it prompted them to want to do something more. *Auction* was one of our vocabulary words, and they didn't have a clue what an auction was. After explaining it to them and demonstrating how it works, they decided that having one and using the money to buy something special for the cleaners would be a fantastic idea. The next day they all brought in items from home that they no longer used. They also brought money to spend. Teaching them not to raise their own bids was another challenge that even the adults who came had a hard time coming to grips with. However, that's another story.

When all was said and done, we had raised a substantial amount of money. There was a holiday coming up, and as a result, there would be no school. If there wasn't any school, the students wouldn't have an opportunity to collect any food or drinks for the cleaners that day. *What will they eat if we aren't here?* they wondered. The solution they came up with was to use the money that had been raised to buy pizzas for the cleaners that day. The class was thrilled with the idea, and needless to say, the cleaners were ecstatic. They sent the class a thank-you note that every one of them signed. It hung on the wall until the end of the year as a testament to the students' thoughtfulness. This was a lesson that would be remembered by everyone, adults and students alike.

Food was another area of major difference and, in this case, a very disappointing one indeed. After teaching in Turkey for seven years, I had become accustomed to eating lunch in the school cafeteria every day. Each and every day the cooks prepared a different culinary delight. Everything was new and different, and although I liked some dishes better than others, I quickly became acquainted with typical Turkish food. Unlike most Turkish schools, this school didn't have a cafeteria. There was a small canteen that was manned by one of the more popular local restaurants. Their offerings consisted primarily of chicken sandwiches, ice cream, and donuts, and more often than not, they ran out of food before the end of the first lunch hour. As a result, most of the students brought their own lunches, or at least something to eat during the first morning break. Therefore, I decided that the only way I was going to learn anything about typical Libyan food was to sit with the students and look at what they brought to eat.

I was amazed to learn that the sandwich of choice was tuna mixed with a hot red pepper sauce on a bun. It was literally the only sandwich that I ever saw a student bring from home, so it appeared to me to be the Libyan version of a peanut-butter-and-jelly sandwich in the States. As much as I like tuna fish, the hot red pepper sauce that was mixed in with it was something I never developed a taste for. In addition, these lunches didn't provide any insight into what people considered to be typical Libyan food. As a result, I left the country still wondering if there are any popular national dishes and, if there are, what are they?

I had also never worked in a school where students were allowed to wear head scarves. In fact, in Turkey, it's forbidden in most schools. When students in Libya are given information regarding their uniforms, the accepted colors for their *hijabs*, or head scarves, are listed. Although most of the students in the lower grades opt not to wear them, there were some girls as young as ten who wore them on a regular basis.

This particular school also did not supply toilet paper or paper towels in any of the restrooms, including those for the adults. Because hand soap was also at a premium, one had to wonder how a person was supposed to relieve themselves in a manner that would be universally accepted and hygienically sound. It was also not uncommon to visit a private home and discover that there was no toilet paper in the bathroom. In fact, it was difficult to purchase packages of four rolls of quality toilet paper anywhere. It was only available in the newest and most modern supermarkets, and they were few and far between. When I had an opportunity to shop at one of the two I frequented, the first item in my cart was toilet paper! Libyans watched, amused and amazed, as I loaded twelve or sixteen rolls of toilet tissue into my cart. I'm sure they were silently judging me and questioning my choice of hygienic practices. However, there are just some habits that are too ingrained to change, and at my age, I was not about to give up toilet tissue in favor of a butt washer.

Perhaps the biggest surprise at this school was that all of the classroom teachers were foreigners and that all classes, except Arabic and Islamic Studies, were taught in English. The exact opposite is true in Turkey. All the classroom teachers are Turkish and English is only offered a few hours a week as a foreign language. In Libya, Arabic is only taught a few hours a week, and it's taught as a foreign language! To me, this was proof positive that Libyans are looking toward the future and are actively doing whatever they can to become a part of the international community.

CHAPTER 57

Foreign Women in Libyan Society

Accustomed as we are to change, or unaccustomed, we think of
a change of heart, of clothes, of life, with some uncertainty.
—Josephine Miles

I have been fortunate enough to have traveled the world. I have been in breathtakingly beautiful mosques, elaborately decorated cathedrals, ancient synagogues, and pagan temples. I've dined with royalty and swallowed whole sea urchins, scraped off the walls of caves on the isle of Capri, that were still wiggling as they slid down my throat. However, nothing I'd ever seen or done could have prepared me for what I would experience as a foreign woman on the streets of a Libyan city.

Libyan women, for the most part, are sequestered inside their apartments or behind the walls of their sprawling concrete villas. That's not to say that they never venture out. However, for the most part, when they do, they all wear the ankle-length, long-sleeved black coats called *abayas* and the accompanying black head scarf called a *hijab*. No self-respecting Libyan woman would be caught dead outside of her home wearing anything else. It's the unspoken outward expression of their faith, and the women who wear them are accorded the respect that comes with being a devout Muslim woman.

Even some of the foreign teachers at the school decided that in an effort to blend in they would wear long coats, slacks, and head scarves. Although they weren't clothed entirely in black, they were covered from head to toe, which they believed would afford them some level of respect and protection from the sexual advances that countless foreign women had been victims of. Perhaps out of curiosity or perhaps because of my tendency to live on the edge, I refused to bow to the pressure. As a result, I was able to see exactly what kind of a response an uncovered foreign woman in an Islamic country could expect. Surprisingly, most of the reactions I received were positive.

When crossing a busy street, it was not uncommon for all traffic to come to a grinding halt and let me pass. However, it was also not uncommon for men to roll down their windows and yell things like, "I love you, honey. Will you marry me?" Men gawked and lost control of their cars at the sight of a pair of uncovered legs. It was, at the very least, comical. Although I was fully clothed, at the sight of me, grown men reacted like teenage boys who were looking at naked women for the first time in a *Playboy* magazine.

Fridays everything is closed, and no one even answers their telephone until the afternoon prayers are finished. Therefore, all major shopping excursions were done on Saturday mornings. The stores were overflowing with men of every age and description shopping for their families. Invariably, I was the only woman in the fruit market or at the butcher shop and, much to my surprise, I was always ushered to the head of the line. The crowd of men parted like God parted the seas allowing me to pass like visiting royalty. In fact, even at the airport, all men wait, sometimes a little impatiently, until every woman has boarded the plane. I was beginning to think that perhaps there may be some advantages to living in a society where women are subservient. They give up much of their freedom, but in return, there are many benefits they enjoy that liberated women in other societies would, I believe, willingly embrace.

One evening another female teacher and I agreed that we were in need of some retail therapy, so we decided to go shopping. Because of the difficulty of getting around, most shopping was limited to the essentials like food and water. It was a daring escapade on our part, because it was after dark, and we were two women alone heading into parts unknown. However, a male friend had dropped us off and agreed to pick us up when we were finished, so the transportation aspect of our adventure was covered. There were only two shops we intended to visit, and they were in the same block, so we weren't worried about getting into serious trouble of any kind. When both our energy and money were spent, we decided to find a quiet place to sit and have something to drink while we waited for our friend to pick us up. Because we were unfamiliar with the area, we unknowingly entered a "men only" café. When we realized our mistake, we expected to be unceremoniously ejected on the spot. However, much to our surprise, the owner instead instructed all of the men present, and there were a lot of them, to move to the other side of the room so he could create a "women only section" especially for us. Even the men were a little surprised at the princess treatment we received as the owner fluffed the couch pillows for us and dropped everything to cater to our every need. When we got up to leave, he bowed, kissed our hands, and asked us to please come again. His door, he said, would always be open for us. As we left, we could hardly contain our glee. How we wished we could share our story with our colleagues the next day. However, we knew that instead of seeing the humor in what had happened, we would be chastised for not being more careful about where we went and what we did. We decided it would be in our best interest to keep our secret to ourselves. We lamented what a shame it was we couldn't share our story.

As we left and started to walk down the street, a group of rather unsavory young men appeared to be following us. Before we had time to plan a course of action, two tall and much older men appeared out of nowhere and offered to escort us to the car that was waiting for us. *Unbelievable—more guardian angels,* I mused.

Eventually, more out of respect than the need to bow to cultural pressure, I decided to buy an abaya. Every abaya comes with a matching hijab, which I stalwartly refused to wear. When I was out on the streets by myself, I wore the abaya but never covered my hair. As a result, it was still obvious I was a foreigner, but the fact that I was covered from my neck down to my ankles seemed to entitle me to an even greater level of respect. Men smiled and bowed their heads as I passed as a gesture of respect. There was nowhere I was afraid to go and nothing I was afraid to do.

Armed with a false sense of courage, I made my first mistake. There are only a handful of legitimate taxis in Libya, so anyone who has a car and happens to be on the road that day is a potential taxi. If a person is standing on the street waiting for a taxi, cars will blink their headlights twice. If you hail them, they stop and take you anywhere in the city for three Libyan dinars. That's approximately $2.37. Since a full tank of gas only costs five dinars, a person can buy half a tank of gas if they pick up one person a week. I was warned repeatedly to *never* take a taxi when I was alone. However, it was a Saturday morning, and I had things to do. Everyone else was busy, so I put on my abaya and headed for the souk. It was too far to walk, so naturally, I would need a taxi. Because kidnappings were commonplace, it was normal practice for men in Libya to ignore the common rules of courtesy that dictate a woman enter a vehicle before the man. The chances that the taxi might drive off with the woman and leave the man standing in the road were just too great. *No problem here*, I mused. *There's not a man with me!*

Thinking that my abaya would afford me the same level of respect as a covered Muslim woman was my first mistake. I was still very obviously a foreign woman and, as such, prey for any oversexed Libyan man. A car blinked its headlights, and I quickly surveyed the man driving it. He looked clean-cut and respectable enough, so I approached the door. He immediately opened the glove box of the car and produced a legitimate-enough-looking ID that identified him as a policeman. *How lucky can I get?* I thought, and I jumped in, never thinking that a policeman could pose a potential threat.

My second mistake was jumping into the front seat. Although the driver didn't speak any English, he understood that I wanted to go to the souk, and off we went. However, it didn't take me long to notice that he was pacing the speed of his car so that he hit every red light on the road. Now I began to wonder what he was up to. As he slowed to a stop at the third light, he put his hand on my thigh. I pushed him away. At the fourth light, he did it again and tried to pull up my abaya. Again, I pushed him away. By the time we had reached the fifth light, he had unzipped his fly and exposed his penis! I jumped out of the cab and ran as fast as my feet would carry me to the nearest large hotel where I knew there would be a legitimate cab waiting. I climbed in and heaved a sigh of relief that I had escaped before anything worse had happened. I had heard horror stories about what happened to people who got into cabs by themselves but, once again, I had to learn the hard way. There were definitely cultural differences here and dangers that couldn't be ignored.

CHAPTER 58

Still More Cultural Differences

Growth is a process of experimentation, a series of trials,
errors, and occasional victories. The failed experiments are
as much a part of the process as the experiments that work.
—Cherie Carter-Scott, *If Life Is a Game, These Are the Rules*

Libya, much like Turkey, is a country of contradictions. Enormous villas are adorned with intricate stonework and secured behind six-foot-high walls with elaborate gilded entrances. Villas the size of boutique hotels enjoy manicured gardens overflowing with magnificent red and purple bougainvillea and mile-long driveways lined with palm trees. Yet, directly in front of them, stand burned-out, rusted, abandoned cars and veritable mountains of uncollected, fly-infested, decaying garbage.

Armed soldiers carrying automatic weapons are everywhere, and trucks with automatic weapons mounted on the back stand guard at every major intersection. The armed military presence and numerous checkpoints give one a false sense of security. To a newcomer such as myself, it appears that one would certainly have to have a death wish to even contemplate breaking the law here. However, despite their sheer numbers, chaos reigns. Not an evening goes by without a bombing, shooting, or assassination attempt of some kind, and more recently, those who are intent on destabilizing the new government have become even more brazen and carry out these atrocities during daylight hours.

Burned-out buildings stand as silent reminders of the success of the revolution. Yet, as of this writing, a stable new government is not yet in place. There is no infrastructure, and public services such as busses, taxis, and garbage collection are almost nonexistent. The police are ineffective, and the army, in many cases, is composed of former Gadaffi supporters. There are rumblings, in many sectors, that things were better before the revolution. At least, people argue, they were safe on the streets.

Many Libyans who fled during the Gadaffi era have returned with their fortunes intact and are building new villas and opening new businesses. Ironically, however, at the moment there is nowhere in their country to spend all of their money. As a result, during the holidays, they fly to Dubai, Tunis, Malta, or Turkey where there are luxurious shops in which they can buy designer clothing and a variety of restaurants where they can enjoy fine dining and expensive wines.

One of my biggest disappointments was the lack of good restaurants. I was anxious to try typical Libyan cuisine. However, Libyans are obsessed with all things Turkish, and the majority of restaurants serve Turkish, not Libyan, food. Unfortunately, what they try to pass off as authentic Turkish food doesn't come even close to the mark. I have often joked that the easiest way to make some fast money would be to open a real Turkish restaurant in Libya. Once people tasted the genuine article, they'd never settle for the Libyan interpretation of Turkish cuisine.

Libya itself is an incredibly beautiful country. It's tropical, so the flowers and palm tree-lined streets are breathtakingly beautiful. The seacoast is completely undeveloped and, with the proper planning and funding, could easily become an international holiday destination. Volunteer organizations composed of concerned citizens are forming in an effort to try to clean things up. However, it's a job of gargantuan proportions, and some sort of master plan is needed in order to do it efficiently and effectively. What they're trying to do is comparable to trying to drain the ocean with a teaspoon.

During the Gadaffi era, if a person had more than one car, or had an especially luxurious one, it was confiscated and given to one of his supporters as a political plum. As a result, the roads are clogged with ancient relics that in any other country would be pulled off the road and towed to the nearest recycling center. Headlights and windows are cracked or broken, bumpers are falling off, and rusted doors hang on by a thread. At the same time, luxury car dealerships are sprouting up like mushrooms after a rain in order to give the people who successfully held onto their fortunes a place to spend them.

Because the sale and consumption of alcohol is illegal, there are no clubs or bars. However, people still drink, but they're forced to buy their liquor on the black market, which is risky and very expensive. It's not uncommon to pay one hundred American dollars or more for a bottle of Scotch whiskey. The other alternatives are to make your own or to buy something called Flash, which is produced illegally in the desert. It's only thirty-five dinars a bottle and is delivered in one-liter water bottles. I drank my share of it while I was there and didn't go blind, so I can thank my angels for sending me a trustworthy supplier. The internet was a good source of recipes for homemade wine and spirits, and there wasn't a foreigner, myself included, who didn't have a special recipe for their own "homemade" brew. However, producing liquor at home was a messy and risky proposition. If a person was discovered, it could mean losing his job and/or being deported so one had to weigh the pros and cons to determine whether or not it was worth the risk.

Social contact between young men and women, what we would refer to as dating, is forbidden. As a result, many young people are eager to enter the workplace, because that may be the only opportunity they have to interact with the opposite sex. Other than that, in the majority of cases, communication is restricted to text messages or e-mails. The movements of young girls are strictly monitored by their families, so it's only the young men who have the freedom to be out on the streets in the evening.

Given the fact that there really isn't anywhere to go, or anything special to do, even they are usually at home with their families before nine thirty or ten o'clock in the evening. There is also the constant threat of being caught up in a shooting or car bombing, which also makes being out at night unadvisable. As a result, there is an entire nation of young people struggling to find a way to interact with one another in a society where such interaction is strictly frowned upon. One can only wonder how long young people will bow to this pressure now that the war is over and Libya is struggling to increase their contacts with the outside world. As Joe Young and Sam M. Lewis wrote in their famous song after World War I, "How Ya Gonna Keep 'Em Down on the Farm after They've Seen Paree?"

Weddings are expensive and extremely elaborate celebrations that normally last for two or three days. Hundreds of people are invited to the actual wedding dinner, but men are not allowed to enter. They are required to pick up the female guests and take them to the reception. However, once they arrive, the men wait in the parking lot for hours until the groom finally arrives to claim his bride. That usually happens three or four hours after the dinner begins and signals the end of it. Women spends hundreds of dollars on exquisite and extremely revealing dresses in order to impress the mothers of eligible single men who are at the dinner. Once they are inside, the abayas come off, and the women dance, prance, and display their "wares." I am an open-minded and free-spirited woman. However, even I was appalled at the blatant display of sexuality that I witnessed at one wedding. I was told in advance that photographs were not allowed, and it didn't take me long to understand why. The amount of flesh that was exposed and the brazen manner in which it was done rendered me speechless. At approximately 11:45 p.m., the groom arrives, the women put their abayas back on, he claims his bride, and the evening ends. Meanwhile, rain or shine, all of the men have spent their evening smoking in the parking lot. Because cigarettes only cost seventy-five cents a pack, it's an inexpensive, although doubtlessly extremely boring diversion.

Television is strictly monitored, and anything considered potentially offensive is deleted. That includes all profanity, kissing, touching of any kind, and anything even slightly suggestive. In fact, when they aired the film *Inglorious Bastards*, I barely recognized the title because they rewrote it and changed so many of the letters that, if I hadn't been familiar with the movie, I wouldn't have recognized the title from what I saw written on the television screen. Ironically, none of the violence is removed from anything, so children grow up only seeing the negative side of life and human relationships. It's not surprising that there's such a shroud of secrecy surrounding male and female relationship.

CHAPTER 59

My Libyan Guardian Angel

Miracles are instantaneous; they cannot be summoned,
but come of themselves, usually at unlikely
moments and to those who least expect them.
—Katherine Anne Porter

It was May 18, and it was my birthday. Three of the teachers I worked with and I had decided to take a little trip to celebrate, so we traveled to a neighboring city for an overnight. Because we all had to work the next day, we decided that we'd better allow ample time to get to the airport and check in for our return trip home. Libyan airlines are notorious for cancelling or rescheduling flights, and we couldn't afford to miss ours.

We arrived at the airport in plenty of time and found ourselves being jostled in a virtual sea of people. The noise was deafening and the heat stifling. It was hours before our flight was scheduled to leave, and we were searching frantically for a place to stand that was out of the mainstream of traffic in order to collect our thoughts. Out of sheer desperation, we finally decided to plant ourselves on one of the luggage conveyor belts. Our throats were parched, so after a few minutes, I volunteered to go and try to find a place where I could buy something for us to drink. I found a newsstand, but when it was obvious the proprietor wasn't selling drinks, I decided to return to my friends.

As I passed a large glass window, I noticed several people waving frantically in my direction. I turned to see whose attention they were trying to get because I knew it couldn't be mine. There was no one behind me, so I continued to fight my way back through the crowds to my friends. As I tried to move, the waving and pounding became more frantic. I stopped again and looked inquiringly. Were they motioning to me? And if so why? Sure enough! They beckoned me to come, but I didn't know where to go or how to get there. Suddenly, a tall, handsome man in an airline uniform grabbed my arm and pulled me along beside him into an invisible office.

It was miniscule and, other than the glass window, completely shielded from the chaos outside. He motioned for me to sit down in an overstuffed leather chair and gave me a bottle of water. I grabbed it and downed it in one gulp. There were several people in the office, but unfortunately, none of them spoke English. After what seemed like an eternity and hundreds of hand gestures, I finally got the message. He realized that I was a foreign woman and, as such, was going to attract a lot of unwanted attention from the throng of people on the outside. He had come to my rescue! I tried to explain that I wasn't alone. I had friends outside. Eventually, he understood and went to retrieve them as well.

Moments later, we were all comfortably situated in the cool, air-conditioned office enjoying our refreshing drinks and the respite from the insanity outside when suddenly the tall, dark stranger disappeared. Just when we were beginning to wonder where he went and what would happen to us now, he reappeared, scooped up my carry-on bag, and motioned for all of us to follow him up the escalator. Suddenly, we found ourselves the only people in a completely secluded private area that we had reached without even going through a security check. The tall, dark stranger turned on the air conditioner for us, asked for our tickets, and disappeared again. He reappeared moments later with more water, juice, and chocolates for all of us. When he eventually returned again, he handed us our boarding passes and asked if everything was all right now.

After examining them, we realized that we were not returning on the flight we were originally scheduled to leave on. If we took this one, we would get home much later than we had originally expected, so we expressed our gratitude but tried to explain that it would be much better if we could get on an earlier flight. The handsome stranger disappeared again, and after what seemed like hours, returned at last with boarding passes for the flight we had originally booked. We were dumbfounded. Who was this man, and how could we have been this fortunate? Surely, the heavens were smiling on us. All of my friends have always told me that Allah loves me. At this point, I was convinced they were right!

When it was time to board our flight, he suddenly reappeared and walked us to the appropriate gate. He watched as we passed through the final security, and when we emerged at ground level to board the bus that would take us to our plane, he was there again. Therefore, I guess it shouldn't have come as a surprise that as we climbed the stairs to actually board the plane, he was there to wave good-bye.

During the course of events, I learned that my new angel's name was Abdallah. He asked for my phone number, which I gave willingly. Since he didn't speak English and I don't speak Arabic, I never imagined that anything more would come of this strange encounter. However, that evening, much to my surprise, my phone rang; it was Abdallah. He was calling to make sure that I had arrived home safely. *What an amazing gentleman,* I thought to myself.

His calls continued, but our conversations were always extremely brief and to the point due to the language barrier. Sometimes he would call five or six times in a day, but the conversation was limited to "Are you okay? No problems?" "Yes, I'm fine. No problems." He had assumed the role of my Libyan protector and guardian angel. Because he worked for an airline, he made it clear that he was willing and able to jump on a plane and come to help me at a moment's notice. *How nice,* I thought. At the time, I was flattered and found the whole thing a little humorous. However, little did I know how helpful he would turn out to be. I'm absolutely certain God brought him into my life that day for a reason. He proved to be an invaluable friend to me up until the time I actually got on the plane and left Libya.

CHAPTER 60

Time to Say Good-Bye

Good-bye may seem forever. Farewell is like the end, but in
my heart is the memory, and there you will always be.
—Walt Disney Company

It was June 29, and the following morning I was scheduled to leave Libya. Abdallah had stayed in contact with me since we first met on my birthday weekend. He had friends and family in Tripoli, so he always made sure that there was a local Libyan connection I could call in the event that I needed help of any kind. He was a thoughtful, polite, and considerate man, and I felt extremely lucky to have met him. It was obvious he was concerned about my welfare and would have been much happier if we had been in the same city, but as fate would have it that was not to be. However, he had promised that when I was actually ready to leave the country, he would come to Tripoli and personally see to it that I got to the airport on time, that my baggage was loaded properly, and that I was safely put on the plane back to Turkey.

He was a man of his word, and early in the afternoon on June 29, he arrived in Tripoli. He came to my apartment and made sure that my bags were properly tagged and met the weight requirements. He helped me with the last-minute things that needed to be done, and when we were finally finished, I suggested that we go out for dinner. The best restaurant in the city was within walking distance of my apartment, and it was a glorious evening. There was a cool breeze blowing in off the sea, and the palm trees were swaying like poetry in motion. It was a perfect evening for a stroll through Martyr's Square and down to the sea.

Abdallah is a devout Muslim, so in order to please him and to show my appreciation for all of the kindness he had shown me I offered to wear my abaya. He was grinning from ear to ear as he watched me take it off the hanger and then helped me to carefully put it on. After he had adjusted the shoulders of it, he put his hands on my upper arms and turned me around to face him. He smiled a smile I will never forget. Without uttering a word, it was obvious to me that, with this gesture, I had touched his heart.

We sauntered like tourists without a care in the world as we covered the short distance to the restaurant. He was the consummate gentleman, holding my hand as we crossed each intersection and protectively putting himself between me and every man we passed on the street. He is an extremely tall and powerful man, and he reminded me of a gentle giant who was instinctively trying to protect his offspring.

We had a leisurely meal that Abdallah enjoyed immensely, and although neither of us spoke the other's language, there was an unarticulated understanding between us. What we weren't able to communicate with words, we were able to express nonverbally through our facial expressions and body language. It was unmistakably clear that we had both thoroughly enjoyed our time together. We walked a little more briskly on the way back to my apartment, because it was getting late and we would need to be up and on our way early in the morning in order to avoid the rush hour traffic and arrive at the airport in time for my flight. We both went to sleep that night dreaming our own dreams and doubtless wondering what the future would have held in store for us were I not returning to Turkey the following morning.

Suddenly, and without warning, morning was upon us. I had forgotten to set the alarm, so we were off to the races. There was no time for a shower and no time for breakfast. We dressed as though the house were on fire and ran down the stairs and into the street hoping to hail a taxi. Although the car that stopped was not an official taxi, at this point, we couldn't be choosey, and I was with my friendly giant, so there was nothing for me to be afraid of.

We arrived at the airport just in time to see that the passengers were starting to board the plane. Fortunately, Abdallah was wearing his ID, which clearly identified him as an employee of a Libyan airline. As a result, we were able to bypass security and eliminate all of the formalities normally associated with check-in. Before I knew it, my luggage was on the conveyor belt, and my boarding pass was in my hand.

Abdallah walked me to passport control and waited as I had exited the building. I was on the tarmac heading toward the plane when I got my last glimpse of him. Because I had been completely focused on Abdallah, I was nearly at the entrance to the plane and I still hadn't actually looked at my boarding pass to check my seat number. Now I was standing at the bottom of the stairs that would take me up and into the plane, so I decided I'd better check to see whether it would be better to board from the front or the rear of the plane. As I looked at my seat number, I thought to myself that there must be a mistake of some kind.

One of my friends was on the same flight, and I asked him if the numbers on the boarding passes were in Arabic or if something was wrong with mine. He looked at me like I was from outer space, mumbled something, and walked away. The reason I asked was because my number was a zero with a dot in the center followed by a number one. *There's no way I'm sitting in first class,* I thought. Perhaps this was supposed to be the number ten, and somehow it was written backward because it's in Arabic. As I entered the plane, I tentatively handed the stewardess my boarding pass, assuming that there was an error of some sort. With a flourish, she led me to the first seat in the first-class section. If I'd been any closer to the cockpit, I could have flown the plane. Now I was truly grinning from ear to ear.

My luggage was on the plane, and so was I—in first class no less! It was a surprise courtesy of Abdallah, my new guardian angel. And that's still not the end of the story. The president of Libya happened to be on the same flight that day, and because of the upgrade Abdallah had given me, he was sitting in the seat in the aisle across from me. After everyone in first class had greeted him and kissed his hand, I got up the courage to cross the aisle and humbly ask him for his autograph. He signed my boarding pass that day, and it now hangs in a prominent place in my salon along with some of my other Libyan memorabilia. I returned to my seat, closed my eyes, and said a little prayer, once again, for all of my blessings. What a wonderful way to end my Libyan adventure!

CHAPTER 61

Picking Up the Pieces

Sometimes the hardest part isn't letting go
but rather learning to start over.
—Nicole Sobon, *Program 13*

I deplaned in Adana on July 1 with a new attitude and a new resolve. The past six months had been an opportunity for me to reflect on my life, my values, and what I needed to change to eliminate the stress and anxiety that had been my constant companions toward the end of the time I spent with Metin. While I was in Libya, we had virtually no contact. However, shortly before I was scheduled to return to Adana, he called and asked whether I wanted him to meet me at the airport. I was cordial and thanked him politely but told him that I had a significant amount of baggage that needed to be delivered to my apartment and that I had already made arrangements for someone to meet me and do that. Although, at the time, he seemed to have accepted what I said, I should have known better.

As I emerged from the terminal, I saw both Metin and my friend Neset waiting for me. Metin looked glum, and Neset looked stunned. I'm sure Neset was wondering why I had called him if I'd already made arrangements for Metin to meet me. It was awkward and uncomfortable, and it seemed like it took an eternity to load my baggage and get on the road to my apartment. However, within less than an hour, I was home and both Neset and Metin had left. It had been an exhausting day both physically and emotionally, so I headed for bed believing, like Scarlett O'Hara, that tomorrow was another day.

For the next six weeks, Metin walked on water. He told me he had suffered immensely in my absence and realized how ungrateful and totally insensitive he had been toward me. He was ready and willing to do whatever I felt was necessary to make our relationship work. I told him, in no uncertain terms, that I was completely unwilling to go down the same road we had traveled so many times before. I also made it perfectly clear that this wasn't the first time he'd had an awakening, and it was always only a matter of time before he slipped back into his old ways. He asked me to make a list of deal breakers, which I did. He carefully perused it and told me that there wasn't anything on it he couldn't do. Having said that, he naturally assumed that he was back in my good graces and we would immediately pick up where we left off.

Much to my surprise, for the first time in the eight years that I had known him, all of his pleas fell on deaf ears. There was nothing he could say or do that could weaken my determination to stay the course I had set out for myself. I knew what kind of a life I wanted now, and unless he proved me wrong, I no longer believed he could be a part of it. Amazingly, the angst and heart-wrenching sense of loss that I had felt in the past were no longer present. In the months we were apart, I'd found my power again, and I wasn't about to be taken in as I had been so many times before. Weeks flew by, and although he continued to try to finagle his way back into my heart, a miracle of sorts had occurred. The distance that our time apart had created between us allowed me to step back and, for the first time in eight years, see him for what he truly was. I was no longer swayed by his ardent professions of undying love or intimidated by his threats to go back to Deniz. For the first time in eight years, I had my power back. I said what I meant, and I meant what I said. I went about establishing a routine of my own and making my own plans. I no longer felt any need to discuss my decisions with him or to ask for his blessing on any of my many endeavors.

By the seventh week, it was clear to him that the age-old ploys he had used on me were no longer getting the desired result, and we parted ways again. As usual, after a few days, he began to call, but I had no desire or time to answer. I had bigger fish to fry. I was packing and preparing to meet my German relatives in Hungary for a weeklong holiday. We were going on a quest. My niece had spent months doing the research necessary to find my paternal grandfather's boyhood home. She had learned it was in Murga, Hungary, and she and her family, as well as her uncle and his family, and I, were all going to meet in Bikal, Hungary, the following week. We would explore the environs, meet some of my other shirttail relatives, and, at the end of the week, travel to Murga to see what we could learn about the family homestead.

CHAPTER 62

Moving On

Within our dreams and aspirations we find our opportunities.
—Sue Atchley Ebaugh

I had begun my search for my long-lost European relatives almost twenty years earlier. It was my dream to find them and, hopefully, to one day actually have the opportunity to meet them face-to-face. Who could have known at the time that not only would I meet them but visit them in their ancestral home in Neideroderwitz, Germany, five times; have dinner together in Vienna, Austria; ski with them in the Italian Alps; and now, after finally having found them thirteen years earlier, be off together in search of our family's homestead in Hungary? It was truly an impossible dream come true.

I boarded a plane in Adana and flew to Istanbul. From there, I flew to Budapest, the capital of Hungary, and there boarded an intercity train for Dombovar, a small village in southern Hungary. My niece Anett and her husband, Egbert, picked me up at the station, and together we drove to Bikal where we had booked rooms at Castle Puchner. This property was originally owned by Antal Szaniszló Puchner who was born in 1779 and died in 1852. However, the new owners bought it in the late 1990s, and since then, they have worked tirelessly to turn it into a popular holiday destination. It has a bowling alley, squash courts, swimming pools, archery, paintball, a theme park, and a jousting area. I felt as though we had been transported back in time. The decor was strictly medieval and great pains had been taken to ensure that the theme was carried out impeccably from the moment we checked in until the day we finally reluctantly departed.

Once again, I luxuriated in the princess treatment. My room was spectacular from the vine-covered, tiled private terrace to the luxurious canopied bed. I was in heaven. The castle was equipped with a spa that offered manicures, pedicures, ten different types of massages, facial treatments, and an array of services guaranteed to pamper even the most discerning clientele. After two pedicures, two manicures, a Cleopatra honey massage, and a facial, I was ready to meet the world.

Dinner every evening was a feast for the senses. The array of mouthwatering Hungarian specialties the chef prepared every evening was overwhelming. After the dearth of good food in Libya, I was ready to sample any and every offering, and I did. Magnificent tapestries decorated with life-size knights in full battle regalia hung from every wall, and an enormous carved stone fireplace was the focal point of the main knight's dining room. Walking in, I felt like an honored dinner guest at Camelot. I actually imagined that, at any moment, Sir Lancelot would saunter in, his helmet held deftly under his arm, and join us at our table.

It is said that Hungarians drink wine like water, so I shouldn't have been surprised to learn that in the mini bar in my room, a split of champagne cost about fifty cents more than a bottle of water. As a result, I raided the mini bar nightly and enjoyed a bag of nuts or a bar of chocolate with my champagne or glass of Epebor, a mouthwateringly delicious fruit-flavored Hungarian wine. I relaxed in my sumptuous surroundings wondering why I hadn't done this sooner. My extended family spent a week or two in Hungary every summer and had repeatedly asked me to join them. It had taken me years, but I was finally here with them. I was in my ancestral homeland, spending hours every day learning about my grandfather's life, taking advantage of the spa services, and enjoying the majestic countryside. Could it get any better than this?

During the course of the week, we went on a carriage ride, attended a medieval reenactment of the Turkish invasion of Hungary complete with men on horseback in suits of armor and professional archers. We walked the roads in the surrounding countryside and picked fruit off the trees. There were apples, miles and miles of grapes, apricots, and juicy, plump, purple plums. We visited scores of distant relatives in the neighboring villages and, although we frequently arrived unannounced, were welcomed with open arms. Homemade Palinka, a traditional fruit-flavored brandy invented in the Middle Ages, flowed like water, and my relatives consumed it like it was water. Unfortunately, to me, it tasted more like grain alcohol, so I definitely didn't share their enthusiasm and sipped my lone glass ever so slowly as they refilled theirs over and over again. One can only imagine the welcome I received when the relatives learned that I was a descendant of the lone family member who had escaped before World War I and gone to America. When I was introduced as Henry Marcz's granddaughter, it was as though they were looking at a ghost.

Finally, the big day arrived, and we hopped into two different vehicles for the trip to Murga. Although Anett had done a meticulous job of researching the village in which my grandfather's house was located, no one was exactly sure how to get there. Even the navigational systems in the vehicles were having a hard time pinpointing the exact location. However difficult, we were not to be deterred. This was our raison d'être for being here, and we were going to persevere no matter what.

Only Hans and his wife, Sigrid, had been to Murga before, and she shook uncontrollably as she retold the story of being chased by a band of itinerant gypsies. She warned us all to hide anything of value, including our passports, because she couldn't be sure what we would find if and when we finally found Murga. I immediately dove into my purse to retrieve my passport and bank cards and frantically began stuffing them into my bra as my nephew Sebastian watched in horror. Certainly, he must have thought his aunt was being slightly overdramatic. However, based on his mother's tone of voice and the fact that the color had completely left her face as she recounted her experience, I thought what I had done was perfectly in line with the potential threat level. In addition, according to Anett, the cousin who had done all of the research, there were rumblings from relatives in the area that my grandfather's house was vacant and that a band of gypsies had moved in and claimed it as their own. As a result, none of us knew exactly what to expect when we finally arrived.

After driving in circles for what seemed like hours, we finally stopped at a gas station to ask for directions. Our GPS system was of little or no help, and we had driven in circles for so long we weren't even sure we could find our way back to the castle. The man on duty didn't have a clue where Murga was, but because our quest must have been divinely inspired, we were fortunate enough to meet a man in the same station who offered to help us. He told us he was heading in that direction, and although he would be turning off before we would, he could at least get us on the right road. *Eureka*, we thought, and off we went.

After what seemed like an interminable amount of time, we finally saw a miniscule sign that said Murga and had an arrow that pointed to the right. We turned off of the main highway onto a single-lane dirt road and prayed for the best. After several kilometers, we saw a much more official-looking sign that announced we had arrived! We were all holding our breath and waiting to see what would come next.

My heart was pounding, and the tears were welling up in my eyes as the realization hit me that I was about to stand in front of the actual house where my grandfather had been born and raised. I wanted to pinch myself, because I never imagined that I would live long enough to be able to visit this place.

As we approached the village, we saw two shabbily dressed, unshaven old men standing by the side of the road. Although they looked extremely intimidating, we were desperate, so we stopped to ask them if they had any information about the Marcz house. They pointed to an imposing granite monument behind them and explained that most of the Marcz family had died long ago and were buried here. This was a special memorial erected to honor those who had died during the war.

They went on to say that one of the Marcz family boys had been fortunate enough to have left for America before the war broke out but that no one had heard from him since. When my relatives heard that, once again, they pointed at me and announced, "This is that man's granddaughter." Once again, I got that she-must-have-just-risen-from-the-grave look. After we'd given the two strangers enough time to compose themselves, we all got out of the van and went to the memorial to read the list of names. It was difficult for Hans, my elder cousin, to hold back his tears. He had heard stories about many of these relatives since he was a small boy, and now he finally he had a chance to come to their last resting place and pay his respects. This was truly a miracle.

Obviously, the next question we asked was whether the men could direct us to the Marcz house. After listening carefully to their directions, we were off to complete our mission. When we arrived, we experienced a wide variety of emotions. We jumped out of the van and began hugging one another. Next, we all grabbed for our cameras or cell phones and began madly photographing the house from every angle. We were thrilled to see that the gypsies had vacated the premises and surprised to see that there was a for-sale sign posted on the fence. There was a neighbor working in his garden, so we approached him and began firing questions like machine gun bullets: Who had lived here? Where did they go? Who owns the house now? Why is it for sale? Where are the property lines? The questions went on and on.

Sebastian and I were the first to approach the front door to see what we could see. The front of the house was still standing. We pulled at the door, but it wouldn't open so we strained our necks to look through the only window that provided a view into the inside. It was obvious that people had lived there recently, so we knew that at least a portion of the house was inhabitable. The back portion of it had collapsed. The vineyards were gone, and the entire property was overgrown with weeds. There was debris everywhere, but the well was still operational. It was what I would later lovingly refer to as a handyman's special.

We all embraced and cried tears of joy. We were, after all of these years, finally reunited as a family and standing on the very ground where my grandfather and their great-grandfather had been born and lived. We were overcome with emotion. After taking what seemed like hundreds of photos, Hans began a serious conversation with the neighbor about the possibility of buying the property. He asked the neighbor for specifics regarding the property lines, taxes, the price, and how to contact whoever had listed the property. I couldn't help but laugh out loud when right there, standing literally in the middle of nowhere, the neighbor announced, "It's listed on Facebook!"

The ride back to the castle was a quiet one. We were all engrossed in our own thoughts and dreaming our own special dreams. I had already agreed that if my nieces and nephews wanted to buy the property, they should count me in. I would be thrilled to own a part of my family's history. We talked about replanting the grapes and once again, as our relatives had done a hundred years ago, producing wine on the land. What they didn't know at the time was that in my heart of hearts I felt like a part of my own personal destiny was being fulfilled.

The high school I attended had a very special tradition, and each year the junior class wrote a last will and testament for the graduating seniors. The juniors met as a group and individually discussed each senior class member in an attempt to determine what they could leave that person that would be beneficial for them in the future. For example, the girl who was considered to be one of the prettiest in the class might have been left a lifetime supply of Avon products. The boy with the nicest car might have been left a lifetime subscription to *Popular Mechanics*. For whatever reason, the junior class decided to leave me "the key to the winery." Perhaps it was because at that time, and ever since, in fact, it has been my drink of choice.

As I lay in my bed in the castle that night, I was overwhelmed with emotion. I felt as if my life had come full circle. Fifty years ago I had been willed a key to a winery, and now my extended family and I were actually in the process of trying to decide how we could buy our family's ancestral home, replant the grapes, and start producing wine again! Was this just an incredible coincidence or another instance of divine intervention? Whichever it was, I believed that my destiny was unfolding in front of my very eyes.

CHAPTER 63

The Death of a Dream, or Was It Just a Girlish Fantasy?

Love never dies a natural death. It dies because we don't
know how to replenish its source. It dies of blindness
and errors and betrayals. It dies of illness and wounds;
it dies of weariness, of witherings, of tarnishings.

—Anaïs Nin

Two days after returning from Hungary I had a private lesson to prepare for. I needed to run some photocopies, but my printer was out of ink. I drove the short distance to the local bookstore to buy a new ink cartridge for my printer. When I opened my wallet to get my bank card, I was shocked to see that it wasn't there! I paid for my purchase with cash and immediately rushed home to check and see if I had left my bank card behind. I ignored all of the traffic lights and rules of the road as I sped back to my apartment. I had a sinking feeling in my stomach.

I am a creature of habit, and I knew it was highly unlikely that I had misplaced the card. However, before jumping to the conclusion that it had been stolen again, I decided I should first check the counter in my apartment and, if it wasn't there, call my bank to check the balance in my account. If I had accidentally misplaced the card, I couldn't have withdrawn any money, and the balance wouldn't have changed. On the other hand, if someone had stolen it, I understood the contrary would most definitely be true. Five days earlier, I had deposited twenty-five hundred American dollars. The current exchange rate was two-to-one, so I prayed with all my heart that when I called my friend at the bank she would tell me that my balance was a little over five thousand liras.

I pulled into my otopark and rushed up the stairs, taking two at a time as though the devil himself was chasing me. I opened the door, threw my purse on the floor, checked the counter where I thought I might have left the card and, not finding it there, frantically dialed my bank. I held my breath and waited anxiously for the response of Mercan, my personal banker. When she told me that my balance was only 162 liras, approximately eighty-one American dollars, my heart stopped beating. Once again, I had been robbed!

My mind was reeling. By the time I returned from Hungary, Metin had rented his own apartment, and as a result, he couldn't have taken it. Who then, I wondered, could the culprit be? At that moment, I didn't know what needed to be done or who to call, so out of desperation, I resorted to calling Metin for help. He was absolutely astounded that something like this could have happened to me again and told me not to worry and that, in his opinion, the bank would be responsible for reimbursing the loss. He told me that in order for that to happen I needed to fill out some paperwork and take it to the prosecutor's office at the courthouse. I had absolutely no idea how to proceed, so I asked him if he would help me. Without a moment's hesitation, he assured me that he would always be there for me and told me to pick him up immediately.

I drove to his apartment, and we went to the city center to find someone who could write a *dilekce* for me. This was the form that the court would need in order to begin their investigation. Metin told the man exactly what to write, paid for the paperwork, and took me to the courthouse where we went from one office to another in an attempt to file everything correctly. One of the courthouse officials told us that the investigation couldn't proceed until we went to the bank and obtained a copy of the transactions that had been made during the last week. If the money was taken from ATM machines, the dates, times, and ATM numbers would be available from the bank. Because all ATM machines are required by law to have cameras installed, catching the culprit would only be a matter of time.

When we arrived at the bank, we got the copy of the transactions and discovered that, indeed, all of the money had been taken from ATM machines. There were four withdrawals, and each was in the amount of one thousand liras. Because it was already almost five o'clock in the evening, the courthouse was closed, so we would have to wait until the following morning to return and submit the necessary documentation.

Sleep didn't come easily that night. The money that had been taken was intended to cover my living expenses for the month. A thousand questions were running through my head. How would I pay my bills? How would I buy my groceries for the month? But, most importantly, how could I have been careless enough to let something like this happen to me again?

Early the next morning I picked Metin up, and once again, we headed to the city center. The streets were jammed with traffic, and there was absolutely no place to park. As a result, Metin offered to run into the courthouse and give the paperwork to the appropriate official. He told me to go around the block and pick him up in front of the courthouse in five minutes. In Adana's city center, there is no such thing as going around the block. There are numerous one-way streets; therefore, I had to drive several blocks before I could turn and make my way back to where I had dropped Metin off.

I hadn't driven more than three blocks when I was stopped at a red light. When it turned green, a white Chevrolet Sierra turned in front of me and ran straight into the right front end of my new car. When we both got out of our cars to inspect the damage, it was obvious that his was slight compared to mine. He took one look at what he had done to my car and began to run back to his in an attempt to drive off. I grabbed him by his arm and started screaming at the top of my lungs for help. Fortunately for me, there was a policeman standing on the sidewalk directly opposite us. He came in response to my frantic calls for help. Ferhat, the man who hit me, started babbling a mile a minute. Although I speak Turkish, it was obvious that I couldn't handle this one on my own, so once again, I called Metin, told him someone had hit my car, and asked him to come as fast as his feet would carry him. Within a few minutes, Metin and the traffic police had both arrived.

I learned that the reason Ferhat, the man who had hit me, tried to run off and afterward wanted to handle the problem without involving the police was because the car he was driving wasn't his. He had borrowed his friend's car, and because the accident was his fault, his friend's insurance would be responsible for paying for my repairs. Ferhat kept talking a mile a minute, trying his best to convince the officer on the scene that I was responsible. The officer finally looked him straight in the eye and in a tone of voice that was so gruff that even I was a little amazed said, "I've been doing this job for twenty-seven years; don't try and fool me. I know you hit this lady, and I know you're trying to get her to pay for the damage you already have from a prior accident." He handed him the police report and barked, "Now stop lying and fill out the accident report."

I smiled sweetly and thanked the officer profusely. Actually, I wanted to kiss him! He recognized Ferhat for the charlatan he was, and he wasn't swayed by his arguments or his professions of innocence. *Smart man*, I thought.

Metin and Ferhat worked together filling out the report. Unfortunately, the traffic police had left by this time, so there was no one to check what had been written on the form. I had told Metin repeatedly that Ferhat had lied, and I explained in graphic detail what had happened so I had no reason to question whether what he had written was accurate. Once again, I should have known better than to trust someone who had betrayed me so many times in the past.

We made multiple copies of the report, and Ferhat and I both signed all of them. Ferhat left, and Metin and I went to the local Chevrolet dealer to see how many days they would need to repair my car and to make sure that we had all of the necessary paperwork in order. When we arrived, we learned that nothing could be done until we had a copy of Ferhat's driver's license, insurance papers, and car registration. Metin told me that he knew where Ferhat worked and that he would take care of getting the necessary documentation from him. In the meantime, he would take me home because he didn't know how I would get home from the Chevrolet dealership without my car. It sounded reasonable to me, so I agreed. We went back to my apartment, and I made copies of the documentation the dealership needed from me and trusted that Metin was meeting Ferhat at two o'clock to get the same paperwork from him.

An hour or two passed, and I hadn't heard from Metin so I began calling his mobile phones. Both of them were closed, which I thought was unusual because he knew that I was expecting to hear from him regarding what had happened. Finally, at four thirty, I went onto the Internet and got the telephone number of the Chevrolet dealership. I called them to inquire whether my car had been dropped off. When they told me they didn't have it, my heart sank. In spite of all the promises that Metin had made regarding turning his life around, I now fully suspected that he was up to his old tricks again. I jumped into the shower and changed my clothes in record time. I went to the restaurant next door and asked them to please call a taxi for me. If Metin was pulling another one of his shenanigans, I fully intended to catch him in the act.

When the taxi pulled up in front of Metin's apartment, I was thrilled to see that my car was not there. Perhaps I had misjudged him after all, and I felt slightly ashamed of myself for being so paranoid. However, given our past history, I felt I had every right to be suspicious. I climbed the stairs to his apartment and knocked on his door. When he answered, it was obvious that he had been sleeping, and I had awakened him. I told him I had called the Chevrolet service department, and they told me that he never brought the car back. He told me that they wanted entirely too much paperwork, so he had taken the car to Mersin to a different dealership. I was flabbergasted!

I wanted to know how in the hell we were going to get the car back from Mersin, a city almost a hundred kilometers away. I told him that Mustafa, my attorney, had told me that we were entitled to a rental car. Metin told me that Mustafa didn't know what he was talking about. I insisted on seeing the insurance papers so that I could check for myself whether what Mustafa had told me was true. Metin told me they were in the car.

"Great," I said, "then you have to call Asli, my insurance agent, and ask her."

We were standing in the kitchen as Metin made the call. The kitchen windows provided an unobstructed view of the driveway below. Suddenly, as if he were swatting a fly, I noticed Metin waving his right hand. I looked out of the window and saw my car pulling into the drive. He was trying to warn the person who was driving it to pull back out again. Fearing that his next move would be to go out onto his balcony and tell the driver to take off with my car, I grabbed my purse and flew down the stairs like a woman who was literally running for her life. As I reached the ground floor, I met his neighbor coming up the stairs. Apparently, he had loaned her my car to do an errand.

Not only had he lied about dropping off the car, but I later learned that he had also filled out a false police report saying that the accident was my fault, which meant that my insurance, not Ferhat's, would have to pay for the damage to both cars. In addition, my car is registered in Turkey as a *misifir* car, which means a visitor's car. If anyone other than myself is caught driving it, the penalty is 1,450 liras, or US$725. Allowing Metin to drive it was risky enough, yet he had seen fit to loan it to his neighbor's wife!

His deceitfulness coupled with his total lack of responsibility was more than I could handle. I had trusted him again only to be betrayed again! I was beside myself. As I sped home, his plan became crystal clear to me. He intended to have one of his friends do the repair work at a fraction of the cost the insurance company would have been asked to pay the Chevrolet dealership. It would have been a small enough amount that he could have paid it out of his own pocket. In return, he would have had a car at his disposal for a minimum of five or six days, which was the amount of time the man at the Chevrolet dealership told me they would need it. By going to a local repair shop instead, the work could've been done in two days, leaving Metin four or five days to go wherever he wanted and use the car as if it were his own.

In the past several months, Metin had admitted to many betrayals. He had admitted to stealing money, jewelry, and many household items from me. He also admitted to lying about things that, in many instances, weren't worth lying about. His willingness to come clean had, to a great extent, convinced me that he really was interested in turning his life around and taking a more honest road.

However, if I needed anymore proof that he was a pathological liar who was incapable of telling the truth, this was certainly it! He had stood, defiantly looking me directly in the eyes, and lied as his neighbor was pulling into the driveway. In the unlikely event that the coffin needed another nail, this was definitely it. I had already distanced myself from him and made a conscious decision to maintain the separation unless there was a significant difference in his behavior. This was a difference all right, but certainly not the one I had expected. I had called him for help simply because I didn't know what to do or where to go to get help about the theft from my bank account. Ironically, the traffic accident that followed simply provided him with another opportunity to take advantage of me. Divine intervention was at work in my life again.

As I drove home, I wondered how a woman who is as intelligent and well educated as I am could have been taken in over and over again by an uneducated, uncultured boy from the streets of old Adana. It wasn't that he was smart or good-looking. It wasn't that he was an outstanding lover. It wasn't that he bent over backward trying to win my heart. On the contrary, I was the one who had turned myself inside out trying to please him.

Once again, I had found my father and was doing everything in my power to win his approval. He hadn't held a gun to my head to get me to agree to some of his outrageous demands. On the contrary, I had been a willing victim. There was no way around it. I had allowed myself to be emotionally, physically, and financially abused. If I needed another reason to beat myself up, this was certainly it. However, although I thought this was the ultimate deception, once again, it still wasn't over. Unbeknownst to me, I still didn't have all the information. The fat lady hadn't sung yet.

Based on what had happened with the car, I now had every reason to suspect the Metin may also have been the culprit who somehow managed to take the money from my bank account. When the bank gave me the list of ATM withdrawals, I racked my brain trying to remember the last time I had used the card. Because I operate primarily on a cash-only basis, it had been weeks since I'd used the card. In fact, it had been weeks since I even remembered seeing it. In addition, I'd been out of the country and had only seen Metin for a few brief moments after I returned. He had called and asked me to drop off a blanket and duvet for him.

Although his new apartment was furnished, they didn't provide any linens and he had left all of his with me when he moved out. I wasn't with him for more than five minutes, so it was inconceivable to me how he could have taken the card in that short amount of time. More importantly than that, however, is the fact that no one, absolutely no one, knew my pin number. In fact, I had a difficult time remembering it because I had used the digits from my home phone as my pin code, and I rarely, if ever, called that number. I was at a total loss.

The following day I called Mustafa and told him what had happened. Given the fact that every one of my friends had warned me repeatedly about how ruthless Metin could be, I was more than a little embarrassed to have to confess that I had called on him for his help again when I needed to write and file the dilekce. I also had to confess that based on the fact that Metin had concocted another fabulous scam about the car, I now fully suspected that he may have been the person who stole the money from my bank account. I asked Mustafa if he would follow up on this for me and go to the courthouse to see whether Metin actually filed the dilekce. Later that day, Mustafa called me and informed me that the dilekce that Metin had helped me write and had supposedly filed for me had never been submitted to the court! Now, in my heart of hearts, I had to admit that it was undoubtedly Metin who had stolen the four thousand liras from my account.

Fortunately, by this time, my feelings for Metin had died, so the losses were purely financial. This final betrayal didn't tear at my heartstrings as so many of the things he had done in the past had. The flame of all-encompassing love that had burned so brightly for him for the past eight years had finally extinguished itself. He had manipulated me like a puppet on a string with his charisma and his gift of gab.

I will never forget the warm summer night that we sat on the terrace of a local restaurant overlooking the lake. He took my hands in his, tenderly kissed each knuckle, and locked his gaze in mine. He professed his undying love and vowed that when I died he would carry my body, wrapped in its plain white shroud, into the sea and die with me because without me his life wouldn't be worth living. Although I knew at the time that this was a gross overexaggeration, I couldn't help but be moved by what seemed to be a sincere expression of his feelings for me. What I understand now is that I was like a fine musical instrument to him, and he knew how to play me to get exactly the results that he wanted. What a silly woman I had been.

In my heart of hearts, I know that part of my destiny was to meet another man like this. He came into my life as a teacher to help me learn the lessons that I had refused to come face to face with over the course of my lifetime. The Universe needed to send me a "professional" in order for me to finally realize that the only person who can give me the love I have been seeking all of my life is me. Metin was a professional manipulator, liar, and thief. When I finally believed I had extricated myself from his chicanery, there was yet another betrayal to deal with. Unfortunately, it was exactly what I needed to force me to open my eyes and see him for what he was.

Now, as I reflect on the past eight years, I have to ask myself whether my love for him was ever real. Perhaps he merely served as the instrument that would eventually help me heal my childhood wounds. Perhaps all of the sacrifices that I made and the pain that I experienced were necessary to help me deal with my unresolved anger toward my father. At any rate, the love has died. Whether it died a natural death, I'll never know. Certainly, the betrayals, the lies, and the manipulations helped turn the tide. All I know at this point is that I have finally filled the hole in my soul. I no longer need a man in my life to take care of me and to make me feel complete. It was an extremely painful and expensive journey to get to this point, but the Universe sent me the perfect teacher. His name was Metin, and unlike all the other men before him, he finally succeeded in bringing me to my knees.

CHAPTER 64

Serenity, Peace, and Contentment

Something inside you emerges . . . an innate, indwelling
peace, stillness, aliveness. It is the unconditioned,
who you are in your essence. It is what you had been
looking for in the love object. It is yourself.
—Eckhart Tolle

I am now alone, and for the first time in more than fifty years, there is no significant other in my life. There are times that I feel terribly alone and vulnerable, and not surprisingly, I sometimes find myself worrying about what I would do if I suddenly became ill or if my cancer recurred. When I have a problem with my car or something in the house, I still find that my first impulse is to call Metin. However, I resist the urge with every cell in my body, and although it may take me longer than I'd like to come up with a solution, I always find another alternative.

I no longer work full-time, which means that I have lots of time on my hands. In the beginning, the days were sometimes long, and the nights often seemed as though they would never end. I stayed up until the wee hours of the morning watching television or reading so that I could sleep late and there would be fewer hours of the day that I needed to fill. The first few weeks I wandered aimlessly around my apartment as I tried to figure out how to fill up the hours in my day.

I missed the drama and the excitement that were my constant companions. I felt like I was dying a slow death. I ate even though I wasn't hungry. I thought about buying a dog, moving to another city, or even leaving the country for a while again. I felt I desperately needed to do something to make me feel alive again. My mind wandered, and I seemed to have little or no control over my thoughts. Often Metin would creep into them like a thief in the night, and again, there was an ache in my heart. However, gradually, this changed. Sleep came more easily, and ever so slowly the thoughts of Metin dissipated like the morning mist when the sun begins to shine.

Slowly but surely, I was finding joy in my life by doing the things that gave me pleasure. I began to pray for help to overcome my addiction to him and to drama. I began to mediate and exercise, and suddenly I found peace and contentment. Admittedly, there were still times when I felt completely alone and longed for a significant other to share my burdens and my joy with. However, the memories of how dearly I had paid for this companionship kept me from ever acting on my thoughts.

My journey to oneness has not been an easy one, and in my heart of hearts, I know that it's not over. There will, undoubtedly, be setbacks and a few missteps along the way. However, for the most part, I feel that for the first time in my life I have gained some genuine insights into what it takes to find true peace, serenity, and contentment.

The first requirement is establishing a relationship with the God of your choice. I finally refused to continue to be a victim in this life. Yes, I had a horrible childhood. Yes, I had parents who failed miserably when it came to launching me into adulthood properly. Yes, I was destined to have trouble finding and maintaining healthy relationships with men because of my childhood issues with my father. However, all of these things were part of God's plan for me. What I've learned is that in order to find peace and contentment I must let go of my plans, because the truth is that there is already a divine plan laid out for me. My challenge is to come to grips with the fact that the plans I had that failed, or that never materialized, were not failures as such. They were lessons that God sent to me in order to help me along my journey to enlightenment.

C. W. Lewis said it best in *A Grief Observed.*

"It was too perfect to last," so I am tempted to say of our marriage. But it can be meant in two ways. It may be grimly pessimistic—as if God no sooner saw two of His creatures happy than He stopped it ("None of that here!"). As if He were like the Hostess at the sherry-party who separates two guests the moment they show signs of having got into a real conversation. But it could also mean "This had reached its proper perfection. This had become what it had in it to be. Therefore of course it would not be prolonged." As if God said, "Good; you have mastered that exercise. I am very pleased with it. And now you are ready to go on to the next."

C. S. Lewis, *A Grief Observed.* (United States of America, Harper Collins, 1961).

The second truth I've discovered is that in order to find peace and contentment I must learn to do the things that make me happy. All of my life I've been a people pleaser. When asked what I wanted to do or where I wanted to go, I always deferred to the other people in the group. I justified my actions by convincing myself that I was eager to try any and every new experience that came my way. The truth is I was afraid of expressing my opinion for fear of being rejected. I have finally learned to express my preferences and to abstain from activities that I'm really not interested in being a part of. Surprisingly, people have not stopped asking me to join them, and they respect my right to accept or refuse their invitations. I no longer waste my time and money doing things that I really don't want to do, and when I do go out, I find that I enjoy myself more than ever because I am now very selective about where I go, what I do, and with whom I go.

My next awakening was that my level of contentment is directly proportional to the amount of gratitude I have expressed on any given day. When I wake up and thank God for the many blessings in my life, the law of attraction seems to bring even more positive things to me that day. It's often said that what we think expands. For example, if I'm on a diet and I dwell on the fact that I'm on a diet and depriving myself of the things that I enjoy, I will remain hungry and crave food until I change my thought processes. Similarly, if I concentrate on thinking kind thoughts, sending positive vibrations into the Universe, and being grateful for all my blessings, I will attract people and experiences that are good for me and that raise my vibrational level and, therefore, my sense of peace and contentment.

Last but not least, I have learned that when I practice random acts of kindness or do something that makes a difference in someone's life, I am filled with a sense of serenity and purpose. I have dedicated my life to working with young people, many of whom I am still in contact with. I know that long after I am dead and gone, my legacy will live on through them. They frequently remind me of things that I said or did that had a significant impact on them. I know in my heart of hearts that when they have children, they will pass these lessons on to them, and I will, as a result, become immortal. When I reflect on this and realize the significance of the contributions I have been able to make, I am ashamed of myself for temporarily losing sight of my purpose in this lifetime and being so sidetracked by my personal agenda. Learning to forgive myself for this is one of the hardest things I've had to do.

Having said all of this, I am happy to report that, although it's taken me more than sixty years to learn my lessons, I finally seem to be on the road to recovery. I have turned my apartment into my sanctuary, and I am blissfully happy here. I have several good friends with whom I can socialize and who are ready and willing to help me simply because they are my friends, not because they expect something in return. My life is uncomplicated and sometimes a little lonely, but that's the price I have to pay for refusing to be caught up in the drama that's a natural accompaniment of the kind of relationships that I've been drawn to all of my life.

I am taking my own advice and have begun doing the things that make me happy. Travel has always been at the top of my list, and as this book goes to press, I am preparing to leave on a short trip to the Ukraine with a Turkish friend of mine. A few months later, I will either entertain some of my Libyan friends at my home in Adana, or I will fly to Venice to ring in the New Year. In February, two of my dear friends from Arizona have invited me to visit them at their vacation home in Thailand, so at long last, Barbara is doing what she wants to do.

I have enjoyed an incredible life, and for that, I am extremely grateful. I have traveled the world and seen and done more things in one lifetime than most people could even imagine. I have dined with everyone from Italian royalty to Turkish prostitutes and felt comfortable. I have tasted food from around the world and embraced different customs and cultures. I have learned to speak three different foreign languages with enough fluency to be clearly understood in most situations. I have survived breast cancer and outlived most of the women in my family. I have loved and been loved. I have laughed and cried, sang and danced.

As I look back on my life, there isn't a lot I would change. The adversity and pain that I've undergone has made me the strong woman I am today. I have undergone a baptism of fire here in Turkey, and it didn't kill me. Quite the opposite, it made me stronger. In 1929, in *A Farewell to Arms*, Ernest Hemingway wrote, "The world breaks everyone and afterward many are strong in the broken places. But those that will not break it kills. It kills the very good and the very gentle and the very brave impartially. If you are none of these you can be sure it will kill you too but there will be no special hurry."

My experience in the past eight years broke me and brought me to my knees, but it didn't kill me. Quite the contrary, I lived to write and tell my story!

Lightning Source UK Ltd.
Milton Keynes UK
UKHW041602301218
334668UK00001B/36/P